Albemarle County, Virginia

Deed Abstracts

1768-1770

Ruth and Sam Sparacio

The Antient Press Collection
from

Colonial Roots
Millsboro, Delaware
2016

Colonial
Roots

Helping You Grow Your Family Tree

ISBN 978-1-68034-114-0

CONTENTS

Albemarle County, Virginia, Deed Abstracts 1768-1770..1

Index 124

[this page intentionally blank]

p.
1

To all well Disposed Christian People to whom these presents shall come Greeting. Now Know ye tht I ARCHIBALD CARVER of Albemarle County in the Colony of Virginia as well for the love and affection I bare to my Sone, WILLIAM CARVER as for many other good causes & considerations myself hereunto moving Espetially for and in consideration of the sum of Five Shillings Curt. money of this said Colony to me the said ARCHIBALD CARVER in hand paid by him the said WILLIAM CARVER and immediately before the delivery of these presents do give release and confirm unto said WILLIAM CARVER his heirs one certain parcel of land whereof he the sd WM. now liveth containing by estimation One hundred acres be it more or be it less situate lying and being in County of Albemarle & bounded beginning at a white Oak corner to me the said ARCHIBALD and my Son, JOSEPH CARVER, & extending thence with the said line to the land of JOSEPH WOOD, thence with his line to the land of NICHOLAS CAINE, thence with his line to the land of THOMAS EASTON, & thence with his line to the land of said ARCHIBALD CARVER & finally thence to the beginning To have and to hold said lands and premises together with every of their appurtenances to him said WILLIAM CARVER In Testimony whereof I the said WILLIAM CARVER have hereunto set my hand and affixed my Seal this Seventh day of August in year of our Lord Christ One thousand seven hundred and Sixty eight

Signed Sealed and Delivered & Quiet and peaceable possession & seizin of the within mentioned land and premises as given by and of the said ARCHIBALD CARVER taken and received by said WILLIAM CARVER the day and year above mentioned according to the true intent and meaning of this present Deed

In the presence of THOMAS EASTIN   ARCHIBALD his mark ⫟ CARVER
    JOHN THOMAS, THOMAS JERRY

Received of WILLIAM CARVER the just sum of Five Shillings Curt. money of Virginia it being in full of the consideration within mentioned I say reced this (blank) day of 1768

pr. me   (no signature)

At Albemarle August Court 1768

This Indenture and Receipt was proved by the Oaths of THOMAS EASTIN & JOHN THOMAS & THOMAS JERRY witnesses thereto and ordered to be recorded

                                   Test HENRY FRY Cl.

pp.
2-
3

THIS INDENTURE made this ninth day of June One thousand seven hundred and Sixty eight Between WILLIAM WAKEFIELD of Parish of St. Anne County of Albemarle Colony and Dominion of Virginia, Planter, and ELIONER his Wife of one part and CHARLES MASSIE of County aforesaid of other part Witnesseth that for sum of Eighty pounds Curt. money to WILLIAM WAKEFIELD in hand paid by CHARLES MASSIE before the sealing and delivery of these presents doth bargain and sell unto CHARLES MASSIE his heirs a certain tract or parcel of land lying & being in said County on the waters of LYNCH CREEK under the RAGGED MOUNTAINS being part of a Tract granted by Letters Patent to one JOHN DOBBINS and by him conveyed to HENRY WAKEFIELD SENR. and by him conveyed to WILLIAM and JOHN WAKEFIELD beginning at pointers in HENRY WAKEFIELD JUNR. line, running thence South sixteen and a half degrees East one hundred and twelve poles to pointers being the Dividing Line between WILLIAM and HENRY WAKEFIELD, thence South fifty degrees East one hundred and two poles to pointers in JOHN WAKEFIELDs land and with the lines in all their courses and

distances till it joyns WILLIAMs Dividing line and with the same until the place of begining on HENRY WAKEFIELD JUNR. containing One hundred and seventy acres be the
same more or less Together with all houses orchards and profits thereto belonging To
have and to hold the land hereby granted and conveyed unto said CHARLES MASSIE his
heirs freeg cleared and discharged of all Incumbrances whatsoever In Witness whereof the said WILLIAM WAKEFIELD and ELIONER his Wife hath hereunto set their hands
and Seals the day and year first above written
Signed Sealed & Delivered in the presence of
            (no witnesses shown)   WILLIAM WEAKFIELD
  Memorandum that on the day and year within mentioned Quiet possession of the within tract of land with all the appurtenances thereunto belonging was by the within
mentioned WM. WAKEFIELD and by him Delivered to the within mentioned CHARLES
MASSIE to be by him his heirs and assigns forever enjoyed according to the within
Deed Signed Seal'd and Delivered in the presence of
            (no witnesses shown)   WILLIAM WEAKFIELD
  Received June the ninth One thousand Sixty Eight the sum of Eighty pounds Curt.
money in consideration of the within tract of land per me
                                                          WILLIAM WAKEFIELD

    At Albemarle August Court 1768
This Indenture memorandum and Receipt were acknowledged by WM. WAKEFIELD party
thereto & ordered to be recorded

pp.   THIS INDENTURE made the Eleventh day of August One thousand seven hundred
3-   and Sixty eight Between HENRY WAKEFIELD of County of Albemarle of one part
5   & FRANS. TURNER of County aforesaid of other part Witnesseth that said HENRY
        WAKEFIELD for sum of Ninty pounds current money of Virginia to him in hand
paid by FRANS. TURNER doth bargain and sell unto FRANCIS TURNER his heirs one
certain tract of land lying and being in Albemarle County on the Branches of LINCHES
CREEK a branch of ROCKFISH RIVER containing Three hundred and Thirty nine acres
and bounded Begining at HENRY WAKEFIELDs SENR. line at a Chesnut Oak and thence
Seven degrees East sixty one poles to pointers, South fifty six degrees East fifty six poles
to a Chesnut Oak, South fifty eight degrees West one hundred and forty four poles to
pointers, South thirty three poles to a Locust, North twenty degrees West twenty eight
poles to a Chesnut tree, North five degrees West Sixty six poles to a Chesnut tree, North
forty three degrees East one hundred and two poles to pointers, North eighty poles to
pointers, North forty six degrees West one hundred and nineteen poles to a Spanish
Oak, North fifty degrees East sixty one poles to pointers, North forty degrees West
Eleven poles to a Hickory, North sixty seven degrees East sixty six poles to pointers
South fifty seven degrees East one and sixteen poles to pointers, South sixteen and a
half degrees East one hundred and twelve poles to pointers, South fifty degrees
East sixty eight poles to the first station and now in the possession of the said TURNER
with all houses and advantages whatsoever to said land and premises belonging and
HENRY WAKEFIELD and his heirs will warrant and ever defend by these presents In
Witness whereof HENRY WAKEFIELD hath hereunto set his hand and Seal the day and
year first above written
Signed Seal'd and Deliver'd in the presence of
            (no witnesses shown)   HENRY WAKEFIELD
  Received of FRANS. TURNER ninety pounds it being the consideration money within
mention'd this Eleventh day of August One thousand seven hundred and Sixty eight
                                                          HENRY WAKEFIELD

At Albemarle August Court 1768
This Indenture & Receipt were acknowledged by HENRY WAKEFIELD party thereto and ordered to be recorded

pp.
5-
6

THIS INDENTURE made the Twenty forth day of October in year of our Lord One thousand seven hundred and Sixty five Between MOSES AGER of County of Albemarle of one part and THOMAS McCOULOUGH of the same County of other part Witnesseth that said MOSES AGER for sum of Ten pounds currant money of Virginia to him in hand paid by said THOMAS McCOULOUGH by these presents doth bargain sell and confirm unto THOMAS McCOULOUGH and to his heirs one certain tract or parcel of land containing <u>Forty one acres</u> be it more or less lying and being in County of Albemarle on the Branches of MICHAMS RUN on both sides ROCKFISH ROAD and thus bounded Beginning at a red Oak and running thence North eighty seven degrees East Sixty poles to pointers round a Great Rock, thence on thence on new lines North twenty three degrees East twenty seven poles to a gum in MIRY BRANCH and down the said Branch by the meanders thereof North Thirty degrees West forty five poles to a red Oak sapling, thence down the said branch by its meanders North Sixty degrees West One hundred and two poles on MOSES AGERs line and with it South ten degrees West eighteen poles to his corner Poplar, thence South Nineteen degrees East ninety poles to the first station And all houses orchards and water courses to the same belonging To have and to hold <u>said forty acres</u> of land be it more or less with every of their appurtenances unto said THOMAS McCOULOUGH his heirs and MOSES AGER and his heirs shall warrant and defend the above sold land against all persons In Witness whereof said MOSES AGER hath hereunto set his hand and assigned his Seal the day and year first above written
Signed Sealed & Delivered in the presence of
    DAVID WHITESIDE,   MOSES his mark ৶ EGER
    RICHARD WOODS, SAML. BOYD
Received of THOMAS McCOULLOUGH the consideration money mentioned this 24th of October 1768
    DAVID WHITESIDE,   MOSES his mark ৶ EGER
    RICHARD WOODS, SAMUEL BOYD
At Albemarle June Court 1768
This Indenture was proved by the Oath of RICHARD WOODS & SAML. BOYD, And at a Court held for the said County the XIIth day of August 1768 was fully proved by the Oaths of DAVID WHITE SIDES a witness thereto & ordered to be recorded

p.
7

KNOW ALL MEN by these presents that I JOHN FRY of Albemarle County in consideration of the sum of Three hundred and nineteen pounds twelve Shillings and nine pence Currt. money of Virginia to me in hand paid by JAMES & ROBERT DONALDS & CO., Merchants of GLASGOW by these presents do bargain sell and deliver unto said DONALDS & CO. one certain parcell of land consisting of Five hundred acres being part of a certain tract by Patent to JOSUA FRY containing 1518 acres lying on the GREEN MOUNTAIN in Albemarle County and joining the tract on which I now live, the said Five hundred acres to be laid off by said DONALDS & CO. in the most convenient manner joining the lines of JOHN COLES's land as far as it extends on the GREEN MOUNTAIN with all houses orchards and other appurtenances thereunto belonging and likewise I bargain and sell unto DONALDS & CO. one Negro fellow named Millford, one Negroe wench Jeany, a young Wench named Betty, a Negroe girl named Sally, a Negroe girl named Milley, a Negro boy named Sam & a Negroe boy named Milford the last five mentioned being the Children of the above named Jeany, and one white horse branded,

To have and to hold unto DONALDS & CO. their heirs and I the said JOHN FRY the said bargained premises unto the said JAMES & ROBERT DONALDS & CO. their heirs shall warrant and forever defend against the claim of any person PROVIDED Nevertheless that if said JOHN FRY or assigns shall well and truly pay or cause to be paid unto said JAMES & ROBT. DONALDS & CO. their heirs the above mentioned sum with lawful Interest from this date on or before the first day of December in year one thousand seven hundred and Sixty Nine this Indenture to be void and of no effect but if default be made in the payment in said Three hundred and nineteen pounds Twelve Shillings and Nine pence in manner and form aforesaid that then this Indenture shall remain in full force & virtue In Witness whereof I have hereunto set my hand and Seal this Twenty sixth day of May in year of our Lord One thousand seven hundred and Sixty eight
Sign'd Seal'd and Deliver'd in presence of us

ISAAC COLES,   JOHN FRY
PETER DAVID, ELISHA COX,
HECTOR McALESTER

At a Court held for Albemarle County the XIIth day of August 1768
This Deed was proved by the Oath of ISAAC COLES, PETER DAVID & ELISHA COX witnesses thereto and ordered to be recorded

pp.   THIS INDENTURE made the Sixth day of January in year of our Lord One thousand
8-   seven hundred and Sixty eight Between THOMAS BALLOW of County of Albemarle
9   of one part and GEORGE RIPPIN and COPY., Merchants in GLASGOW of other part
         Witnesseth that said THOMAS BALLOW for sum of Forty five pounds Ten Shillings
Virginia Currency to him in hand paid by GEORGE RIPPIN & CO. by these presents doth
bargain and sell unto GEORGE RIPPIN & CO. their heirs one certain tract or parcel of
land lying and being in County of Albemarle and containing One hundred and nineteen acres be the same more or less being the same land granted to LEONARD BALLOW
by Patent from WILLIAMSBURG bearing date the Twentieth day of August One thousand
seven hundred and Forty eight and also all the Right title and Interest of said THOMAS
BALLOW in said tract of land and THOMAS BALLOW shall warrant and forever defend
Provided Always and it is agreed between the parties to these presents that if said THO-
MAS BALLOW his heirs shall pay or cause to be paid unto said GEORGE RIPPIN & CO. the
aforementioned sum on or before the first day of July next Insuing the date of these
presents that then from thenceforth this present Indenture shall be null & void notwithstanding anything to the contrary contained therein but after default shall be
made then this Indenture to take place according to the true intent and meaning thereof In Witness whereof said THOMAS BALLOW hath hereunto set his hand and affixed his
Seal the day and year first above written

LEONARD BALLOW,   THOMAS BALLOW
JOHN OLD, CLOUGH SHILTON

Albemarle County Jany. 6 1767. Then received of GEORGE RIPPIN & CO. Forty five
pounds Ten Shillings Virginia currency being the consideration money in this Deed
mentioned I say received by me

NEILL CAMPBELL,   THOMAS BALLOW
JOHN OLD, CLOUGH SHILTON

At Albemarle July Court 1768
This Indenture was proved by the Oath of JOHN OLD Witness thereto, And at another
Court held for said County the XIIth day of August 1768 was further proved by the Oath
of NEILL CAMPBELL & CLOUGH SHILTON witnesses thereto and Ordered to be recorded

pp.
9-
11

THIS INDENTURE made the Seventeenth day of May in year of our Lord One thousand seven hundred and Sixty Eight Between SAMUEL KARR of County of Albemarle of one part and THOMAS STEVENSON of County of AUGUSTA of other part Witnesseth that said SAMUEL KARR for sum of Fifty nine pounds Nineteen Shillings and nine pence Curt. money of Virginia to him in hand paid by said THOMAS STEVENSON at and before the sealing and delivery of these presents doth bargain sell and confirm unto said THOMAS STEVENSON his heirs one certain tract or parcel of land containing Three hundred and Thirty one acres lying and being in County of Albemarle on both sides of the South Fork of ROCKEY CREEK bounded Beginning at HENRY BUNCHes Corner of two white Oaks running thence on his line North sixty degrees West fifty one poles to MOSIAS JONES corner of several marked trees in BUNCHes, thence on JONES line North eighty four degrees West one hundred and thirty poles to his Corner Pine, thence on his line South nineteen degrees West eighty two poles to ROCKEY CREEK continued Twenty poles to his Corner Pine, thence South thirteen degrees West one hundred and four poles, thence South thirteen degrees West one hundred and forty four poles to a Corner white Oak by the side of a Branch thence South seventy degrees East one hundred and twenty four poles to a scrubby white Oak thence North sixty five degrees East one hundred and seventy four poles crossing the Creek to a white Oak on the line of HENRY BUNCH, thence on his line North twenty nine degrees West eighty eight poles to his Corner Pine, thence on his line North ten degrees East ninty seven poles to the beginning; Likewise hath bargained and sold another tract or parcel of land lying and joining to the above said tract mentioned Tract of land and being the same tract the above mentioned SAMUEL KARR now Dwells and resides on containing Two hundred and fifty nine acres Together with all houses orchards & gardens and all improvements whatsoever belonging To have and to hold said Two tracts of land and every of their appurtenances unto said THOMAS STEVENSON his heirs and SAMUEL KARR will warrant and defend the said bargained and sold premises against the claims of all manner of persons In Witness whereof said SAMUEL KARR hath hereunto set his hand and Seal the day and year first above written
Sign's Seal'd & Deliver'd in presence of

SAMUEL BOYD, WM. HOWARD,   SAMUEL KARR
THOMAS ANDERSON, JAMES BOWER

Received of THOMAS STEVENSON the sum of Fifty nine pounds Nineteen Shillings and Nine pence Curt. money of Virginia it being the consideration money of the within written Deed reced by me
Signed & Delivered in presence of

WM. HOWARD, THOS. ANDERSON,   SAML. KARR

Memorandum the Quiet and peaceable possession of the within premises is as given by the within SAMUEL KARR to the within THOMAS STEVENSON by delivery of Turf and Twig of the same as the usual sybols of Livery and Seizin In Witness whereof I have hereto set my hand and Seal the day and year within written
Signed Sealed and Delivered in presence of

WM. HOWARD, THOS. ANDERSON,   SAMUEL KARR
SAML. BOYD, J. BOWER

At Albemarle August Court 1768
This Indenture memorandum and Receipt was proved by the Oath of WM. HOWARD, THOS. ANDERSON & JAMES BOWER witnesses thereto and ordered to be recorded

p.   TO ALL TO WHOM these presents shall come Greeting. Know ye that I JOHN JOHN-
11   SON, Planter, of County of Albemarle for and in consideration of the love and
    affection that I do bare unto my Son, WM. JOHNSON, of County of BUCKINGHAM, I
the said JOHN JOHNSON being in perfect mind and memory do freely give unto said WM.
JOHNSON one Bay Horse named Buck whose property was that of one BOLENS, I do likewise from and after my decease give unto my Son, WM. JOHNSON, one certain tract of
land lying in Albemarle County being 100 acres more or less on the North Branch of
JAMES RIVER being the land I now live To have hold possess and enjoy said land and
premises and all appurtenances thereunto belonging to said WM. JOHNSON his assigns
and I said JOHN JOHNSON will warrt. and defend the same against the claim of all persons In Witness whereof I have hereunto set my hand and Seal this 29th day of May One
thousand seven hundred and Sixty eight
Sign'd Seal'd & deliver'd in presence of
    JOHN MARTIN,   The mark of $\mathcal{F}$
    HUDSON MARTIN   JOHN JOHNSON
  At Albemarle August Court 1768
This Indenture was proved by the Oath of JOHN MARTIN & HUDSON MARTIN witnesses
thereto & ordered to be recorded

pp.   THIS INDENTURE made the Tenth day of August in year of our Lord One thousand
11-   seven hundred and Sixty eight Between WILLIAM TERRELL LEWIS of St. Anns
13   Parish in Albemarle County of one part and SAMUEL DEDMAN of County of
    LOUISA of other part Witnesseth that said WILLIAM TERRELL LEWIS for sum of
Forty pounds Curt. money of Virginia to him in hand paid by said SAMUEL DEDMAN by
these presents doth bargain and sell unto said SAMUEL DEDMAN and to his heirs one
certain tract or parcel of land lying and being in the Parish and County aforesaid Two
hundred acres it being a tract of land granted to said WILLIAM TERRELL LEWIS by
Letter Patent bearing date at WILLIAMSBURG the fourth day of March 1756 it lying and
being in County of Albemarle on North Branch of MOORS CREEK and bounded beginning at a white Oak and running thence South sixty six degrees East eight poles to pointers North fifty six degrees East one hundred and fifty four poles to a white Oak, North
forty eight degrees East eighty two poles to pointers, North eight degrees West forty
poles to a Gum, North twenty three degrees West sixty six poles to a forked white Oak,
South sixty one degrees West fifty four poles to pointers, North five degrees East thirty
eight degrees West one hundred and twenty eight poles to pointers, South twenty nine
degrees West Thirty eight poles to pointers and South seven degrees East one hundred
and forty six poles to the beginning with the rights members and appurtenances and
all houses orchards profits and advantages whatsoever to said parcel of land belonging
To have and to hold said land with the appurtenances to the said SAMUEL DEDMAN his
heirs In Witness whereof said WILLIAM TERRELL LEWIS hath hereunto set his hand
and Seal the day and year first above written
Signed Sealed and Delivered in presence of
    (no witnesses shown)   WILLIAM TERRELL LEWIS
  Memorandum that full peaceable & Quiet possession & Seizen was this day given and
delivered by the within mentioned WILLIAM TERRELL LEWIS to the within mentioned
SAMUEL DEDMAN of the land and premises within mentioned In Witness whereof he
hath hereunto set his hand and affixed his Seal the day and year within written
Signed Sealed & Delivered in presence of
    (no witnesses shown)   WILLIAM TERRELL LEWIS

At Albemarle August Court 1768

This Indenture & memorandum was acknoweldged by WM. TERRELL LEWIS party thereto and ordered to be recorded; SARAH the Wife of said WM. TERRELL LEWIS appearing in Court voluntarily relinquished her right of Dower in the Estate conveyed by her said Husband

pp.
13-
15

THIS INDENTURE made the Eighth day of April in year of our Lord one thousand seven hundred and Sixty eight Between LEONARD BALLOWE SENR. of County of Albemarle and JANE BALLOWE his Wife of one part and WILLIAM COX of County of Albemarle of other part Witnesseth that for sum of three hundred pounds Virginia currency to said LEONARD BALLOWE in hand paid by said WILLIAM COX by these presents doth bargain and sell unto WILLIAM COX and his heirs the following tract of land containing in the whole Four hundred acres be the same more or less lying and being in County of Albemarle on North side of JAMES RIVER; one tract containing One hundred and fifty acres being the same said LEONARD BALLOWE got by his said Wife, JOHANNA BALLOWE, by a Deed made to the said JOHANNA by her Father, THOMAS GOOLSBEE, bearing date the Fifteenth day of July in year of our Lord One thousand seven hundred and Forty which Deed is recorded in GOOCHLAND COUNTY; Also one other tract of land containing fifty acres joining the former being the same said LEONARD BALLOWE purchased of THOMAS GOOLSBEE by a Deed record to him in Albemarle County from the said GOOLSBEE bearing date the Ninth day of October in the year of our Lord One thousand seven hundred and forty six and bounded Beginning at a Spanish Oak on the River bank, thence running on the River to a white Hickory, from thence runing cross the low grounds to the back line, a white Oak, thence down said line to a red Oak and from thence to the RIVER to the place it begun at; Also one other tract of land containing Two hundred acres granted to said LEONARD BALLOWE by Patent from WILLIAMSBURG bearing the third day of March one thousand seven hundred and Sixty, Together with all houses fences, water courses and all other appurtenances whatsoever belonging to have and to hold the aforesaid tract of land and every of their appurtenances unto WILLIAM COX his heirs and LEONARD BALLOWE and JANE BALLOWE his Wife their heirs shall warrant and forever defend In Witness whereof said LEONARD BALLOWE and JANE BALLOWE his Wife have hereunto set their hands and Seals the day and year before mentioned

Signed Sealed & Delivered in presence of us

NEILL CAMPBELL,   LEONARD his mark + BALLOWE
RICHD. FARRER, THOMAS UPTON   JANE her mark ⊘ BALLOWE

Memo. That on the Eighth day of April one thousand seven hundred and Sixty eight quiet and peaceable possession & seizen of the land and premises within mentioned was had and taken by said LEONARD BALLOWE and JANE BALLOWE his Wife and by them delivered to the within named WM. COX to the form and effect of the within written Indenture Signed & Delivered in presence of

NEILL CAMPBELL,   LEONARD his mark ✝ BALLOWE
RICHD. FARRAR, THOMAS UPTON   JANE her mark ◯ BALLOWE

April the 8th 1768 Then received of the within named WM. COX three hundred pounds Virginia currency it being in full for the consideration money in this Deed mentioned I say reced by me   LEONARD his mark ⊥ BALLOWE

Signed & Delivered in presence of us

NEILL CAMPBELL, RICHD. FARRAR,
THOMAS UPTON

At Albemarle April Court 1768
This Indenture memorandum and Receipt was proved by the Oaths of NEILL CAMPBELL
& THOMAS UPTON Witnesses thereto & at a Court held for the said County the XIIth day
of August 1768 was further proved by the Oath of RICHARD FARRAR witness thereto
and ordered to be recorded

pp.   THIS INDENTURE made the Eighth day of September in year of our Lord One
15-   thousand seven hundred & Sixty eight Between JOHN KINDKEAD & ELIZABETH
17   his Wife of County of Albemarle of one part and JAMES TURK of County of
        AUGUSTA of other part Witnesseth that for sum of Seventy five pounds current
money of Virginia to said JOHN KINDKEAD & ELIZABETH his Wife in hand paid by said
JAMES TURK at or before the sealing and delivery of these presents doth bargain and
sell unto JAMES TURK (in his actual possession now being by Virtue of a Bargain and
Sail to him thereof made by JOHN and ELIZABETH KINKEAD for one whole year and by
force of Statute for transferring uses into possession) and his heirs one certain tract or
parcel of land containing Two hundred acres being part of a larger tract of Four hundred acres made over to said JOHN KINDKEAD by his Father, DAVID, & WINIFRED his Wife
by Deeds of Lease & Release dated the twenty eighth & twenty ninth days of May one
thousand seven hundred and Sixty five lying and being in County of Albemarle and
bounded beginning at a Chesnut Oak on STOCKTONS BRANCH and thence South one hundred and sixty four poles to two read Oak bushes, thence East One hundred and twenty
four poles to pointers on the corner of a Hill between two branches, thence on a new
line & running through a field crossing STOCKTONS BRANCH North one hundred and
forty three poles to a white Oak sapling in a field, thence North forty one degrees West
Eleven poles to a Hicory sapling, thence North fifteen West sixteen poles to pointers on
the Old Line and with the same West one hundred and fifty eight poles to the first station and all houses orchards profits and appurtenances whatsoever to the same belonging and all Deeds evidences and writings touching the same To have and to hold
the land hereby conveyed and every of their appurtenances unto said JAMES TURK his
heirs free and clear of and from all Incumbrances whatsoever the Quit rents hereafter
to grow due and payable to our Sovereign Lord the King his heirs only excepted and
foreprized and said JOHN & ELIZABETH KINDKEAD and their heirs will warrant and defend by these presents In Witness whereof said JOHN & ELIZABETH KINDKEAD hath
hereunto set their hands and Seals the day and year first above written
Sealed & Delivered in presence of
        ROBERT LOGAN, JAMES LOGAN   JOHN KINDKEAD
        BETHEAH LOGAN, WILLIAM JONES   ELISBETH KINKEAD
    At a Court held for Albemarle County the IXth day of Septr. 1768
This Indenture was proved by the Oath of ROBT. LOGAN, BETHEAH LOGAN and JAMES
LOGAN Witnesses thereto and ordered to be recorded

pp.   THIS INDENTURE made the Eighth day of September in year of our Lord One
17-   thousand seven hundred & Sixty eight Between JOHN KINKEAD of County of
18   Albemarle of one part and JAMES TURK of County of AUGUSTA of other part Wit-
        nesseth that said JOHN KINKEAD for and in consideration of sum of Five Shil-
lings current money of Virginia to him in hand paid by said JAMES TURK at or before
the sealing and delivery of these presents doth bargain & sell unto JAMES TURK and to
his heirs one certain tract or parcel of land containing Two hundred acres being part
of a larger tract of Four hundred acres made over to said JOHN KINKEAD by his Father,
DAVID, & WINIFRED his Wife, by Deeds of Lease and Release dated the Twenty eighth and

twenty ninth days of May One thousand seven hundred and Sixty four and being in the County of Albemarle & bounded begining at a chesnut Oak on STOCKTONS BRANCH and thence South one hundred and Sixty four poles to two red Oak bushes thence East one hundred and ninety four poles to pointers on the Corner of a hill between two branches North one hundred and forty three poles at a red Oak sapling in a field, thence North forty one degrees West eleven poles to a Hiccory sapling, thence North fifteen degrees West sixteen poles to pointers in the old line and with the same West one hundred and fifty poles to the first station and all houses orchards profits and appurtenances whatsoever to the premises hereby granted belonging To have and to hold the lands hereby conveyed with the appurtenances unto said JAMES TURK his heirs from the day before the date hereof for the full term of one whole year paying therefore the rent of one Pepper Corn on Lady Day next if the same shall be lawfully demanded to the intent that by virtue of these presents and the Statute for transferring uses into possession said JAMES TURK may be in actual possession of the premises and be thereby enabled to take a release of the Reversion and Inheritance thereof to him and his heirs In Witness whereof said JOHN KINKEAD hath hereunto set his hand and Seal the say and year first above written
Sealed & delivered in presence of

ROBERT LOGAN, BETHIAH LOGAN,   JOHN KINKEAD
WILLIAM JONES, JAMES LOGAN   ELISBETH KINKEAD

At a Court held for Albemarle County the 9th day of September 1768
This Indenture was proved by the Oath of ROBT. LOGAN, BETHIAH LOGAN, & JAMES LOGAN, witnesses thereto, and ordered to be recorded

pp.   THIS INDENTURE made the Eighth day of September in year of our Lord One
18-   thousand seven hundred and Sixty eight Between BENJAMIN McCORD of County
19   of Albemarle of one part and JAMES KERR of aforesaid County of other part Witnesseth that BENJAMIN McCORD for sum of Thirty pounds of Virginia currency to him in hand paid at or before the sealing and delivery of these presents doth bargain and sell unto JAMES KERR his heirs a certain tract of land lying and being in Parish of Fredricksville in Albemarle County containing by estimation two hundred acres more or less bounded Beginning at a white Oak running thence North thirty five degrees, West two hundred poles to a Stake North fifty five degrees East one hundred and sixty poles to a Stake in the Muster Field Meadow South thirty two degrees East Two hundred poles to a white Oak in the Patent Line and along the same South fifty five degrees West one hundred and sixty poles to the first station Together with every of the appurtenances to the same belonging To have and to hold said tract or parcel of land unto said JAMES KERR his heirs and BENJAMIN McCORD his heirs shall warrant and forever defend by these presents. In Witness whereof said BENJAMIN McCORD hath hereunto set his hand and affixed his Seal the day above written
Sealed & delivered in the presence of

REUBEN LINDSAY,   BENJAMIN McCORD
CHRISTOPHER JOHNSON, THOMAS BALLARD

Received the day and year within written of JAMES KERR the sum of (blank) current money of Virginia the consideration money within mentioned for the within granted & sold according to the true intent and meaning of these presents   (no signatures)
Albemarle September Court 1768
This Indenture and receipt was acknowledged by BENJAMIN McCORD party thereto and ordered to be recorded. AGNES the Wife of said BENJAMIN personally appeared in Court & being first privily examined as the Law directs Voluntarily relinquished her right of Dower in the Estate conveyed by her said Husband

pp.   TO ALL TO WHOM these presents shall come, I JOHN FRY of County of Albemarle
19-   send Greeting. Whereas I have by Indenture bearing equal date with these
20   presents made over to HENRY FRY, JOHN SCOTT & JOHN NICHOLAS among other
Estate the following Negroe slaves (none named) the said HENRY FRY, JOHN SCOTT
& JOHN NICHOLAS lay claim to their proportionate part of being the Estate of WILLIAM
FRY deced NOW KNOW ye that I said JOHN FRY for myself my heirs do covenant and
agree to and with HENRY FRY, JOHN SCOTT & JOHN NICHOLAS that they nor their heirs
shall be barred from claiming their part of the said slaves anything in the said Inden-
ture contained to the contrary notwithstanding. In Witness whereof I have hereunto
set my hand and Seal the thirtieth day of August in year of our Lord One thousand
seven hundred and Sixty eight
Sealed & delivered in presence of
    RICHARD GILLIAM,   JOHN FRY
    MARY GILLIAM, BENJAMIN his mark ✝ WHITE
At Albemarle September Court 1768
This Deed was proved by the Oath of RICHARD GILLIAM, BENJAMIN WHITE & MARY
GILLIAM, Witnesses thereto, & ordered to be recorded

pp.   THIS INDENTURE made the thirteenth day of August One thousand seven hun-
20-   dred and Sixty eight Between JOHN FRY of County of Albemarle and SARAH his
22   Wife of one part and HENRY FRY, JOHN SCOTT of the same County and JOHN
NICHOLAS of County of BUCKINGHAM of other part. Whereas JOHN FRY stands
indebted to several persons in divers and many large sums of money by Bills of Exchange, Mortgage, Bonds and open accounts, and finding it impossible to discharge the
same without disposing of his Estate or the greatest part thereof is minded of giving
satisfaction to his several Creditors some of whom have signified that in case the said
JOHN FRY would make over his Estate to the said HENRY FRY, JOHN SCOTT & JOHN
NICHOLAS that they may have the disposing of the Estate and the profits thereof they
will wait some time for their Debts due from said JOHN FRY in consideration thereof
inasmuch as said HENRY FRY, JOHN SCOTT & JOHN NICHOLAS have severally undertaken
to manage and dispose of the Estate of JOHN FRY and of Five Shillings to him in hand
paid by said HENRY FRY, JOHN SCOTT & JOHN NICHOLAS said JOHN FRY and SARAH his
Wife by these presents do grant alien and confirm and make over to said HENRY FRY,
JOHN SCOTT & JOHN NICHOLAS all that tract or parcel of land containing One thousand
five hundred and Eighteen acres being part of the land whereon said JOHN FRY now
lives be the same more or less lying and being in County of Albemarle joining the land
of JOHN COLEs and the land of which JOSHUA FRY deced purchased of HUDSON at the
GREEN MOUNTAIN, Also all those several tracts or parcels of land lying and being in
County of Albemarle on or near a branch of HARDWARE RIVER containing by estima-
tion nine hundred acres more or less as appears by several Patents granted to the said
JOSHUA FRY & JOHN FRY, also the following Negroe slaves to wit Bob, Peter, Joe, Ned,
Quan, Dick, MIlford, Old Dick, Harry, Tom, Beck, Jenny, Annakey, Kate, Salley, Betty,
Judy, Sally, Pharaoh, Milly, Pat, Letty, Milford, Joshua, Sam, Fanny, Hannah, Anthony,
Lucy, Boson, Kate, Lucy, Rose, Adam, York, Nat, Abraham, and the Increase of the said
Female slaves, Also sixty head of cattle, one hundred hogs, forty sheep all marked with a
swallow fork in each ear and an underkeel in the right, one large gelding, one whole
gelding, one young bay Stone horse, one young bright bay Mare and Colt, one Sorrel
mare, one small black mare, one old black mare, one old bay mare one old white horse,
one bay Gelding all branded F R Y one black gelding and one bay gelding, one desk and
book case, Rifled Gun, two smooth bore guns, one Silver watch, one twenty three gallon

Still, six Feather beds and furniture, one old Bed and furniture, one riding Chair & harness, China, coffe and tea ware, two bedsteads, two dressing glasses, two iron pots, two frying pans, one grid Iron, two pine Chests, one Hogshead of Tobo. marked F R Y together with the Crop of Tobacco now growing upon the land and the reversions, remainders, rents issues & profits of all the lands slaves and other Estate above mentioned all houses outhouses woods ways and water courses to the same lands belonging To have and to hold the several tracts of land and premises, slaves and personal Estate together with the increase of the female slaves to HENRY FRY, JOHN SCOTT & JOHN NICHOLAS for the intent and purpose of raising money to pay off and discharge the Debts at present owing and due from said JOHN FRY and said HENRY FRY, JOHN SCOTT & JOHN NICHOLAS to pay the several Debts In Witness whereof the parties to these presents have hereunto set their hands and Seals the day and year first within written
Sealed & delivered in presence of

RICHARD GILLIAM,   JOHN FRY
BENJAMIN his mark + WHITE,   SARAH FRY
MARY GILLIAM

At Albemarle September Court 1768
This Indenture was proved by the Oath of RICHARD GILLIAM, BENJAMIN WHITE & MARY GILLIAM witnesses thereto & ordered to be recorded

pp. 22-23 THIS INDENTURE made this (blank) day of (blank) in year of our Lord Christ One thousand seven hundred and Sixty (blank) Between JOHN CLARK and ANN his Wife of County of (blank) of one part and WILLIAM TANDY of County of Albemarle of other part Witnesseth that said JOHN CLARK and ANN his Wife for sum of Three hundred pounds current money of Virginia to him in hand paid by WILLIAM TANDY by these presents doth bargain sell and confirm unto WILLIAM TANDY his heirs one certain tract or parcel of land situate in County of Albemarle containing Four hundred and Ten acres be the same more or less it being part of a larger tract of land taken up by JOHNATHAN CLARK, JOSEPH SMITH, EDWIN HICKMAN & THOS. GRAVES containing Three thousand two hundred and Seventy seven acres as by the Patent for the said land will more fully appear which said Four hundred and Ten acres more or less is bounded Begining at three Beaches standing on the North side of RIVANNA RIVER or North Fork of JAMES RIVER by LINCHES FORD, one of the Beaches marked H T and Corner to the land that THOMAS GRAVES sold to MEREWETHER running thence South eighty eight degrees East two hundred & thirty eight poles to three red Oak saplins standing on East side of a branch between two small Mountains in the line of the aforesaid GRAVES, also a corner to BENJAMIN CLARK's part of this land runing thence North twenty four Degrees West two hundred & twenty six poles to a white Oak on a branch, a corner to BENJAMIN CLARKs land, runing thence Thirty one degrees East forty four poles to a Hickory Grub by two small white Oaks in the head of a Valley, also a Corner to BEN CLARKs land runing thence North East two degrees West seventy two poles to a branch on the River a Corner to the Patent runing thence up the said RIVANNA or NORTH RIVER being the North Fork of JAMES RIVER according to its meanders to the begining together with all houses Orchards profits and hereditaments whatsoever to the same belonging To have and to hold said Four hundred and Ten acres of land more or less with the appurtenances unto WILLIAM TANDY his heirs and JOHN CLARK and ANN his Wife will warrant and forever defend by these presents In Witness whereof said JOHN CLARK & ANN his Wife hath hereunto set their hands and Seals the day and year first above written

Signed Seal'd & Delivered in presence of us
WM. DABNEY,   JOHN CLARK
WILLIAM GOOCH,, WM. his mark ✝ SMITH
Memorandum that on the day and year first above written Quiet possession & Seisen of
the land and premises within granted was had & taken by the within named JOHN
CLARK and by him delivered over to the within named WILLIAM TANDY to hold to him
his heirs forever according to the contents and true meaning of the within written
Indenture in Confirmation of which said JOHN CLARK hath hereunto set his hand
In presence of us WM. DABNEY,   JOHN CLARK
WM. GOOCH
Then received of Mr. WILLIAM TANDY the sum of Three hundred pounds current
money of Virginia it being the consideration money for the lands and premises men-
tioned , I say reced the same pr. me   JOHN CLARK
Witness WM. DABNEY, WILLIAM GOOCH
At a Court held for Albemarle County the XIth November MDCCLXVIII
This Indenture memorandum & receipt was proved by the Oath of WILLIAM SMITH &
the same having been before proved by two other witnesses was ordered to be recorded

p.   THIS INDENTURE made the Tenth day of November One thousand seven hundred
24   & Sixty Eight Between PETER DAVIE on behalf of JAMES & ROBERT DONALDS & CO.
Merchants in GLASGOW & NICHOLAS MATLOCK of Albemarle County Witnesseth
that said PETER DAVIE for sum of Fifty current money of Virginia to him in hand paid
by NICHOLAS MATLOCK by these presents doth bargain sell and confirm unto NICHOLAS
MATLOCK his heirs one certain tract or parcel of land in County of Albemarle on the
Long Branches of MOORES CREEK bounded begining at a Spanish Oak and runing South
One hundred and fifty poles to pointers, South Seventy one degrees West sixteen poles to
a white Oak, South ten degrees East seventy poles to a white Oak, South twenty four degrees West One hundred & eighty poles to pointers, North seventy three degrees West
two hundred & fifty eight poles to a white Oak and North forty more degrees East three
hundred & ninety two poles to the begining the same land purchased of JOHN HARGIS
with all the appurtenances thereunto belonging To have and to hold said land unto said
MATLOCK his heirs and said DAVIE for himself his heris doth covenant to warrant and
defend agains the claims of any person In Witness whereof said DAVIE doth hereunto
set his hand and Seal the day & year above written
Signed Seald & delivered in the presence of
JOHN MARTIN,   PETER DAVIE
WILLIAM HOPKINS, JOHN COLEMAN
Memorandum That on the Tenth day of November in the year of our Lord One thou-
sand seven hundred & sixty eight Livery & Seizen of the within land & premises was
made & done by PETER DAVIE to NICHOLAS MATLOCK according to Law
Teste JOHN MARTIN,   PETER DAVIE
WILLIAM HOPKINS, JOHN COLEMAN
At Albemarle November Court 1768
This Indenture & Memorandum was acknowledged by PETER DAVIE party thereto and
ordered to be recorded

Test TUCK: WOODSON Dy. Clk.

pp.   THIS INDENTURE made the Twenty first day of March in year of our Lord One
24-   thousand seven hundred & Sixty eight Between JOHN HOLLAND JUNR. of the
25   Parish of Saint James Northam and County of GOOCHLAND of one part and JOHN
BAKER of the same parte of the said Parish and County Witnesseth that said JOHN

BAKER for sum of Twenty pounds current money of Virginia to him in hand paid by
said JOHN HOLLAND JUNR. at or before the delivery of these presents doth bargain sell
and confirm unto JOHN HOLLAND and his heirs one certain tract or parcel of land lying
and being in County of Albemarle on both sides of the BYRD CREEK and bounded beginning at a small Pine on West side of the BYRD, SAMUEL DAVIS's Corner, thence new
lines North twenty degrees West two hundred and ten poles to a Pine, North fifty seven
degrees East One hundred & forty poles crossing two forks of said Creek to pointers,
South thirty five degrees East two hundred and six poles to pointers, South forty five
degrees West One hundred & forty seven poles to SAMUEL DAVIS's Corner pointers,
thence on DAVIS's line West Sixty poles crossing the Creek to the first station Together
with all houses gardens and all manner of appurtenances thereunto belonging To have
and to hold said Two hundred & Thirty acres of land be the same more or less with the
appurtenances unto said JOHN HOLLAND JUNR. his heirs and JOHN BAKER his heirs doth
warrant to be clear and free from all manner of Incumbrances whatsoever In Witness
whereof said JOHN BAKER hath hereunto set his hand and affixed his Seal the day and
year first above written
Signed Seald. & Delivered in presence of

    JAMES MOSLEY,   JOHN BAKER
    HENRY NASH, MARTHA HOLLAND JUNR.   SUSANAH her mark ✝ BAKER

Memorandum that on the day and year of the within Indenture Quiet & peaceable possession and Seizen of the land and premises within mentioned was had and taken by the
within named JOHN BAKER and by him given & delivered unto the within named JOHN
HOLLAND according to the true intent tenor and effect and meaning of the within
written Indenture   JOHN BAKER
                                        SUSANAH her mark ✝ BAKER

Received the day and year of the within Indenture of JOHN HOLLAND JUNR. the sum of
Twenty pounds current money of Virginia it being the full satisfaction for the within
sold land & premises, I say reced pr. me   JOHN BAKER
                                        SUSANAH her mark ✝ BAKER

At a Court held for Albemarle County the Xth day of November 1768
This Indenture memorandum & receipt was proved by the Oath of JAMES MOSLEY,
HENRY NASH and MARTHA HOLLAND JUNR. witnesses thereto & ordered to be recorded

pp.   THIS INDENTURE made this Twenty first day of March in year of our Lord One
25-   thousand seven hundred & Sixty eight between JOHN HOLLAND JUNR. of the
26   Parish of Saint James Northam and County of GOOCHLAND of one part and JOHN
         BAKER of the same part of the same Parish & County Witnesseth that said JOHN
BAKER for sum of Twenty pounds current money of Virginia in hand paid by said JOHN
HOLLAND JUNR. at or before the sealing and delivery of these presents doth bargain
and sell unto JOHN HOLLAND & to his heirs one certain tract of land lying and being in
County of Albemarle on the Branches of the GREAT BYRD CREEK left to me by my Father
Four hundred acres of land thus bounded Begining at pointers in his said line and
running thence a new line North sixty three West at eighty poles a branch sixty two
poles to pointers in TIMOTHY (   ) line & with his line South forty West at thirty two &
one hundred & forty poles (the lower right hand corner and lower part of this Deed blurred) a
red Oak the same course continued on ROBERT ADAMS line Sixty poles to pointers a new
line South seventy two West One hundred & forty four poles to pointers in THOMAS
HARBOURs line and with it South Forty West eighty two pole to a Pine the same Course
continued at fifty six poles a branch one hundred and forty six poles in all two hundred
and twenty six poles to a Chesnut Oak a new line North eighty four East five hundred &

eighty four poles to pointers in his own line and with his lines North twenty West
ninety three to a Pine & North fifty East crossing a branch one hundred & forty poles to
the first station Together with all houses orchards and all manner of appurtenances
thereto belonging To have and to hold said Four hundred acres of land be the same
more or less and every of their appurtenances unto said JOHN HOLLAND JUNR. his heirs
and JOHN BAKER his heirs doth warrant to be clear from all manner of Incumbrances
In Witness whereof said JOHN BAKER hath hereunto set his hand and affixed his Seal
the day and year first above written
Signed Seald. & Deliverd. in presents of
         JAMES MOSLEY,   JOHN BAKER
         HENRY NASH, MARTHA HOLLAND   SUSANAH her mark † BAKER
   Memorandum That on the day and year of the within Indenture Quiet & peaceable pos-
session and Seizen of the land & premises within mentioned was taken up by the within
named JOHN BAKER and by him given and delivered unto the within named JOHN HOL-
LAND JUNR. according to the true meaning tenor and effect of the within written
Indenture   JOHN BAKER
                                                 SUSANAH her mark † BAKER

   Received the day and year of the within Indenture of JOHN HOLLAND JUNR. the sum of
Twenty pounds current money of Virginia it being the full satisfaction for the within
sold land & premises I say reced pr. me   JOHN BAKER
                                                 SUSANAH her mark † BAKER
   At a Court held for Albemarle County the Xth day of November 1768
This Indenture memorandum & receipt was proved by the Oath of JAMES MOSLEY,
HENRY NASH and MARTHA HOLLAND witnesses thereto & ordered to be recorded

pp.   THIS INDENTURE made this second day of April in year of our Lord One thousand
27-   seven hundred & Sixty eight Between JAMES HILTON of County of Albemarle of
28   one part and RICHARD BENNETT of same County of other part Witnesseth that
         said JAMES HILTON for sum of Seventy five pounds of good & lawful money of
Virginia to him in hand paid bysaid RICHARD BENNETT before the sealing & delivery of
these presents doth bargain sell and confirm unto RICHARD BENNETT his assigns one
certain tract or parcel of land containing Three hundred acres lying & being in County
of Albemarle on both sides of CUNINGHAM CREEK bounded Begining at pointers near a
branch of the said Creek on the East side thereof thence North twenty five degrees East
ninety two poles crossing a branch to pointers, North sixty five degrees West twenty
four poles to pointers, thence North fifty degrees West one hundred poles crossing
CUNINGHAM CREEK to pointers, thence South sixty degrees West two hundred poles to
pointers South ninety poles to an Hickory, thence North eighty three degrees crossing
CUNINGHAM CREEK to a Poplar on INDIAN CAMP BRANCH, thence up the said Branch to
a Maple on the said branch in WILLIAM AMOSS's line, thence on his line to pointers,
thence new lines to first station containing Three hundred acres be the same more or
less Together with all manner of proffits thereof with the appurtenances unto the same
belonging To have and to hold said tract of land with the appurtenances unto the same
belonging unto RICHARD BENNETT his heirs and JAMES HILTON doth agree to and with
said RICHARD BENNETT he will warrant and forever defend against the claim of all persons clear from all Incumbrances and will make other Deeds necessary in the Law if
required within Twenty years from the date of these presents at the cost of him the said
RICHARD BENNETT In Witness whereof said JAMES HILTON hath hereunto set his hand &
affixed his Seal the day and year first above written

Signd. Seald. & Delivd. in the presence of
    WM. AMOSS,   JAMES HILTON
    WILLIAM his mark W BRADSHAW,   LUCY HILTON
    ROBT. his mark R HARDIE

Memorandum that on the day and date of the within written Deed full & peaceable possession of the land & premises with the appurtenances within mentioned was had & taken & by me the within named JAS. HILTON & by me given & delivered unto the within named RICHARD BENNETT according to the Tennor form & effect of the within written Deed In the presents of
    WM. AMOSS,   JAMES HILTON
    WM. his mark W BRADSHAW,   LUCY HILTON
    ROBT. his mark R HARDIE

At Albemarle November Court 1768
This Indenture & memorandum was proved by the Oath of WM. AMOSS, WM. BRADSHAW & ROBERT HARDIE witnesses thereto & ordered to be recorded

p.   THIS INDENTURE made this Eight day of November in year of the Reign of our
28   Sovereign Lord King George the Third by the grace of God of Grate Britain
          France and Ireland, King Defender of the faith &c. and in the year of our Lord One thousand seven hundred and Sixty eight Between SAMUEL STOCKTON of County of Albemarle of one part and THOMAS STOCKTON of the County aforesaid of other part Witnesseth that said SAMUEL STOCKTON for the sum of Five pounds current money of Virginia to him in hand paid at or before the sealing & delivery of these presents doth bargain sell and confirm unto said THOMAS STOCKTON his heirs all that Dividend tract or parcel of land containing Fifty acres lying and being in County of Albemarle on both sides of CAMPING CREEK and bounded Begining at a Pine, thence South Sixty two degrees East sixty eight poles to pointers, thence North Forty degrees East one hundred & thirty nine poles to pointers, thence North sixty two degrees West fifty six poles to a Pine surrounded by pointers, thence South forty five degrees West One hundred and thirty nine poles to the first station Together with all houses priviledges and commodities whatsoever to the same belonging To have and to hold said tract of land to said THOMAS STOCKTON his heirs and SAMUEL STOCKTON will warrant and forever defend In Witness whereof the said SAMUEL STOCKTON hath hereunto set his hand & fix his Seal the day & year first above written
Signd Seald & deliverd. in presents of
    (no witnesses shown)   SAMUEL STOCKTON

Memorandum that on the day and year within written full satisfaction & Seizen was had and taken of the land and premises within granted by the within named SAMUEL STOCKTON & by him delivered over unto the within named THOMAS STOCKTON to hold to him his heirs & according to the intent & true meaning of the within Indendure in presence of   SAMUEL STOCKTON

At Albemarle November Court 1768
This Indenture was acknowledged by SAMUEL STOCKTON party thereto & together with the memorandum thereon endorsed was ordered to be recorded. PRUDENCE the Wife of said SAML. personally appeared in Court & being first privily Examined as the Law directs voluntarily relinquished her right of Dower in the Estate conveyed by her said Husband

pp.   THIS INDENTURE made the Twenty second day of October in year of our Lord
29-   Christ Seventeen hundred & Sixty eight Betweeen BENJAMIN HARRISON of the
30   County of GOOCHLAND, Planter, & SARAH his Wife of one part & EDWARD RICE
       JUNR. of other part Witnesseth that BENJAMIN HARRISON & SARAH his Wife for
divers good causes and considerations them thereunto moving but more especially in
consideration of the sum of Five thousand pounds of Merchantable Tobo. to them in
hand paid at or before the ensealing & Delivery of these presents doth give sell & confirm unto said EDWARD RICE & to his heirs all that tract Seat or parcel of land of said
BENJAMIN HARRISON & SARAH his Wife lying & being in the Fork of the JAMES RIVER
& County of Albemarle & bounded Begining at a red Oak in JOHN COBBs line & runing
thence on COBBs line North thirty five degrees West One hundred & fifty six poles to a
Pine & South fifty degrees West Sixty eight poles to pointers in the said line, thence
new lines thence North forty five degrees West one hundred poles to a Pine, North sixty
eight degrees East three hundred and thirty four poles crossing four branches to pointers on EDWARD PIE CHAMBERLAINs line & on the same South Twenty eight degrees East
one hundred and forty eight poles to pointers and North sixty degrees East seventy
poles to a white Oak in the said line, thence a new line South sixty degrees East thirty
two poles crossing a branch to pointers in BENJAMIN & RICHARD COCK's line and on the
same South forty five degrees West two hundred & twenty two poles crossing two
branches to a white Oak saplin on the bank of the said Creek, thence up the same as it
meanders to the first station with all woods marshes low grounds and share of all mines
& Quarries as well discovered as not discovered within the bounds aforesaid and being
part of said Four hundred acres of land To have and to hold the said tract of land with
every of their appurtenances unto said EDWARD RICE his heirs and BENJAMIN HARRI-
SON & SARAH his Wife & their heirs shall warrant & for ever defend by these presents
In Witness whereof the parties to these presents their hands & Seals have Interchang-
ably sett and affixed the day & year above written
Signd Seald & Delivered in presence of
       EDWARD RICE,   BENJAMIN HARRISON
       CHAS. RICE, WM. RICE
 Memorandum that on the day & year within written full possession & seizen was had &
taken of the within granted lands & premises by the within named BENJAMIN HARRI-
SON & by him delivered unto the within named EDWARD RICE to hold to him the sd
EDWD. RICE his heirs &c. according to the contents of the within written Indenture
In the presence of EDWARD RICE   BENJAMIN HARRISON
       CHAS. RICE, WM. RICE
 October 22d Then received of EDWARD RICE the sum of Five thousand pounds of Tobo.
being the consideration in the within mentioned pr. me BENJAMIN HARRISON
 At Albemarle November Court 1768
This Indenture memorandum and receipt was acknowledged by BENJAMIN HARRISON
party thereto and ordered to be recorded

pp.   THIS INDENTURE made this Tenth day of November One thousand seven hundred
30-   and Sixty (blank) Between ROBERT THOMPSON of County of Albemarle and
31   Parish of Fredericksville of the one part and JOHN OGG of the Parish of Saint
       Thomas and County of ORANGE of other part Witnesseth that said ROBERT
THOMPSON for sum of fifteen pounds current money to him in hand paid by said JOHN
OGG at or before the ensealing and delivery of these presents do bargain sell and confirm unto said JOHN OGG his heirs a certain tract or parcel of land containing by supposition Sixty five acres more or less lying and being in Albemarle County on the head

branches of BUCK MOUNTAIN CREEK near the BLUE RIDGE of Mountains and bounded
Begining at a Corner Hickory in ROBERT THOMPSONs line running thence North twelve
degrees East seventy poles to a Chesnut red Oak, thence North twenty six degrees West
forty six poles to a red Oak, thence North fifty two degrees West twenty six poles to a
Chesnut red Oak, thence South seventy nine degrees West thirty two poles to a Chesnut
red Oak saplin, thence South fifty two degrees East fifty eight poles to a Chesnut red Oak
& Poplar in THOMPSONs line, thence on his line South sixty degrees East thirty two poles
to the beginning, Together with all houses orchards woods thereunto belonging To
have and to hold the said land with the appurtenances whatsoever to the same
belonging to him said JOHN OGG his heirs and ROBERT THOMPSON for himself and his
heirs shall warrant and forever defend by these presents In Witness whereof said
ROBERT THOMPSON hath hereunto set his hand & Seal the day & year above written
Signd Sealed & Deliverd in the presence of
     (no witnesses shown)   ROBERT THOMPSON
  Memorandum that Quiet & peaceable possesion and Seizen of the within mentioned
lands and premises was had & taken by the within named JOHN OGG of and from the
within named ROBERT THOMPSON on the day and year within written according to the
form and Effect of the within written Deed   ROBT. THOMPSON
  At Albemarle November Court 1768
This Indenture was acknowledged by ROBERT THOMPSON party thereto together with
the memorandum thereon endorsed was ordered to be recorded

PP.   THIS INDENTURE made the tenth day of November in year of our Lord One thou-
31-   sand seven hundred & Sixty Eight Between THOMAS MURRAY of County of Albe-
32   marle and Colony of Virginia of one part and ROBERT LOGAN of the County and
        Colony aforesaid of other part Witnesseth that said THOMAS MURRAY for sum of
Twenty four pounds current money of Virginia to him in hand paid by said ROBERT
LOGAN by these presents doth bargain sell and confirm unto ROBERT LOGAN his heirs
one certain tract or parcel of land lying & being in County of Albemarle on the Waters
of IVY CREEK and bounded Begining at a Hickory JOHN WOODS line running thence
South thirty five degrees East Sixty two poles to a Chesnut thence South thirty five degrees East to a white Oak, corner tree twenty two poles thence South seventy five degrees West twenty poles to a white Oak thence South seventy five degrees West eighteen
poles to a Hickory thence a Hickory Corner joining JOHN WOODS & WILLIAM LEWIS,
thence North sixty five degrees East eighty poles to a black Oak North fifty five degrees
East twenty two poles to a Hickory, thence North fifty five degrees East thrity one poles
to the beginning containing Thirty four acres be the same more or less being part of a
tract of land of two hundred acres granted by Deed to ALEXANDER MURRAY, Father of
the said THOMAS MURRAY, by THOMAS WRIGHT, with all houses orchards fences to the
same in any wise appertaining To have & to hold said Thirty four acres of land with
their appurtenances unto ROBERT LOGAN his heirs and THOMAS MURRAY doth covenant
with ROBERT LOGAN that said THOMAS MURRAY his heirs will forever warrant & defend
the above sold land unto said ROBERT LOGAN againSt all persons In Witness whereof the
said THOMAS MURRAY hath hereunto set his hand & Seal the day & year first above
written Signd. Seald. & Deliverd in presence of
     JAS. LOGAN,   THOMAS MURRAY
     JAMES BOWER
  Memorandum That on the Twenty forth day of June in the year of our Lord One thousand seven hundred and Sixty Eight Quiet & peaceable possession and seizen of the lands
and premises within mentioned was had & taken by the within named THOMAS MUR-

RAY & by him was delivered unto the within named ROBERT LOGAN and his heirs & assigns forever
Signed Sealed & Deliv'd in presence of
    (no witnesses shown)   THOMAS MORROW
  Then received of ROBERT LOGAN the sum of Twenty four pounds current money of Virginia being in full of the consideration money in this Deed mentioned
          I say reced by me   THOMAS MORROW
   At Albemarle November Court 1768
This Indenture Memorandum & receipt was acknowledged by THOMAS MORROW party thereto and ordered to be recorded

pp.   THIS INDENTURE made this Seventh day of November in the Eight year of the
32-   Reign of our Sovereign Lord George the Third by the grace of God of Great
33   Britain France & Ireland King defender of the faith &c. & in the year of our
        Lord Christ MDCCLXVIII Between GEORGE HOLLAND of GOOCHLAND COUNTY of one
part and JOHN SHEPPERD of the other part Witnesseth that said GEORGE HOLLAND for and in consideration of sum of Ten pounds Current money of Virga. to him in hand paid by JOHN SHEPPERD at and before the ensealing and delivery of these presents doth bargain and sell unto JOHN SHEPPERD his heirs all that tract or parcel of land containing One hundred acres lying & being in County of Albemarle on the Branches of the GREAT BIRD being part of a greater tract containing One thousand acres by Patent bearing date March 26th 1739 to THOMAS BANKS and conveyed by him to Majr. JOSEPH STEPHENS deced, and ROBERT FARISH as Executor of said STEPHENS is empowered to sell the said land to pay off debts and Legatees and the said FARISH has Impowered me the said GEORGE HOLLAND to convey the same to said JOHN SHEPPERD which said tract of land is bounded Beginning at a red Oak in his own line, thence crossing the BIRD CREEK to a Hickory, thence up the said Creek to pointers of Oaks on BANKS old line, thence on his line to a red Oak in the said line and so to the first station with all the appurtenances thereunto belonging and GEORGE HOLLAND for himself his Executors the above sold land to warrant & defend against the claim of any person whatsoever In Witness whereof said GEORGE HOLLAND hath hereunto sett his hand Seal the day & year first above written
Signed Seald & Deliverd in the presence of
    JAMES JOHNSON, JOHN WILLIAMS,   GEORGE HOLLAND
    WILLIAM HUMPHREY, JOSEPH HADEN
  Memorandum that on the day & year first within mentioned peaceable & Quiet possession and Seizen of the land & premises within granted was had taken by the within named GEORGE HOLLAND and by him delivered unto the within mentioned JOHN SHEPPERD according to the form and effect of the within Deed
In presence of JAMES JOHNSON,   GEO: HOLLAND
    JOHN WILLIAMS, WILLIAM HUMPHREY
Received the Seventh day of November MDCCLXVIII of JOHN SHEPPERD the sum of Ten pounds currt. money of Virginia being the consideration money within mentioned for the land and premises within granted and sold according to the purport and true intent and meaning of the within Deed I say reced p. me   GEO: HOLLAND
   At Albemarle November Court 1768
This Indenture memorandum & receipt was proved by the Oath of JAMES JOHNSON, WILLIAM HUMPHREY and JOSEPH HADEN witnesses thereto & ordered to be recorded

pp.   THIS INDENTURE made this second day of August in the eighth year of the Reign
33-   of our Sovereign Lord George the third by the grace of God of Great Britain,
34   France and Ireland King Defender of the faith &c. in the year of our Lord
       MDCCLXVIII between GEORGE HOLLAND of GOOCHLAND COUNTY of one part and
JOSEPH HADEN of Albemarle County of other part Witnesseth that said GEORGE HOLLAND
in consideration of sum of Five pounds current money of Virginia to him in hand paid
by said JOSEPH HADEN at and before the ensealing and delivery of these presents doth
bargain & sell unto JOSEPH HADEN & his heirs all that tract or parcell of land containing seventy acres lying & being in the County of Albemarle on the branches of the
GREAT BIRD being part of a greater tract containing One thousand acres by Patent
bearing date March 26th 1739 to THOMAS BANKS and conveyed by him to Majr. JOSEPH
STEPHENS deced and ROBT. FARISH as Executor of said STEPHENS is impowered to sell the
said land to pay off Debts and Legatees and said FARISH has impowered me said GEORGE
HOLLAND to convey the same to said JOSEPH HADEN which said tract of land is bounded
Beginning at a red Oak in THOMAS BAILEYs line and running a new line parting him
and JAMES JOHNSON S. 30 E. 280 poles to a white Oak near VENABLEs line, thence at his
line S. 66 W. 80 poles to pointers in VENABLEs line, from thence N. 14 W. 280 poles to the
Beginning and all the Estate, right, title & demand of him the said GEORGE HOLLAND his
heirs unto the premises To have and to hold to the said JOSEPH HADEN & his heirs free
and clear of all Incumbrances whatsoever and GEORGE HOLLAND will for ever warrant
& defend by these presents In Witness whereof I have hereunto set my hand & Seal the
day & year first above written
Signd Seald & Deliverd in presence of
    JOHN WILLIAMS,   GEORGE HOLLAND
    WM. HUMPHREY, JOHN his mark SHEPPERD,
    JAMES JOHNSON
  Memorandum that on the day & year first within mentioned peaceable & Quiet possession & Seizen of the land & premises within granted was had & taken by the within
named GEORGE HOLLAND & by him delivered unto the within named JOSEPH HADEN
according to the form & effect of the within Deed
In presence of JAMES JOHNSON,   GEO: HOLLAND
    JOHN his mark SHEPPERD,
    WM. HUMPHREY, JOHN WILLIAMS
  Received the second day of August MDCCLXVIII of JOSEPH HADEN the sum of Five
pounds current money of Virginia being the consideration money within mentioned
for the lands & premises within granted & sold according to purport & true meaning &
intent of the within Deed I say reced p me   GEO: HOLLAND
  At Albemarle November Court
  This Indenture memorandum & receipt was proved by the Oaths of JOHN WILLIAMS,
WILLIAM HUMPHREY & JAMES JOHNSON witnesses thereto and ordered to be recorded

pp.   THIS INDENTURE made this ninth day of November in the Eighth year of the
34-   Reign of our Sovereign Lord George the third by the grace of God of Great
35   Britain France & Ireland King defender of the faith &c. and in the year of our
       Lord Christ One thousand seven hundred & Sixty eight Between THOMAS BAILEY
of County of Albemarle of one part & JOSEPH HADEN of the same County of other part
Witnesseth that THOMAS BAILEY for sum of Ninety pounds current money of Virginia to
him the said THOMAS BAILEY in hand paid by these presents doth bargain and sell unto
JOSEPH HADEN his heirs one certain tract or parcel of land containing by estimation
Two hundred acres and is lying & being on the Branches of the GREAT BYRD called

BAILEYs CREEK and bounded Beginning at a red Oak in BANKS's Line running thence
on his line South Seventeen degrees East one hundred & fifty five poles to pointers in
VENABLEs line, thence on his line South sixty two degrees West ninety five poles to the
Creek, thence up the Creek as it meanders to a large white Oak upon the bank of the
Creek in BAILEYs Line, thence on his line South Seventy eight degrees West eighty one
poles to pointers in GOOCHes line thence on his line North twenty one and a half degrees West one hundred & seventy four poles to an Old Pine in LOWRYs line thence on
his line North seventy degrees East fifty poles to a forked Maypole North nineteen degrees West seventy three poles to a Pine in THOMASONs line thence along his line North
seventy six & a half degrees East ten poles to a red Oak Bush thence a new line South
fifty two & a half degrees East One hundred & ninety two poles to the beginning To have
and to hold the aforesaid Two hundred acres of land with the appurtenances unto
JOSEPH HADEN his heirs free and discharged of all Incumbrances and THOMAS BAILEY
the aforesaid land with the appurtenances will forever warrant & defend from any
person In Witness whereof said THOMAS BAILEY hath hereunto set his hand & Seal the
date above mentioned
Seald & Deliverd. in presents of
          JOHN WILLIAMS, JAMES JOHNSON,   THOMAS BAILEY
          JOHN his mark ‡ SHEPPERD
  Memorandum that Livery & Seisen of the lands & appurtenances within mentioned
were given to the within JOSEPH HADEN by the within named THOS. BAILEY this ninth
day of November One thousand seven hundred & sixty eight
Test   JOHN WILLIAMS,   THOMAS BAILEY
        JAMES JOHNSON, JOHN SHEPPERD
  Received of JOSEPH HADEN Ninety pounds current money being the consideration
within mentioned   THOMAS BAILEY
  At Albemarle November Court 1768
This Indenture memorandum & receipt was proved by the Oaths of JOHN WILLIAMS,
JAMES JOHNSON & JOHN SHEPPERD witnesses thereto & ordered to be recorded

pp.   TO ALL TO WHOM these presents shall come Greeting. Know ye that I ROBERT
36-   FARISH of CAROLINE COUNTY, Executor for the Estate of Majr. JOSEPH STEPHENS
37   deced pursuant to his Will for and in consideration of the sum of Forty eight
        pounds currt. money of Virginia to him in hand paid before the ensealing and
delivery of these presents doth bargain and sell unto JAMES JOHNSON of Albemarle
County and to his heirs four hundred being part of a larger tract lying and being in
the aforesaid County on SMITHS CREEK and bounded Beginning at a black Oak near the
Creek and running thence North sixty three degrees East One hundred poles to a Pine,
thence North forty three degrees West three hundred & eighty poles to a red Oak saplin
South fifty six and a half degrees West one hundred and thirty two poles to pointers of
Oak in THOMAS BAILEYs line, thence on his line South thirty degrees East One hundred
& seventy poles to a red Oak on BAILEYs Line the same course two hundred & sixty poles
to a white Oak in or near VENABLEs line, and North sixty six degrees East sixty poles to a
white Oak and North five degrees East sixty poles to the first station with all houses orchards & other appurtenances thereto belonging To have and to hold the said tract or
parcel of land according to the bounds aforesaid with there and every of their appurtenances unto said JAMES JOHNSON and his heirs and ROBT. FARISH Exr. for the Estate of
Majr. JOSEPH STEPHENS deced will warrant and defend the right & title of the said land
In Witness whereof I have hereunto set my hand & Seal this Seventeenth day of March
One thousand seven hundred and Sixty eight

Signd Seald & Deliverd in presence of
JOHN WILLIAMS,   ROBERT FARISH
JOHN his mark ⟂ SHEPPERD,
WILLIAM HUMPHREY, REUBIN his mark X CARDIN
   Memorandum that on the Seventeenth day of March One thousand seven hundred &
Sixty eight Quiet & peaceable possession was had & given with the Livery of Seizen of
the lands and premises within mentioned by the within named ROBT. FARISH, Exr. for
the Estate of Majr. JOSEPH STEPHENS deced, unto the within named JAMES JOHNSON
according to the true intent & meaning of the within Indenture as Witness my hand &
Seal in the presence of
JOHN WILLIAMS, WILLIAM HUMPHREY,   ROBERT FARISH
JOHN his mark ⟂ SHEPHERD,
REUBIN his mark X CARDIN
   Then received of JAMES JOHNSON Forty eight pounds Currt. money of Virginia in
satisfaction for the within lands & premises I say recd ROBERT FARISH
Test   JOHN WILLIAMS, WM. HUMPHREY,
        JOHN his mark ⟂ SHEPHERD, REUBIN his mark X CARDIN
   At Albemarle November Court 1768
This Indenture Memorandum & receipt were proved by the Oath of JOHN WILLIAMS,
JOHN SHEPHERD & WILLIAM HUMPHREY witnesses thereto & ordered to be recorded

pp.   THIS INDENTURE made this second day of June in year of our Lord One thousand
37-   seven hundred & Sixty eight Between WILLIAM DABNEY & JANE his Wife of
38   County of Albemarle of one part & WM. SHELTON of the said County of other part
        Witnesseth that said WM. DABNEY & JANE his Wife for the sum of Two hundred
pounds current money of Virginia to them in hand paid by said WM. SHELTON doth bargain and sell unto said WM. SHELTON & to his heirs one certain tract or parcel of land
lying on MECHAMS RIVER in County of Albemarle and is bounded Beginning at a red
Oak a Corner to WM. WALLACE & running thence new lines North thirty nine degrees
East two hundred & eighteen poles to pointers by the River, thence up the River according to its meanders sixty eight poles to pointers, thence crossing the River South thirty five degrees East two hundred & thirteen poles to a white Oak, South forty four degrees West two hundred & one poles to pointers, North sixty four degrees West two hundred poles to a Pine in WM. WALLACEs line and thence on his line North fourteen degrees East one hundred & sixteen poles crossing MECHAMS RIVER to the first station To
have and to hold the aforesaid tract of land and the apurtenances unto said WM. SHEL-
TON & to his heirs and WM. DABNEY and JANE his Wife & their heirs will warrant and
forever defend the aforesd. lands unto sd WM. SHELTON and to his heirs In Witness
whereof said WM. DABNEY & JANE his Wife hath hereunto set their hands & affixed
their Seals the day & year first above written
Signd Seald & Deliverd in the presence of
THOMAS GRUBBS   WM. DABNEY
ELIZABETH JONES, CHRISTOPHER HARRIS,
ROBERT HARRIS, TYRE HARRIS
   Memorandum that on the second day of June One thousand seven hundred & Sixty
eight Quiet & peaceable possession and Seizen of the lands within mentioned was had &
taken by WM. DABNEY and JANE his Wife and by them was delivered to WM. SHELTON
according to the tenor & effect of the within written Deed
In the presence of us THOMAS GRUBBS,   WM. DABNEY
ELIZABETH JONES, CHRISTOPHER HARRIS,
ROBERT HARRIS, TYRE HARRIS

Then received of WM. SHELTON the sum of Two hundred pounds current money of Virginia which is in full the considertion money in the Deed mentioned
    THOMAS GRUBBS,   reced by me   WM. DABNEY
    ELIZABETH JONES, CHRISTOPHER HARRIS,
    ROBERT HARRIS, TYRE HARRIS
At Albemarle November Court 1768
This Indenture memorandum & receipt was proved by the Oath of THOS. GRUBBS, ROBT. HARRIS & TYRE HARRIS witnesses thereto & ordered to be recorded

pp.   THIS INDENTURE made this tenth day of November in year of our Lord One thou-
38-   sand seven hundred & sixty eight Between JAMES McNEELY of Albemarle County
39   and Parish of Fredricksville of one part and WILLIAM McNEELY of AMHERST
    COUNTY and Amherst Parish of other part Witnesseth that said JAMES McNEELY
for sum of Twenty pounds current money of Virginia to him in hand paid by said WIL-LIAM McNEELY by these presents doth bargain and sell unto WILLIAM McNEELY his heirs one certain tract of land containing Ninety four acres lying in the County of Albemarle on both side of MEACHUMS RIVER being part of a tract formerly granted to ROBERT McNEELY and now the property of JAMES McNEELY thus bounded Beginning at WILLIAM WOODS Corner pointers thence running North thirty six degrees West at sixty eight MEACHEMS RIVER in all eighty two poles to pointers on both side of the RIDGE ROAD to BEAVER CREEK, thence a new line and up BEAVER CREEK, RIDGE ROAD & by the meanders thereof South forty six degrees West two hundred & six poles to pointers on South side of said Road, North fifty five degrees East forty six poles to a Pine, South sixty five degrees East fifty four poles to a Pine on the North of MEACHEMS RUN thence down & across the same in a streight line East eighty poles to a Hiccory Saplin, North fifty degrees East sixty eight poles to pointers, North thirty degrees West thirty nine poles to pointers & North twenty five degrees East thirty poles to the first station & now in the possession of said JAMES McNEELY To have and to hold the said land & premises and the appurtenances unto said WILLIAM McNEELY his heirs and JAMES McNEELY & his heirs will warrant & forever defend by these presents In Witness whereof the said JAMES McNEELY doth hereunto set his hand & Seal
Seald & Delivered in presence of
    JAMES WOODS,   JAMES McNEELY
    ADAM WALLACE, MICHAEL McNEELY
Received this the tenth day of November One thousand seven hundred & Sixty eight the within consideration money in full
Test SAMUEL WOODS,   JAMES McNEELY
    ADAM WALLACE, MICHAEL McNEELY
At Albemarle November Court 1768
This Indenture was acknowledged by JAMES McNEELY party thereto with the receipt thereon endorsed was ordered to be recorded

pp.   THIS INDENTURE made this sixth day of July in year of our Lord One thousand
39-   seven hundred & Sixty eight Between DAVID NOWLIN of ye Parish of St. Anne
40   County of Albemarle Colony & Dominion of Virginia, Planter, & MARY his Wife
    of one part and WILLIAM BURRUSS of Parish & County aforesaid, Overseer, of
the other part Witnesseth that for sum of Thirty pounds current money to him the said DAVID NOWLIN in hand paid by the sd BURRUS before the sealing & delivery of these presents doth bargain and sell unto said BURRUS his heirs a certain tract or parcel of land lying and being at the head of TAYLORS CREEK & LYNCHES in Albemarle being part

of a tract by Letters Patent to CHARLES WINGFIELD as by his Patent may more fully appear Beginning on a deviding line at a pair of Barrs and running thence North new lines South West to a Hiccory, thence to the old line, thence a South East Course upon the old line, thence North to the place of beginning containing Ninety nine acres be the same more or less Together with all houses orchards & appurtenances thereunto belonging and DAVID NOWLIN will warrant & forever defend the same unto sd BURRUS his heirs In Witness whereof sd DAVID NOWLIN & MARY his Wife hath to these presents set their hands & Seals the day & year first written
Signed Sealed & Delivered in the presence of

CLAUDIUS BUSTER,   DAVID NOWLIN
CHAS. MARTIN, PETER GILLUM   MARY her mark ⚔ NOWLIN

Memorandum that the day & year within mentioned peaceable & Quiet possession of the within tract of land with the appurtenances thereunto belonging was had by DAVID NOWLIN & MARY his Wife & by them delivered to within BURRUS to be by him his heirs forever enjoyed according to the within written Deed
Signed Sealed & Delivered in the presence of

CLAUDIUS BUSTER,   DAVID NOWLIN
CHAS. MARTIN, PETER GILLUM

Reced this 6th day of July in the year of our Lord One thousand seven hundred & Sixty eight the sum of Thirty pounds current money being in full consideration for the within tract of land p me   DAVID NOWLIN
Test   CLAUDIUS BUSTER,
CHAS. MARTIN, PETER GILLUM
At Albemarle November Court 1768
This Indenture memorandum & receipt were proved by the Oath of CLAUDIUS BUSTER, CHAS. MARTIN & PETER GILLUM witnesses thereto & ordered to be recorded

pp.   THIS INDENTURE made this Eighth day of October in the Eighth year of the
40-   Reign of our Sovereign Lord George the third by the grace of God of Great
41   Britain, Frances & Ireland King Defender of the faith &c. & in the year of our
         Lord MDCCLXVIII between WILLIAM & JAMES HOPKINS of Parish of St. Anns in
County of Albemarle of one part and WILLIAM ASHLEY of the same Parish & County of other part Witnesseth that WILLIAM HOPKINS & JAMES HOPKINS for sum of Thirty two pounds current money of Virginia to them in hand paid by WILLIAM ASHLEY at and before the Ensealing and delivery of these presents doth bargain & sell unto said WILLIAM ASHLEY & to his heirs all that tract or parcel of land containing Two hundred & fourteen acres lying & being in Albemarle County which by the Last Will & Testament of ARTHUR HOPKINS deced, their Father, they the said WILLIAM & JAMES HOPKINS were appointed & impowered as Trustees to sell the remainder of a tract of land containing One thousand seven hundred & fifty acres commonly called the DRY BRANCH TRACT and said WILLIAM & JAMES HOPKINS by virtue of said Will and in pursuance of said Trust, & in consideration of the above sum have bargained & sold the above quantity of land which is bounded Beginning at a large Pine in the line of the said ARTHUR HOPKINS deced which was made a corner & running thence a new line North 50 East ninety four poles to two corner red Oaks, thence another new line North twenty three West two hundred & sixty poles to a Pine at the head of a Branch, then another new line South sixty four West One hundred & sixty poles to a Corner white Oak in the said HOPKINS old line, then along the said Old Line South thirty seven East Two hundred & eighty six poles to the beginning & all the Estate, right, property claim & demand whatsoever of them the said WILLIAM & JAMES HOPKINS their heirs unto the premises To have and to

hold to the said WILLIAM ASHLEY his heirs and WILLIAM & JAMES HOPKINS their heirs
will forever warrant & defend by these present In Witness whereof the parties to these
presents their hands and Seals Interchangeably have set the day & year first above
written Signed Sealed & Delivered in presence of

   BENNETT HENDERSON,   WILLIAM HOPKINS
   HENRY MARTIN, SOLOMON BRYANT   JAMES HOPKINS

Memorandum that on the day & year within written peaceable & Quiet possession with
livery & seizen of the land and premises within granted was had & taken by WILLIAM &
JAMES HOPKINGS delivered unto WILLIAM ASHLEY according to the true sence form &
effect of the within Deed   WILLIAM HOPKINS
                  JAS. HOPKINS

Received the day & year within written the sum of Thirty two pounds Currt. money of
Virginia being the consideration money within mentioned
                  WILLIAM HOPKINS
                  JAS. HOPKINS

 At Albemarle November Court 1768
This Indenture memorandum & Receipt was acknowledged by WM. & JAMES HOPKINS
parties thereto & ordered to be recorded

p.   THIS INDENTURE made this Thirteenth day of October in year of our Lord One
41   thousand seven hundred & Sixty eight Between ROBT. MILLER of County of Albe-
    marle of one part and RICHARD WOODS of said County of other part Witnesseth
that said ROBT. MILLER for Twenty two pounds current money of Virginia by these presents doth bargain and sell unto RICHARD WOODS his heirs two lotts containing half an
acre each in a certain Town called CHARLOTTESVILLE lately laid of in the County aforesaid which lotts is marked in the plan of the said Town No. 37 & 38 To have and to hold
the said Lotts together with the previledges & appurtenances thereunto belonging unto
RICHARD WOODS his heirs and said ROBT. MILLER for himself his heirs warrant said
lotts to RICHARD WOODS In Witness whereof I have hereunto set my hand & Seal the day
& year above written
Signed Sealed & Delivered in the presence of
   RICHARD TINSLEY,   ROBERT MILLER
   SAML. BOYD, DANL. SMITH
   ANDW. WALLACE

 Memo. That full possession & seizen was had & taken of the within Lotts by (blank) &
by him delivered to within RICHD. WOODS according to the within Indenture
           (no signatures)
 At Albemarle November Court 1768
This Indenture was acknowledged by ROBERT MILLER party thereto & ordered to be
recorded

p.   THIS INDENTURE made the Fifteenth day of November in year of our Lord One
42   thousand seven hundred & Sixty eight Between RICHARD WOODS of Parish of
    Saint Anne in County of Albemarle of one part and JAMES REID of the Parish &
County of AMHERST of other part Witnesseth that said RICHARD WOODS for sum of five
pounds current money by these presents doth bargain & sell unto JAMES REID & to his
heirs a Lott marked No. 47 lying & being in CHARLOTTSVILLE, a Town lately laid off in
County of Albemarle which said lott is also bounded by GEORGE DUDLEY & SAMUEL BOYD
together with all appurtenances thereunto belonging To have and to hold the aforesaid
Lott with its appurtenances unto said JAMES REID his heirs and RICHARD WOODS for

himself his heirs will warrant and defend the said lott unto JAMES REID against the
claims of every person whatsoever In Witness whereof I have hereunto set my hand &
Seal the day & year first above written
Signed Sealed & Delivered in presence of
      (no witnesses shown)   RICHARD WOODS
  At Albemarle November Court 1768
This Indenture was acknowledged by RICHARD WOODS party thereto & ordered to be
recorded

pp.   THIS INDENTURE made this XVth day of November in year of our Lord One thou-
42-   sand seven hundred & Sixty eight Between JOHN HARGISS & PENELOPE his Wife
43   of County of Albemarle & Parish of Saint Anns of one part and JAMES & ROBERT
       DONALDS of other part Witnesseth that JOHN HARGISS & PENELOPE his Wife for
and in consideration of Fifty pounds current money of Virginia to him in hand paid by
JAMES & ROBT. DONALDS by these presents doth bargain and sell unto said JAMES &
ROBT. DONALDS his heirs one certain tract or parcel of land lying & being in the County
aforesaid on the Long Branch of MOORES CREEK containing Three hundred acres more
or less granted by Patent to ROBERT EDGES bearing date the thirteenth day of September
MDCCLIII and conveyed by Deed to MICHAEL JONES & by said JONES conveyed the same to
JOHN HARGIS & PENELOPE his Wife by Deed now remaining of record in the Clerks
Office of County Court of Albemarle bounded Beginning at a Spanish Oak & running
thence South one hundred & fifty poles to pointers, South seventy one degrees West sixteen poles to a white Oak, South ten degrees East Seventy poles to a white Oak & North
fifty nine degrees East three hundred & ninety two poles to the beginning with all
woods feedings orchards houses and appurtenances whatsoever to the said tract of land
belonging and JAMES HARGIS & PENELOPE his Wife their heirs will warrant & forever
defend by these presents In Witness whereof we have hereunto set our hands & Seals
the day & year above written
Signed Sealed and Delivered in the presence of
      (no witnesses shown)   JOHN his mark _John_ HARGIS
                                PENELOPE her mark / HARGIS
  At Albemarle November Court 1768
This Indenture was acknowledged by JOHN HARGIS & PENELOPE his Wife parties thereto
& ord.d to be recorded, she being first privily Examined as the Law directs voluntarily
relinquished her right of Dower in the Estate conveyed by her said Husband

pp.   THIS INDENTURE made the Eleventh day of November in year of our Lord One
43-   thousand seven hundred and Sixty Eight Between JAMES WOODS & LUCY his Wife
44   of Albemarle County of one part and BEN BROWN of HANOVER COUNTY of other
       part Witnesseth that said JAMES WOODS & LUCY his Wife in consideration of One
hundred pounds current money of Virginia to them in hand paid by said BEN BROWN by
these presents doth bargain & sell unto said BEN BROWN & to his heirs one certain tract
or parcel of land & Plantation by Estimation three hundred & fifty two acres be the
same more or less lying & being in County aforesaid at the foot of the RAGED MOUNTAIN
and on both sides DOYLE RIVER & bounded by the lines of the land of said BEN BROWN,
BINAJAH BROWN, BEZELIA BROWN & some others according to a Deed from BEN BROWN
deced unto the said JAMES WOODS Wife LUCY & ARCHIBALD EAGLE To have and to hold
the aforesaid Three hundred & fifty acres of land with the appurtenances thereto belonging all houses privilidges & appurtenances whatsoever In Witness whereof we
have hereunto set our hands & Seals the day & year first above written

Seald Signd & Deliverd in presence of
     BARTLETT ELLIS,   JAMES WOODS
     JOHN EPPERSON, JOHN CAVE   LUCY WOODS

Memorandum that upon the Eleventh day of November 1768 that full & peaceable possession & Seizen was given and delivered by JAMES WOODS & LUCY his Wife of the within Dividend of land with all the appurtenances whatsoever belonging unto BEN BROWN for and unto his use according to the true purport & meaning of the within Indenture Seald, Signd & Deliverd in presence of
     BARTLETT ELLIS,   JAMES WOODS
     JOHN CAVE, JOHN EPPERSON   LUCY WOODS

At Albemarle November Court 1768
This Indenture & Memorandum was proved by the Oath of BARTLETT ELLIS, JOHN EPPERSON & JOHN CAVE, witnesses thereto, & ordered to be recorded

pp.   THIS INDENTURE made this Twelth day of November One thousand seven hun-
44-   dred & Sixty eight Between JOHN HARGIS & PENOLEPE his Wife of one part of the
45   County of Albemarle and DAVID ROSS of County of GOOCHLAND of other part Witnesseth that said JOHN HARGIS & PENOLEPE his Wife for sum of Thirty pounds to them in hand paid by said DAVID ROSS before sealing and delivery of these presents do bargain sell & confirm unto DAVID ROSS his heirs a certain tract or parcel of land lying & being in County of Albemarle on the North side of a South Branch of MOORES CREEK commonly known by the name of EDGES CREEK containing Three hundred & Twenty sevin acres bounded Begining at a Spanish Oak MICHELL JONES's line on the North side of EDGES CREEK, then on said JONES's line North seventy five degrees West two hundred & thirty eight poles to a white Oak, then new lines South twelve degrees West One hundred & twenty eight poles to pointers, then South fifty degrees East thirty two poles to pointers, then South six degrees East sixty poles to a red Oak saplin, then South forty six degrees East fifty six poles to a Chesnut Oak, then South fourteen degrees East thirty nine poles to pointers, then South seven degrees West forty five poles to a Chesnut Oak, thence South sixty degrees East fifty six poles to a Chesnut tree, then North sixty degrees East thirty four poles to a Chesnut tree Seventeen degrees East one hundred and thirty poles to station To have and to hold said tract of land & premises with the appurtenances to said DAVID ROSS his heirs &c. and said HARGIS & PENELOPE his Wife shall warrant & for ever defend by these presents

N.B. the land herein contained was granted to the said JOHN HARGISS by Letter Patent bearing date the 20th July 1768 as may more fully appear by referring thereto
Signd Seald & delivered in the presence of
    (no witnesses shown)   JOHN HARGISS
                                PENELOPE HARGISS

Received 12th November 1768 Thirty pounds in full of the consideration money within mentioned from the said DAVID ROSS   JOHN HARGISS

Memorandum That on the day & year within mentioned Quiet & peaceable possession of the within mentioned land & premises was had & taken by JOHN HARGISS & by him delivered to DAVID ROSS according to the true effect & meaning of these presents
                                JOHN HARGISS

At Albemarle November Court 1768
This Indenture memorandum & receipt was acknowledged by JOHN HARGISS & PENELOPE his Wife parties thereto & ordered to be recorded, she being first privily Examined as the Law directs voluntarily relinquished her right of Dower in the Estate conveyed by her Husband

pp.   THIS INDENTURE made the (blank) day of (blank) in year of our Lord One thou-
46-   sand seven hundred & Sixty eight Between SAMUEL DAVIDSON of Albemarle
47   County & Colony of Virginia of one part and JOSIAS HUNTSMAN of County &
        Colony aforesaid of other part Witnesseth that SAMUEL DAVIDSON for sum of
Forty five pounds current money of Virginia to him in hand paid by JOSIAS HUNTSMAN
doth bargain sell & confirm unto said JOSIAS HUNTSMAN & to his heirs one certain tract
or parcel of land containing Two hundred & thirty eight acres lying & being in County
of Albemarle & on the Branches of STONEY RUN and bounded Beginning at a white Oak
North thirty one degrees East eighty eight poles to a Pine, new lines North forty seven
degrees West eighty four poles to a red Oak, North fifty five degrees West one hundred &
fifty four poles to pointers, North eighty three degrees West one hundred & Eleven
poles to the Old Line, with it South thirty degrees West eighty eight poles to a red Oak,
South sixty degrees East three hundred poles to the first station, the same being a track
which formerly belonged to JOEL TERRELL and all houses orchards fences to the same
belonging and SAMUEL DAVIDSON & his heirs will for ever warrant & defend the above
sold land & premises unto said JOSIAS HUNTSMAN In Witness whereof said SAMUEL
DAVIDSON hath hereunto set his hand & afixed his Seal the day and year first above
written Signed Sealed & Delivered in presence of
      ABRAHAM MUSICK,   SAML. DAVIDSON
      NIEL McCLEASTER, WILLIAM HUNTSMAN
  Memorandum that on the day of the year of our Lord One thousand seven hundred &
sixty eight Quiet & peaceable possession & seizen of the lands within mentioned was had
& taken by SAMUEL DAVIDSON and by him delivered to JOSIAS HUNTSMAN and his heirs
& assigns forever
In presence of ABRAHAM MUSICK,   SAML. DAVIDSON
      NEIL McCLEASTER, WILLIAM HUNTSMAN
  Then reced of JOSIAS HUNTSMAN the sum of Forty five pounds current money of Vir-
ginia being in full for the consideration in this Deed mentioned
      ABRAHAM MUSICK   I say reced by me SAML. DAVIDSON
      NEIL McCLESTER, WILLIAM HUNSTMAN
  At Albemarle January Court 1769
This Indenture memorandum & receipt was proved by the Oath of ABRAHAM MUSICK,
NEILL McGLESTER & WILLIAM HUNTSMAN witnesses thereto and ordered to be recorded

pp.   THIS INDENTURE made the Twentyeth day of September in year of our Lord One
47-   thousand seven hundred & Sixty eight Between BENJAMIN WHEELER of Albe-
48   marle County of one part and BENJAMIN BURGER of the same County of other
        part Witnesseth that BENJAMIN WHEELER in consideration of the sum of Twenty
pounds current money to him the sd BENJAMIN WHEELER in hand paid by him the sd
BENJAMIN BURGER before the sealing & delivery hereof doth bargain and sell unto
BENJAMIN BURGER and his heirs one certain tract of land lying in Albemarle County
containing three hundred acres on the West Branches of MEACHUMS CREEK on North
side of RIVANNA and bounded begining at a Pine ROBERT ADAMS's Corner, running
thence new lines South sixty five degrees West one hundred & eighty two poles to a
Pine, North twenty five degrees West One hundred & ninety poles to a Pine, North sixty
five degrees East three hundred & twenty four poles to a white Oak and thence on
ROBERT ADAMS's line South twelve degrees West two hundred & thirty eight poles to the
first station with all woods marshes low grounds meadows and his due share of all veins
mines & Quarries as well discovered as not discovered within the bounds aforesaid and
being part of said quantity of three hundred acres of land To have & to hold said tract of

land and every of their appurtenances unto said BENJAMIN BURGER & his heirs In Witness I have hereunto set my hand & Seal

Signed Seald in presence of MICAJAH WHEELER,   BENJAMIN his mark /ß WHEELER
    BENJA. DOD WHEELER, BARTLETT BENNETT

Memorandum that on the day of date of within Indenture full & peaceable possession & Seizen was had & by BENJAMIN WHEELER delivered to BENJAMIN BURGER according to the intent and purpose of the within Indenture

Test MICAJAH WHEELER   BENJAMIN his mark /ß WHEELER
    BENJA. DOD WHEELER, BARTLETT BENNETT

Received on the day of the date of the within Indenture twenty pounds current money of Virginia it being the consideration money within mentioned I say reced p. me

Test MICAJAH WHEELER   BENJAMIN his mark /ß WHEELER

At Albemarle January Court 1769
This Indenture memorandum & receipt was proved by the Oath of MICAJAH WHEELER, BENJAMIN DOD WHEELER & BARTLETT BENNETT witnesses thereto and ordered to be recorded

pp.   Albemarle Sct.
48-   GEORGE the third by the grace of God of Great Britain France & Ireland, King de-
49   fender of the faith &c. to SAMUEL DUVALL & DANIEL PRICE. Whereas RICHARD
        ADAMS of County of HENERICO by his Indenture of Feoffment bearing date the
third day of March One thousand seven hundred & sixty two I have conveyed the fee
simple Estate of Eight hundred acres of land lying and being in County of Albemarle
unto ROBERT LEWIS and Whereas ELIZABETH the Wife of said RICHARD cannot
conveniently travel to our County Court of Albemarle to make acknowledgment of the
said conveyance Therefore we give unto you or any two of you power to receive the
acknowledgment which the said ELIZABETH shall be willing to make before you and
when you have received her acknowledgment & examined her as aaforesaid that you
distinctly & openly certify our Justices thereof in our said County Court under your
Seals sending then there the said Indenture & this Writ Witness JOHN NICHOLAS Clk. of
our said Court the XXIVth day of November in the ninth year of our Reign
                                                    TUCK: WOODSON Dy. Clk

    Henerico Sct
Pursuant to the within order of the worshipfull Court of Albemarle we have Examined
ELIZABETH ADDAMS Wife of RICHARD ADDAMS privily and apart from the said RICHARD
and she the said ELIZABETH freely & willingly acknowledged her wright and Dower to
the said land Given under our hands & Seals this 5th day of January One thousand
seven hundred & Sixty nine   SAML. DUVALL
                                                    DANIEL PRICE JUNR.

    At Albemarle February Court 1769
This acknowledgment was returned to Court and ordered to be recorded

pp.   THIS INDENTURE made this 12th day of June in year of our Lord One thousand
49-   seven hundred & Sixty eight Between THOMAS POWERS of GOOCHLAND COUNTY
50   of one part and ROBERT MIDDLETON of Albemarle County of other part Witness-
        seth that said THOMAS POWERS for sum of Nineteen pounds current money of
Virginia to him in hand paid by said ROBERT MIDDLETON at & before the Insealing &
delivery of these presents doth bargain and sell unto ROBERT MIDDLETON his heirs all
that parcel of land containing Three hundred acres lying & being in County of Albemarle lying on the hed branches between RIVANNA RIVER & MEACHUMS CREEK and

bounded Beginning at a red Oak near ADAMS's Road & running thence new lines South
fifty four degrees East ninety eight poles to a Pine, then South five degrees East ninety
two poles to a Pine on JAMES ADDAMS's line, thence with his line South forty seven degrees East sixty eight poles to pointers, then new lines South twenty nine degrees West
one hundred & twenty poles to a red Oak, then due West one hundred & ten poles to
pointers, then North ten degrees West one hundred and eighty poles to pointers, then
North fifty two degrees East two hundred & two poles to the last station To have and to
hold to said ROBERT MIDDLETON and his heirs free and clear of all Incumbrances whatsoever and THOMAS POWERS & his heirs will forever warrant & defend by these presents In Witness whereof the parties to these presents their hands & Seals Interchangeably have set the day & year first above written
Signd Seald & Deliverd in presents of
          ROBERT SHARP JUNR.,   THOMAS POWERS
          EDITH SHARP, ROBERT his mark R SHARP SENR.
  Memorandum that on the day & year within mentioned peaceable possession of within
land with its appurtenances was sold by THOMAS POWERS to ROBERT MIDDLETON according to the true intent & meaning of these presents
          ROBERT SHARP JUNR.,   THOMAS POWERS
          EDITH SHARP, ROBERT his mark R SHARP SENR.
  Received of ROBERT MIDDLETON nineteen pounds being full satisfaction for the within
land & premises with the appurtenances Reced p me the day & year within written
          ROBERT SHARP JUNR.   THOMAS POWERS
          EDITH SHARP, ROBERT his mark R SHARP SENR.
  At Albemarle February Court 1769
This Indenture memorandum & receipt was proved by the Oath of ROBT. SHARP JUNR.
EDITH SHARP, & ROBT. SHARP SENR. witnesses thereto & ordered to be recorded

pp.   THIS INDENTURE made the ninth day of February in year of our Lord Christ One
50-   thousand seven hundred & Sixty nine Between ROBERT LEWIS of Parish & Coun-
51   ty of Albemarle of one part and SAMUEL MARTIN, Mercht., in WHITEHAVEN
        Gent. of other part Witnesseth that said ROBERT LEWIS for sum of Four hundred
pounds current money of Virginia to him in hand paid at or before the Ensealing &
delivery of these presents doth bargain sell and confirm unto SAMUEL MARTIN his
heirs one certain tract of land cald MOUNT SAMUEL containing Eight hundred acres
lying & being in County of Albemarle on the BYRD CREEK & bounded as by Patent
granted to one RICHARD ADAMS bearing date the fifth day of May One thousand seven
hundred & Fifty four remaining of record in the Secretaries Office in this Colony refer-
rence thereunto being had may fully & at large appear with all houses woods and water
courses thereon standing growing or being together with all profits commodities &
hereditaments thereunto belonging To have and to hold said tract of land & premises
with the appurtenances unto said SAML. MARTIN his heirs and ROBERT LEWIS his heirs
will warrant & defend at all times forever hereafter In Witness whereof said ROBERT
LEWIS hath hereunto set his hand & affixed his Seal the day & year first above written
Signd Seald & Delivered in presence of
          THOMAS HARRISON   ROBERT LEWIS
  Feby. 9th 1769 Reced of SAMUEL MARTIN Four hundred pounds current money by the
hands of THOS. HARRISON being the consideration money above mentioned
                                                            ROBERT LEWIS

  At Albemarle Febry. Court 1769
This Indenture was acknowledged by ROBERT LEWIS party thereto and together with a
Receipt thereon endorsed was ordered to be recorded

pp.   THIS INDENTURE made and agreed on this Eighth day of March One thousand
51-   seven hundred & Sixty nine Between ABRAHAM ALLEN of Albemarle County of
52   one part and MARY ALLEN of County aforesaid of other part Witnesseth that
        said ABRAHAM ALLEN for the consideration that MARY, his Wife, hath to his
Estate doth give up and deliver unto MARY, his Wife, the following articles Vizt. one
Feather bed, bedstead & furniture, one cotton wheel, two new Pewter Plates, one old do.,
one large Pewter Bason, one small do., one large Pewter Dish, one large Mugg, one stone
Jugg, one small pott, one pair of Cotton cards, one black Walnut table, one small chest,
six & a half pound of spun cotton & five pound of wool, one small trunk, two red Cows,
one Sow, two barrows & two sheep, one Sorril horse branded on the near Buttock thus A
and for the consideration above mentioend have given up the above mentioned articles
unto my said Wife her heirs freely & clearly To have and to hold the said goods &
chattles to her the said MARY ALLEN her heirs and ABRAHAM ALLEN will warrant &
forever defend by these presents In Witness whereof said ABRAHAM ALLEN hath hereunto set his hand & Seal the day and year above written
Signed Sealed & Delivered in the presence of
        THOMAS DICKASON,   ABRAHAM his mark A ALLEN
        MICAJAH ALLEN, EDWARD COFFEY
  At Albemarle March Court 1769
This Indenture was acknowledb y ABRAHAM ALLEN party thereto & ordered to be
recorded

pp.   THIS INDENTURE made the tenth day of November One thousand seven hundred
52-   & sixty eight Between THOMAS SHIELDS of County of AUGUSTA in Colony of Vir-
53   ginia of one part & ADAM SMITH of County of Albemarle & Colony aforesaid of
        other part Witnesseth that THOMAS SHIELDS for sum of Forty two pounds Ten
Shillings current money of Virginia to him in hand paid before the sealing & delivery
of these presents doth bargain sell & confirm unto said ADAM SMITH his heirs one certain tract or parcel of land containing Two hundred acres lying & being in County of
Albemarle on the VIRGIN SPRING BRANCH & bounded beginning at pointers & running
thence South eighty degrees West twenty poles to pointers, thence South seventy six
degrees West One hundred & forty poles to CHISWELLs Black Oak corner, thence North
one hundred & sixty poles to pointers, thence East one hundred & twenty two poles to a
red Oak, thence on new lines South fifty three degrees East one hundred & thirty five
poles to a red Oak, thence South sixty one poles to the first station To have & to hold said
tract of land with all houses buildings Emoluments whatsoever unto said ADAM SMITH
his heirs and THOMAS SHIELDS his heirs the premises with the appurtenances unto said
ADAM SMITH will warrant & forever defend by these presents free and discharged of
all Incumbrances whatsoever In Witness whereof the said THOMAS SHIELDS hath here-
unto set his hand and affixed his Seal the day & year first above written
Signed Seald & delivered in the presence of
        JAMES CULL, ARCHIBALD WOODS,   THOMAS SHIELDS
        JOSEPH his mark Jn ANDERSON
  Memorandum on the tenth day of November One thousand seven hundred & sixty eight
Livery & Seizen of within sold land & premises was made by THOMAS SHIELDS to said
ADAM SMITH
In presence of JAMES CULL, ARCHIBALD WOODS   THOMAS SHIELDS
        JOSEPH his mark Jn ANDERSON
  November 10th 1768 Then received of ADAM SMITH forty two pounds Ten shillings
current money of Virginia being the consideration money for the within mentioned

land & premises
Witness present JAMES CULL, ARCHIBALD WOODS   THOMAS SHIELDS
      JOSEPH his mark ᒐₘ ANDERSON
 At Albemarle March Court 1769
This Indenture memorandum & receipt was proved by the Oath of JAMES CULL, & the
same having been before proved by ARCHIBALD WOODS and JOSEPH ANDERSON wit-
nesses thereto was ordered to be recorded

p.   THIS INDENTURE made this ninth day of November in year of our Lord God One
54   thousand seven hundred & Sixty & Eight Between JOSEPH WOODS of County of
       Albemarle and Colony of Virginia, Planter, of one part and NATHAN WOODS of
the Parish of Fredericksville and County of Albemarle & Colony of Virginia, Planter, of
other part Witnesseth that said JOSEPH WOODS in consideration of the sum of Thirty
pounds current money of Virginia to him in hand paid by these presents doth bargain
and sell unto NATHAN WOODS and his heirs all that tract or parcel of land lying & being
in the Parish and County of Albemarle and on the Branches of MOREMANS RIVER and
bounded beginning at a corner Pine in sd NATHAN WOODS line, running thence North
eighty degrees East forty two poles, thence South sixty five degrees East twenty eight
poles, thence South twenty eight degrees East one hundred & forty two poles, thence
South thirty two degrees West one hundred & sixty poles, thence South five degrees
West ten poles, thence North two degrees West two hundred & sixty two poles to the beginning, containing One hundred acres more or less and all houses gardens orchards
profits and hereditaments whatsoever with every of their appurtenances belonging To
have & to hold said tract or parcel of land hereby granted unto NATHAN WOODS his
heirs for the use benefit and behoof of said NATHAN WOODS and no other use intent or
purpose whatsoever In Witness whereof the parties to these presents their hands &
Seals interchangably have set the day & year first above written
Sealed & Delivered in the presence of us
     ROBERT MILLER,   JOSEPH WOODS
     PATRICK WOODS, WILLIAM NORIES
 Memorandum That on the day & year within mentioned peacable & Quiet possession &
seizen of the lands and premises within mentioned was had & taken by within named
NATHAN according to purport of within Deed   JOSEPH WOODS
 Received the ninth day of November 1768 of NATHAN WOODS the sum of Thirty pounds
current money of Virginia being the consideration money for the within mentioned
lands & premises I say reced p me   JOSEPH WOODS
 At Albemarle March Court 1769
This Indenture memoranum & receipt was proved by the Oath of ROBT. MILLER,
PATRICK WOODS & WM. NORIES Witnesses thereto & ordered to be recorded

pp.   THIS INDENTURE made the thirteenth day of October in year of our Lord One
55- thousand seven hundred & Sixty eight Between JAMES WOOD and LUCY his Wife
56   of County of Albemarle and Colony of Virginia of one part and JOSEPH BUSH of
     County & Colony aforesaid of other part Witnesseth that for and in considera-
tion of Thirty pounds current money of Virginia to him in hand paid by said JOSEPH
BUSH at or before the sealing & delivery of these presents doth bargain sell & confirm
unto said JOSEPH BUSH and to his heirs one certain track or parcell of land containing
One hundred acres be it more or less lying and being in County of Albemarle on BEA-
VER CREEK, a branch of MECHUMS RIVER, and bounded Begining at pointers by the said
Creek and running thence North forty five degrees West one hundred & sixteen poles

to a Pine, thence new lines South thirty seven degrees West One hundred & eighty nine poles to a white Oak saplin, thence South eighty four degrees East one hundred and nine poles to pointers by the Meeting House, thence North thirty degrees East forty one poles to a white Oak saplin, then South forty degrees East twenty five poles to pointers, thence North thirty five degrees East eighty two poles to pointers, thence North twenty degrees West sixteen poles to the first station, and all houses orchards and water courses to the same belonging To have & to hold said One hundred acres of land be it more or less and every of their appurtenances unto said JOSEPH BUSH his heirs and JAMES WOODS and LUCY his Wife and their heirs will forever warrant anddefend the above sold land & premises unto said JOSEPH BUSH his heirs In Witness whereof JAMES WOODS & LUCY his Wife have hereunto set their hands & assigned their seals the day & year above written

Signed Sealed & delivered in the presence of

DAVID ALLEN, JOEL TERRELL,   JAMES WOODS
HENRY his mark R RANDOLPH,   LUCY WOODS
MICHAEL WALLACE

Memorandum that on the thirteenth day of October in year of our Lord One thousand seven hundred & Sixty eight Quiet & peaceable possession and Seizen of the land & premises was had and taken by JAMES WOODS & LUCY his Wife and by them delivered to JOSEPH BUSH and his heirs & assigns forever

In presence of JOEL TERRELL, DAVID ALLEN,   JAMES WOODS
HENRY his mark R RANDOLPH,   LUCY WOODS
MICHAEL WALLACE

October thirteenth 1768 Then received of JOSEPH BUSH the sum of Thirty pounds current money being in full for the consideration money in this Deed mentioned I say reced by me   JAMES WOODS

Test DAVID ALLEN, MICHAEL WALLACE

At Albemarle March Court 1769

This Indenture memorandum & receipt was proved by the Oaths of DAVID ALLEN, MICHAEL WALLACE & JOEL TERRELL, witnesses thereto, & ordered to be recorded

pp. 56-57 THIS INDENTURE made the second day of August in year of our Lord One thousand seven hundred and Sixty eight Between PRESLEY DOLLINS of Albemarle County of the one part and THOMAS WALKER of the aforesaid County of other part Witnesseth that said PRESLEY DOLLINS for and in consideration of the sum of Fourteen pounds twelve Shillings & seven pence three farthings current money to him in hand paid by said THOMAS WALKER doth bargain & sell to said THOMAS WALKER and his heirs one tract of land lying in aforesaid County on the Watters of PRETTYS CREEK containing One hundred & ten acres be the same more or less and bounded Beginning at a Pine & Chesnut on JAMES ISBELs line, thence with said ISBELs line South fifty six & a half degrees East one hundred and nine poles to a Gum in a valley on THOMAS DOUGLASS line, thence with said DOUGLASSes line South thirty seven degrees West one hundred & twenty poles to pointers in ROBERT GRENOLDs line, thence with said GRENOLDs line North thirty six degrees West one hundred & thirty eight poles crossing a branch of PRETTYS CREEK twice to a Pine, thence a new line North forty eight degrees East one hundred & twenty five poles to the beginning, Together with the appurtenances thereto belonging To have & to hold said land with its appurtenances unto said THOMAS WALKER & his heirs and PRESLEY DOLLINS & his heirs the said tract of land with its appurtenances to said THOS. WALKER and his heirs will for ever warrant & defend In Witness whereof said PRESLEY DOLLINS hath hereunto Subscribed his name

and affixed his Seal the day & year first above written
Signed Sealed & delivered in the presence of
       WILLIAM SIMS, GEO: MARTIN,   PRESLE DOLLINS
       WILLIAM SUMPTER, DANL. SMITH
  Memorandum that on the day & year within written peaceable & Quiet possession of
the within mentioned land & premises was given by PRESLEY DOLLINS to THOMAS WAL-
KER according to the true intent and meaning of these presents Witness my hand
Test WILLIAM SIMS, WILLIAM SUMPTER,   PRESLE DOLLINS
       GEO: MARTIN, DANL. SMITH
  August 2d 1768 Received of Mr. THOMAS WALKER the consideration of Fourteen
pounds twelve Shillings & seven pence three Farthings & I do acquit said THOMAS WAL-
KER & his heirs of every part thereof
Test WILLIAM SIMS, WILLIAM SUMPTER,   PRESLE DOLLINS
       GEO: MARTIN, DANL. SMITH
  At Albemarle March Court 1769
This Indenture memorandum & receipt was proved by the Oaths of WILLIAM SUMPTER
& GEO. MARTIN & the same having been before proved by DANIEL SMITH a witness
thereto was ordered to be recorded

pp.   THIS INDENTURE made this twenty third day of Feby. in year of our Lord One
57-   thousd. seven hund.d & Sixty nine Between ANDREW KINKEAD of County of Albe-
58   marle of one part & THOMAS SMITH SENR. of said County of other part Witnesseth
       that said ANDREW KINKEAD for & in consideration of sum of Forty pounds Currt.
money of Virginia to him in hand paid by said THOMAS SMITH SENR. by these presents
doth bargain sell & confirm unto sd THOMAS SMITH SENR. his heirs one certain tract or
parcel of land containing One hundred acres more or less lying & being in ye County of
Albemarle & Parrish of St. Ann on the Branches of MECHUMS RIVER, it being part of a
tract of land conveyed by WILLIAM GRAYSON to said ANDREW KINKEAD this sd One
hundred acres being part of five hund.d & twenty acres which was conveyed by JOHN
ROBINSON Esqr. to ye sd GRAYSON & SAML. TINCKER, then South ten deg. East on HUGHES
line One hundred & eighty poles to two white Oaks and black Oak, thence South seventy
six deg. West one hundred & thirty poles to a Corner Stone & pointers, thence partly a
North course on a line of markt. trees of ye sd ANDREW KINKEAD & JOHN KINKEAD own
making to a Locust post in the field, thence partly a North course on a line of markt.
trees to a Corner white Oak on or near WALKER's Line, thence East on WALKER's line to
ye Beginning corner white Oak Together with all houses ways & advantages whatsoever
to ye sd land belonging To have & to hold ye sd land & premises with the appurtenances
unto said THOMAS SMITH SENR. his heirs & ye Estate, right & demand whatsoever of
ANDREW KINKEAD & MARY his Wife of in and to the same & said ANDREW KINKEAD and
his heirs clear of all Incumbrances whatsoever will warrant & forever defend by these
presents In Witness whereof said ANDREW KINKEAD hath hereunto set his hand & Seal
the day and year first above written
Signed Sealed & Delivered in the presence of
       JOHN SMITH, THOS. COFFEY,   ANDREW KINKEAD
       BENJAMIN COFFEY, THOMAS SMITH
Received this Twenty third day of Feby. One thousand seven hundred & Sixty nine of
THOMAS SMITH the sum of Forty pounds currt. money of Virginia it being ye consider-
ation money within mentioned I say reced p me   ANDREW KINKEAD
  At Albemarle March Court 1769
This Indenture was acknowledged by ANDREW KINKEAD & Together with a receipt en-
dorsed was ordered to be recorded

pp.   THIS INDENTURE made the first day of March in year of our Lord Christ One
58-   thousand seven hundred and Sixty nine Between GEORGE KEY of County of BED-
59   FORD of one part and ROBERT ADAMS of County of Albemarle of other part Wit-
        nesseth that said GEORGE KEY for and in consideration of the sum of One hun-
dred pounds to him in hand paid hath bargained & sold unto ROBERT ADAMS one certain tract or parcel of land lying & being in County of Albemarle containing Four hundred and thirty acres and is the same that was granted by Letters Patent unto JOHN KEY
bearing date the Sixth day of July One thousand seven hundred & forty one lying on
KEYS MILL SWAMP and bounded beginning at pointers in Collo. MERIWETHERS line
(now NICHOLAS LEWIS's) thence on the same seventy six degrees West at four KEYS
MILL SWAMP and so on one hundred & thirty four poles to two Pines, thence North
sixty four degrees West One hundred & twenty nine poles to pointers, thence North
twenty six degrees East fifty four poles to pointers, North twenty degrees West one
hundred & sixty five poles to two Pines, North forty five degrees East one hundred &
sixty four poles to pointers, South sixty five degrees East one hundred & thirty six poles
to pointers, thence South four degrees East two hundred & nineteen poles to the first
station & the Reversions & Remainders with every appurtenances to the same belonging To have and to hold said Four hundred & thirty acres of land unto ROBERT
ADAMS his heirs and GEORGE KEY his heirs will forever warrant by these presents In
Witness whereof said GEORGE KEY hath set and affixed his hand & Seal the day & year
above written
Signd Seald & deliverd in presence of
        JANE TANDY, MATHA. BOSWELL,   GEORGE KEY
        WM. TANDY, WM. JOHNSON
 Memo. That on the day and year within written full possession & Seisen was had &
taken of the within lands & premises by GEORGE KEY and by him delivered to ROBERT
ADAMS to hold to him said ROBERT ADAMS his heirs &c. according to the true meaning
of this Indenture
In presence of JANE TANDY, MATHA. BOSWELL,   GEORGE KEY
        WM. TANDY, WM. JOHNSON
 Received of ROBERT ADAMS one hundred pounds current money in hand paid it being
in full consideration of the said land Reced this first day of March One thousand seven
hundred & sixty nine Given under my hand & Seal   GEORGE KEY
Test   JANE TANDY, MATHA. BOSWELL,
        WM. TANDY, WM. JOHNSON
 At Albemarle March Court 1769
This Indenture memorandum & receipt was proved by the Oath of MATTHEW BOSWELL,
WILLIAM TANDY & WILLIAM JOHNSON Wits. thereto & ordered to be recorded

p.   THIS INDENTURE made this 14th day of Feby. One thousand seven hundred &
60   Sixty nine Between WILLIAM & JOEL HARLOW of County of Albemarle of one part
        and ROBERT ADAMS of the same County of other part Witnesseth that WILLIAM &
JOEL HARLOW for and in consideration (blank) (being the award from a Settlement
yesterday made by Messrs. NICHOLAS LEWIS, JOEL TERRELL & REUBEN LINDSAY upon
the several differences between the above said ROBERT ADAMS & the above said JOEL
HARLOW wch said award is lodg'd with the Clk. of the Court to be found a Judgment agst.
the said JOEL HARLOW) do sell make over and convey to said ROBERT ADAMS one Negro
boy named Sam now in possession of said ROBERT to him the said ROBERT ADAMS his
heirs and assigns forever and WILLIAM & JOEL HARLOW for themselves their heirs &c.
do undertake to warrant and defend the said Negro Samm against all and every person

Nevertheless the said HARLOWs reserve unto themselves their heirs that if at any time
within eleven months next to come that they their heirs shall pay or cause to be paid to
said ADAMS his heirs the above said award with lawful Interest on the same without
fraud or deceit that then this Indenture with its contents shall utterly cease and be void
as Witness the hands & Seals of said WILLIAM & JOEL HARLOW the day & year above
written Signed Sealed & Delivered in presence of

      JNO. MOORE,   W: HARLOW
      JAS. ADDAMS, WM. TANDY   JOEL HARLOW

At Albemarle March Court 1769
This Indenture was proved by the Oath of MOORE, JAMES ADDAMS & WILLIAM TANDY
Wits. thereto & ordered to be recorded

pp.   THIS INDENTURE made the fifth day of January in year of our Lord One thou-
60-   sand seven hundred & Sixty nine Between DAVID LEWIS JUNR. of County of
61   Albemarle of one part and ALEXANDER CLEVELAND of the same County Wittnes-
        seth that said DAVID LEWIS for and in consideration of sum of One hundred &
fifty pounds currant money of Virginia to him in hand paid by said ALEXANDER CLEVE-
LAND by these presents doth bargain sell and confirm unto said ALEXANDER and to his
heirs one certain tract or parcel of land containing One hundred and fifty three acres
lying and being in County of Albemarle and on the Branches of LICKINGHOLE and
bounded Beginning at pointers in MICHAEL WOODS line, South nine degrees East two
hundred & fifty five poles, North sixty eight West two hundred and twenty poles to
pointers in the hed of a Branch, a Dividing line, North forty five degrees East two hundred & forty four poles to the first Station which said One hundred & fifty three acres of
land was granted unto WILLIAM WOODS by a Pattent bearing date the tenth day of June
One thousand seven hundred & Thirty seven and all houses orchards and water courses
to the same belonging and to hold the said One hundred & fifty three acres of land &
every of their appurtenances unto said ALEXANDER CLEVELAND his heirs and said
DAVID LEWIS his heirs will warrant and defend the above sold land In Witness whereof
said DAVID LEWIS hath hereunto set his hand and affixed his Seal the day and year
above written & mentioned
Sign'd Seal'd & Deliver'd in presents of us
      MICHAEL ISRAEL,   DAVID LEWIS JUNR.
      JOHN JONES, THOMAS COFFEY
Memorandum that on the fifth day of January in year of our Lord One thousand seven
hundred & sixty nine Quiet and peaceable possession & Seisen of the land & premises
within mentioned was had and taken by said DAVID LEWIS and by him was delivered to
ALEXANDER CLEVELAND and his heirs & assigns forever
      MICHAEL ISRAEL,   DAVID LEWIS JR.
      JOHN JONES, THOMAS COFFEY
At Albemarle March Court 1769
This Indenture & memorandum was acknowledged by DAVID LEWIS JUNR. party thereto
& ordered to be recorded

pp.   THIS INDENTURE made the second day of November in year of our Lord One thou-
62-   sand seven hundred & Sixty eight Between JOHN KINKEAD & ELIZABETH his Wife
63   of County of Albemarle and Colony of Virginia of one part and WILLIAM TEAS of
        AUGUSTA COUNTY & Colony aforesaid of other part Witnesseth that for the sum
of Fifty pounds to said JOHN KINKEAD & ELIZABETH his Wife in hand paid by WILLIAM
TEAS at or before the sealing and delivery of these presents doth bargain sell release &

confirm unto said (blank) (in his actual possession now being by virtue of a bargain & sale to him thereof made by JOHN KINKEAD & ELIZABETH his Wife for one whole year & by force of the Statute for transferring uses into possession) and his heirs one certain tract of land containing two hundred acres be it more or less lying and being in the County of Albemarle on both sides of STOCKTONS BRANCH of MECHUMS RIVER and bounded Begining a red Oak running thence Wt. 190 poles to a Chesnut Oak, thence South 164 poles to a white Oak, thence East 156 poles to a red Oak, thence North on a new line 164 poles to the first station And all houses orchards profits and appurtenances whatsoever to the said premises and all Deeds evidences and writings touching the same To have & to hold the said two hundred acres of land be it more or less and every of their appurtenances unto said WILLIAM TEAS his heirs said premises shall remain and be free & clear of all Incumbrances whatsoever and JOHN KINKEAD & ELIZABETH his Wife their heirs shall warrant & forever defend by these presents In Witness whereof said JOHN KINKEAD & ELIZABETH his Wife hath hereunto set their hands & Seals the day & year first above written

Signed Sealed and Delivered in presence of

ROBERT his mark X LOGAN, JOHN KINKEAD
BETHIAH her mark X LOGAN ELIZABETH her mark E KINKEAD
JAMES LOGAN

At Albemarle March Court 1769

This Indenture was proved by the Oath of ROBERT LOGAN, BETHIAH LOGAN & JAMES LOGAN witnesses thereto & ordered to be recorded

pp. 63-65   THIS INDENTURE made this twentieth day of February One thousand seven hundred & Sixty nine Between JOHN GILLUM of Albemarle County Colony & Dominion of Virginia, Planter, of one part and JOEL TERRELL of the County aforesaid of other part Witnesseth that said JOHN GILLUM for sum of Thirty one pounds current money aforesaid to him the said GILLUM in hand paid by said TERRELL before the sealing & delivery of these presents doth bargain sell and confirm unto said JOEL TERRELL his heirs a certain tract or parcel of land lying and being in Albemarle County in the North & South Garden containing twenty five acres and a half, the said land surrounding and including a conveyance already made to GILES WEBSTER & WILKINSON which lands is hereby conveid altho included in these lines Beginning at a Chesnut bush running thence North eighty degrees West eighteen poles to a Dogwood, thence South seventeen degrees West eighty six poles to a red Oak, South thirteen degrees West forty two poles to a Chesnut Oak among the rocks, thence North seventy five degrees East one hundred & twelve poles to a white Oak, North ten degrees West thirty four poles to the first Station, Together with all houses barnes stables profits and appurtenances whatsoever to said land belonging Except what is above excepted In Witness whereof the said GILLUM hath hereunto set his hand and Seal the day & year above written

Signed Sealed & Delivered in presence of

JACOB MOON, JOHN GILLUM
JOHN SWANN, JOHN PRINCE

Memorandum that the day and year within mentioned peaceable & Quiet possession of the within mentioned tract of land with the appurtenances thereunto belonging was had of JOHN GILLUM & by him delivered to JOEL TERRELL to be by him his heirs & assigns forever Injoyed according to the foregoing Deed

In presents of JACOB MOON, JOHN GILLUM
JNO. SWANN, JOHN PRINCE

Received February the Twentieth day one thousand seven hundred & Sixty nine of the
within JOEL TERRELL the sum of thirty one pounds current money being in full for the
within mentioned Deed p me   JOHN GILLUM
   At Albemarle March Court 1769
This Indenture memorandum & receipt were acknowledged by JOHN GILLUM party
thereto & ordered to be recorded

pp.   THIS INDENTURE made this twenty first day of February One thousand seven
65-   hundred & Sixty nine Between DAVID COOKE of Albemarle County & Colony &
66   Dominion of Virginia, Planter, of one part and JOHN OLD of the Province of
         PENSYLVANIA and JOHN WILKINSON of Albemarle aforesaid of other part Wit-
nesseth that for sum of Eleven pounds Ten Shillings current money aforesaid to him
the said COOKE in hand paid by said OLD & WILKINSON before the sealing & delivery of
these presents doth bargain sell & confirm unto said JOHN OLD & JOHN WILKINSON their
heirs a certain tract or parcel of land lying and being in Albemarle County on the
RAGGED MOUNTAIN Beginning on a large Pine, South fifty degrees West twenty poles to
a red Oak saplin, South fourteen degrees forty three poles to a Pine, North thirty five
degrees East forty five poles to the first Station containing Five acres & three fourths
Together with all profits commodities and appurtenances whatsoever to said lands &
premises belonging In Witness whereof sd. COOK hath hereunto set his hand & Seal the
day & year above written
Signed Sealed and Delivered in the presence of
         JNO. SWANN, JACOB MOON,   DAVID his mark   COOKE
         WM.. WATSON, JOHN PRINCE
 Memorandum this day and year within mentioned Peaceable & Quiet possession of the
within mentioned tract of land with the appurtenances thereunto belonging was had of
DAVID COOKE and by him delivered to JOHN OLD & JOHN WILKINSON to be by them &
their heirs & assigns enjoyed according to the within mentioned Deed
Signed Sealed & Delivered in presence of
         JNO. SWANN,   DAVID his mark   COOKE
         JACOB MOON, WM. WATSON
 Received February the twenty first day the sum of Eleven pounds Ten Shillings current money being in full consideration of the within mentioned tract of land per me
                                                   DAVID his mark   COOKE

   At Albemarle March Court 1769
This Indenture memorandum & Receipt was acknowledged by DAVID COOKE party thereto & ordered to be recorded

pp.   THIS INDENTURE made this third day of March in year of our Lord One thousand
66-   seven hundred & sixty nine Between FOSTER WEBB Gent. of NEW KENT COUNTY
67   and JOHN WEBB & JUDITH his Wife of County of HANOVER of one part and ISAAC
         DAVIS Gent. of County of Albemarle of other part Witnesseth that said FOSTER
WEBB of NEW KENT COUNTY and JOHN WEBB & JUDITH his Wife of County of HANOVER for
sum of Two hundred pounds current money of Virginia to them in hand paid by said
ISAAC DAVIS before the insealding & delivery of these presents do bargain sell and
confirm unto said ISAAC DAVIS one certain tract or parcel of land containing Seven
hundred & ninety seven acres situate in Albemarle County on both sides of the North
Fork of the North Fork of JAMES RIVER joining BUFFALO MEADOW and bounded begin-
nming at a Pine in the County Line corner to GEORGE THOMAS and JOHN EARLEY, then
South sixty five degrees West One hundred & two poles to a Pine and white Oak saplin,

thence South twenty three degrees East twenty four poles to two Hiccorys and a white
Oak by the River, thence South ninety two poles to two Pines on the top of a Hill, thence
South forty six degrees East ninety two poles to a white Oak & two Hiccorys in a Valley,
thence South twenty three degrees East three hundred and ten poles to three white Oak
saplins, thence forty three & a half degrees East four hundred & thirty two poles to a
small Pine in JACKSONs line and the County Line, thence North sixty five degrees West
along the County Line four hundred & fifty eight poles to the begining Together with
all houses orchards & water courses thereunto belonging To have & to hold the said
lands and premises with all the appurtenances whatsoever to the same belonging to
said ISAAC DAVIS his heirs and FOSTER & JOHN WEBB for themselves & their heirs will
warrant and forever defend by these presents against any person whasoever In Witness whereof they the said FOSTER & JOHN WEBB and JUDITH his Wife hath hereunto set
their hands & Seals the day & year above written
Signed, Sealed & Delivered in presence of
    P. HENRY JUNR.,
    W. BELL, DAVID his mark X SPRADLING   FOSTER WEBB
                                     JOHN WEBB
  At Albemarle March Court 1769
This Indenture was proved by the Oath of PATRICK HENRY JUNR., WM. BELL & DAVID
SPRADLING wits. thereto & ordered to be recorded

pp.   THIS INDENTURE made this third day of March in year of our Lord One thousand
68-   seven hundred and Sixty nine Between FOSTER WEBB Gent. of NEW KENT COUNTY
69   and JOHN WEBB & JUDITH his Wife of HANOVER COUNTY of the one part and WIL-
LIAM BELL of County of ORANGE of other part Witnesseth that FOSTER WEBB of
NEW KENT COUNTY and JOHN WEBB & JUDITH his Wife of HANOVER COUNTY for sum of
fifty pounds current money of Virginia to them in hand paid by said WILLIAM BELL by
these presents do bargain sell & confirm unto WILLIAM BELL his heirs one certain
tract or parcel of land containing Four hundred acres lying & being in Albemarle
County on both sides of LINCHES RIVER joining the lands of the said BELL, EPHRAIM
SEMONDS and ORANGE COUNTY line and bounded beginning at the said BELLs Corner
three red Oaks in the County Line and running thence with the County Line North sixty
five degrees West two hundred & ninety eight poles to a large white Oak an Old Corner
of said WEBBs, thence South three hundred & Eighty two poles to pointers, three white
Oaks, thence North sixty five degrees East two hundred & Tenn poles to several small
Pines corner of the said BELLs, thence with BELLs line North twenty five degrees East
One hundred & eighty six poles to the begining, Together with all houses orchards &
water courses thereunto belonging To Have & to hold said lands & premises with all the
appurtenances whatsoever to the same belonging to said WILLIAM BELL his heirs and
FOSTER and JOHN WEBB for themselves and their heirs will warrant and forever defend
by these presents against any person In Witness whereof said FOSTER & JOHN WEBB &
JUDTH his Wife hath hereunto set their hands & Seals the day & year above written
Signed Sealed & Delivered in presence of
    P. HENRY JUNR.,   FOSTER WEBB
    ISAAC DAVIS, DAVID his mark X SPRADLING   JOHN WEBB
  At Albemarle March Court 1769
This Indenture was proved by the Oath of PATRICK HENRY JUNR., ISAAC DAVIS & DAVID
SPRADLING, wits. thereto & ordered to be recorded

p.   THIS INDENTURE made the ninth day of March in year of our Lord One thousand
69   seven hundred & Sixty nine Between NICHOLAS LEWIS of Albemarle County of
one part and JOHN WALKER of same County of other part Witnesseth that said
NICHOLAS LEWIS for sum of Six hundred pounds current money to him in hand
paid by said JOHN WALKER doth bargain and sell unto JOHN WALKER and his heirs one
tract of land containing sixteen hundred acres lying on South East side of the LITTLE
MOUNTAIN whereon Colo. ROBERT LEWIS lately lived bounded on the North West and
South East by MERIWETHERs Old Grant lines, on the South West MRS. KETURAH WILLS's
land and on the North East by JOHN WALKERs land bought of JOHN LEWIS together with
the appurtenances thereto belonging To have & to hold the said tract of land with the
appurtenances unto JOHN WALKER his heirs and NICHOLAS LEWIS & his heirs the said
tract of land & appurtenances to said JOHN WALKER and his heirs against all persons
forever will warrant & defend In Witness whereof the said NICHOLAS LEWIS hath hereunto subscribed his name & affixed his Seal the day & year above written
Signed Sealed & Delivered in presence of
    (no witnesses shown)   NICHOLAS LEWIS
 At Albemarle March Court 1769
This Indenture was acknowledged by NICHOLAS LEWIS party thereto & ordered to be
recorded

p.   THIS INDENTURE made on the ninth day of March in year of our Lord One thou-
70   sand seven hundred & sixty nine Between JOHN WALKER of County of Albemarle
on the one part and THOS. WALKER, MOSIAS JONES, ISAAC DAVIS, WILLIAM
BARKSDALE, THOS. CARR, NICHOLAS LEWIS, NICHOLAS MERIWETHER, (blank)
RODES, MORDECAI HORD, THOS. JEFFERSON & WM. SIMS, Church Wardens & Vestrymen of
the Parish of Fredericksville in the same County Witnesseth that said JOHN WALKER for
sum of Forty Shillings to him in hand paid doth bargain & sell unto said THOS. WALKER
& others, Vestrymen of the said Parish and their Successors, one parcel of land in the
Parish & County aforesaid containing Two acres being the same whereon the BELLVOIR
CHURCH is situated and bounded beginning at the Northern post of a Gate near the
highway (the Northwest Corner of the Church) and running from the said post due East
12 po. 16 1/2 links along marked trees to a Corner, then due South 12 po. 16 1/2 links
along marked trees to a Corner, thence due West 12 po. 16 1/2 links along marked trees
to a corner, thence due North 2 po. 20 lines along marked trees to a corner, thence
South 76 d. 3o" West 22 po. 12 1/2 links along marked trees to a corner, thence North 13
d. 30" West 6 po. 3 1/2 links along marked trees to a Corner, thence due North 2 po. 20
links to the beginning Together with all its appurtenances To have & to hold the said
parcel of land with its appurtenances to the said THOS. WALKER & others Vestrymen of
said Parish and their Successors and JOHN WALKER will warrant & defend In Witness
whereof said JOHN WALKER hath hereunto subscribed his name & affixed his Seal the
say & year above written
Signed Sealed & Delivered in presence of
    (no witnesses shown)   JOHN WALKER
 At Albemarle March Court 1769
This Indenture was acknowledged by JOHN WALKER party thereto & ordered to be
recorded

p.   THIS INDENTURE made the fourth day of February in year of our Lord One thou-
71   sand seven hundred and Sixty nine Between JOHN JONES of County of Albemarle
in the Colony of Virginia of one part and ROBERT FIELDS of the County & Colony

aforesaid of other part Witnesseth that JOHN JONES for and in consideration of Twenty five pounds current money of Virginia to him in hand paid by ROBERT FIELDS by these presents doth bargain sell & confirm unto ROBERT FIELDS and to his heirs a certain tract or parcel of land lying and being in County of Albemarle and Parish of St. Anne in the Colony of Virginia on the branches of MECHIMS RIVER being part of a tract of land granted by Patent to HENRY TERRILL deceased and bounded Beginning at a Spanish Oak sapling on a line of TERRILLs Old Patent on the North side of the above mentioned ROBERT FIELDS Plantation and running thence a North course to pointers saplings on a Road called ROCKFISH ROAD & from thence running along the said Road a North East Course and then a South Course to TERRILLs line joining the aforesaid ROBERT FIELDS, and thence continuing the same a South course to the beginning containing by estimation Forty acres be the same more or less Together with the appurtenances thereto belonging and JOHN JONES his heirs shall warrant and forever defend In Witness whereof said JOHN JONES hath hereunto set his hand and affixed his Seal the day & year above written
Signed Sealed & Delivered in presence of us
          (no witnesses shown)   JOHN JONES
   Memorandum that on the fourth day of February in year of our Lord One thousand seven hundred and Sixty nine Quiet & peaceable possession and Seisen of the lands & tenements within mentioned was had & taken by JOHN JONES in his proper person and by him was delivered unto ROBERT FIELDS according to the form and effect of the within written Deed   JOHN JONES
   4th of February 1769 Then received of the within named ROBERT FIELDS the sum of twenty five pounds the consideration money in the within Deed mentioned
                                                        JOHN JONES

   At Albemarle March Court 1769
This Indenture memorandum & receipt were acknowledged by JOHN JONES party thereto & ordered to be recorded

p.   THIS INDENTURE made this Twenty Eight day of Sept. in year of our Lord One
72   thousand seven hundred & Sixty & Eight Between CHARLES CREASEY of County
          of Albemarle and RENE WOODSON of the same County of other part Witnesseth
that for sum of Twenty pounds Currt. money in hand paid by said RENE WOODSON to sd CHAS. CREASEY by these presents doth bargain sell & confirm unto said RENE WOODSON one certain parcel of land by estimation Two hundred acres bounded by the lines of a Survey made by WM. CREASEY SENR. to contain Four hundred acres the bargained premises being the lower two hundred of the tract Including the plantation whereon the said WILL CREASEY SENR. now lives as far up the Creek in the line of Division run by the Surveyor of the County lying & being in County of Albemarle & on both sides LITTLE RACOON CREEK and was granted to WM. CREASEY SENR. to WM. CREASEY JUNR. & by him to the said CHAS. CREASEY, Together with all woods ways houses & appurtenances thereon being or thereunto belonging together with all Deeds evidences or writings touching the same To have & to hold said bargained premises with every of their appurtenances unto said RENE WOODSON his heirs In Witness whereof sd CHAS. CREASEY hath set his hand & affixed his Seal the day & year above written
Signed Sealed & Delviered in the presence of
     PATK. NAPIER, WM. his mark — CREASEY   CHARLES his mark G CREASEY
     GEO: THOMPSON, GEO: his mark CREASEY
     BENNETT HENDERSON, ROGER THOMPSON

At Albemarle March Court 1769
This Indenture was proved by the Oath of ROGER THOMPSON, GEO: THOMPSON & THOS. NAPIER witnesses thereto and ordered to be recorded

p.   GEORGE the Third by the Grace of God of Great Britain France & Ireland, King
73   Defender of the faith &c. To RICHARD JONES & ROBERT MUNFORD Gent. Greeting
       JAMES HINES and MARIMIAT his Wife of County of AMELIA by their Indenture
bearing date the XIIIth day of May 1765 have conveyed the fee Simple Estate of two
hundred acres of land lying and being in County of Albemarle unto GEORGE TWYMAN
And Whereas the said MARIMIAT cannot conveniently travel to our said County Court of
Albemarle to make acknowledgment of the said Conveyance, Therefore we do give unto
you power to receive the acknowledgement which the said MARIMIAT shall be willing
to make before you and that you distinctly & openly certify our Justices in our said
County Court under your Seals sending then there this Writ and Indenture Witness
JOHN NICHOLAS Clk. of our said Court XXVth day of June in the fifth year of our Reign
                                                    HENRY FRY Clk.
   The Execution of this Writ appears in a certain Schedule hereunto annexed by Virtue
of the within Commission to us directed we did personally go to the within named
MARIMIAT Wife of said JAMES HINES & did examine her privately and apart from her
said Husband that she did the same freely & willingly without the persuations or threats
of her said Husband & that she is willing the same should be recorded in the County of
Albemarl Give under our hands & Seals this 31st day of October 1767
                                                    RICHARD JONES
                                                    ROBT. MUNFORD

At Albemarle March Court 1769
This Acknowledgment was returned to Court and ordered to be recorded

p.   March 11th 1769
74   I DAVID LEWIS JUNR. of County of Albemarle do give and Bequest to ELIZABETH
       LOCKHEART of the same County and to her heirs forever the following things to
Will. Item. One bay Mair branded on two quarters (JS), two side sadles, two cow, one
Brindle one the other a brown, one feather bed, three Chaff beds, three shirts, two
blankets, two ruggs, one counterpin, four bedsteads & cords, eight wallnut chears,
twelve pewter plates, one pewter dish, four putter basons, twelve knives & forks, two
meal baggs, three pails, two iron potts, one Skillet, eighteen spoons, one gray horse
branded on near Buttock W G & on the off Buttock R one Waggon, two collers and
Harneses, two lining wheels, two wollen wheels, two pair cotton cards, two axes, one
broad ax, three chiswells, three augers, one Gouge, two iron pott racks, her drawing
knives, one hand saw, as Witness my hand and Seal this Eleventh day of March One
thousand seven hundred & Sixty nine
                                                    DAVID LEWIS JR.

At Albemarle March Court 1769
This (--ghting) was acknowledged by DAVID LEWIS JUNR. party thereto, & ordered to be
recorded

pp.   THIS INDENTURE made the tenth day of November in year of our Lord One thou-
74-   sand seven hundred & Sixty eight Between JOHN SPENCER of County of Albe-
75   marle & ROSANNA his Wife of one part and JOHN WOODSON of County of GOOCH-
       LAND of other part Witnesseth that said JOHN SPENCER & ROSANNA his Wife for
sum of Fifty pounds current money of Virginia to them in hand paid by said JOHN

WOODSON by these presents do bargain sell & confirm unto JOHN WOODSON his heirs one certain tract or parcel of land containing by Estimation One hundred & Seventy five acres be the same more or less lying and being in County of Albemarle on the head of IVY CREEK and bounded beginning at a white Oak of SAMUEL ARNOLDs and with his line South thirty seven degrees East forty poles to a Hiccory, new lines South thirty degrees West ninety poles to a Locust in ROBERT DAYs line & with his line West seventy four poles to a white Oak, South nineteen degrees West twenty six poles to pointers & South thirty three degrees East twenty poles to a red Oak, new lines South forty seven degrees West eighty poles to a Hiccory, North forty seven degrees West twenty poles to pointers, North twelve degrees West seventy six poles to pointers, North thirty nine poles to a black Oak, North forty three degrees West sixty two poles to a red Oak, North twenty four degrees West eighty poles to pointers, North forty three degrees East fifty four poles to a white Oak in WILLIAM WOODS's line and with his line South forty degrees East eighty poles to the first station with all woods commons pastures profits & appurtenances whatsoever to said tract of land belonging To have & to hold said tract of land with the appurtenances unto JOHN WOODSON his heirs & JOHN SPENCER his heirs shall warrant & forever defend by these presents In Witness whereof said JOHN SPENCER & ROSANNA his Wife have hereunto interchangeably set their hands & affixed their Seals the day & year first above written
Sealed & Delivered in presence of

     JNO. MOORE,   JOHN SPENCER
     RICHARD GILLIAM, NICHS. CABELL,   ROSANNA SPENCER
     MICAJAH CHILES, DAVID GRAVES
     JOHN WOODS

Received the day & date of the within written Deed of the within named JOHN WOODSON the sum of fifty pounds current money of Virginia it being the consideration of the within mentioned lands & tenements
Witness JNO. MOORE   JOHN SPENCER
 At Albemarle April Court 1769
This Indenture was acknowledged by JOHN SPENCER & ROSANNA his Wife parties thereto & Together with a receipt thereon endorsed were ordered to be recorded

pp.   THIS INDENTURE made the 12th day of Appril in year of our Lord God One thou-
76-   sand seven hundred & sixty nine Between WILLIAM MAXWELL & ANN his Wife of
77   County of Albemarle & Colony of Virginia of one part & BAZELEAL MAXWELL of
       other part of sd County & Colony Whereas by one Pattent under the Great Seal of
the Colony & Dominion of Virgnia bearing date the fourteenth day of February One thousand seven hundred & Sixty one in the first year of the Reign of our Sovereign Lord George the third by the Grace of God of Great Britain France & Ireland, King defender of the faith &c., there was granted unto WILLIAM MAXWELL one certain tract or parcel of land containing Fifty acres lying and being in County of Albemarle in the RICH COVE near the head of the RICH CREEK by Virtue of the said Pattent remaining of record in the Secretaries Office of this Colony relation thereunto being had may more fully appear. Now This Indenture Witnesseth that said WILLIAM MAXWELL & ANNE his Wife for sum of Ten pounds current money of Virginia to them in hand paid by BAZALEEL MAXWELL by these presents doth bargain & sell unto BAZELEEL MAXWELL his heirs Fifty acres of land it being the aforesaid tract and bounded Beginning at the said MAXWELLs Corner Spanish Oak on the side of a Mountain at the head of PINEY BRANCH and running thence new lines North forty degrees West fifty one poles to a Hickory, then South fifteen Degrees West forty six poles to pointers, then South Seventy nine

degrees West sixty six poles to a Poplar, then South thirty four degrees East Eighty two poles to a Chesnut Oak, thence North eighty eight degrees East forty one poles to pointers on the said MAXWELLs line, then in his line North Nineteen degrees East one hundred & seven poles to the first station with all houses gardens orchards meadows whatsoever to sd land belonging free and clear of all Incumbrances whatsoever and WILLIAM MAXWELL and ANNE his wife by these presents will forever defend In Witness whereof the said parties have Interchangeably set their hands & Seals the day and year above written

Signed Sealed & Delivered in presents of

(no witnesses shown)   WILLIAM MAXWELL

Memorandum that the day and year within written peaceable & Quiet possession of the within mentioned tract of land & appurtenances thereto belonging was had of WILLIAM MAXWELL & ANNE his Wife and by them delivered to BEZALEEL MAXWELL to be by him his heirs enjoyed according to the within mentioned Deed

WILLIAM MAXWELL

Reced of BEZALEEL MAXWELL this twelvth day of April One thousand seven hundred & sixty nine the sum of Ten pounds Currt. money being in consideration of the within tract of land p me   WILLIAM MAXWELL

At Albemarle April Court 1769

This Indenture memorandum & receipt was acknowledged by WILLIAM MAXWELL party thereto & ordered to be recorded

p.   THIS INDENTURE made this Tenth day of March in year of our Lord One thousand
78   seven hundred and Sixty nine Between RICHD. WOODS of Albemarle County of
       one part and JAMES REID of AMHERST COUNTY of other part Witnesseth that sd
RICHD. WOODS for sum of Five pounds Currt. money the payment whereof he doth hereby acknowledge doth bargain and sell unto JAMES REID his heirs one lot containing half an acre of land in the Town called CHARLOTTSVILLE in County of Albemarle which said Lot is marked in the plan of said Town, Forty Eight To have and to hold said Lot containing half an acre of land to said JAMES REID his heirs with the appurtenances thereunto belonging and Rd. WOODS will warrant and defend unto said JAMES REID his heirs free and discharged from all Incumbrances whatsoever In Witness whereof said RICHARD WOODS hath set his hand and Seal the day and year above written

Signed Sealed and Delivered in presence of

(no witnesses shown)   RICHARD WOODS

Memorandum that on the day and year within written Quiet and peaceable possession of the within Lot was given by said RICHARD WOODS unto JAMES REID in presence of us

RICHARD WOODS

At Albemarle April Court 1769

This Indenture and memorandum were acknowledged by RICHARD WOODS party thereto and ordered to be recorded

p.   THIS INDENTURE made the Twenty Seventh day of October in year of our Lord
79   One thousand seven hundred and Sixty Eight Between JOHN MABE of County of
       Albemarle of one part and CHARLES FERGUSON of same County of other part
       Witnesseth that said JOHN MABE for sum of fourteen pounds current money to
him in hand paid by said CHARLES FERGUSON hath bargained and sold unto CHARLES FERGUSON and his heirs one tract of land in the aforesaid County on the West side of the SOUTH WEST MOUNTAINS being part of a Patent granted to WILLIAM MABE and the same on which said JOHN MABE now lives containing by estimation Fifty acres be the same

more or less together with all the appurtenances thereto belonging To have and to hold the said tract of land unto said CHARLES FERGUSON and his heirs and JOHN MABE his heirs will forever warrant and defend In Witness whereof said JOHN MABE hath hereunto subscribed his name and affixed his Seal the day and year first above written Signed Sealed & Delivered in presence of

GEORGE MARTIN,   JOHN his mark R MABE
SAMUEL SIMPSON, DANL. SMITH

 Memorandum that on the day and year within written Peaceable and Quiet possesstion of the within mentioned land and its appurtenances was given by JOHN MABE to CHARLES FERGUSON according to the true intent and meaning of these presents Witness GEORGE MARTIN,   JOHN his mark R MABE
SAMUEL SIMPSON, DANL. SMITH

 27th October 1768 Received of CHARLES FERGUSON the within mentioned sum consideration of Fourteen pounds and I do hereby acquit him and his heirs of every part thereof Witness

GEORGE MARTIN   JOHN his mark R MABE
SAMUEL SIMPSON, DANL. SMITH

 At Albemarle May Court 1769
This Indenture memorandum and receipt were proved by the Oath of GEORGE MARTIN, SAMUEL SIMPSON and DANL. SMITH witnesses thereto and ordered to be recorded

pp.   THIS INDENTURE made this Twentyeth day of February One thousand seven hun-
80-   dred and Sixty between BENJAMIN WHITE of Parish of St. Anne County of Albe-
81   marle and Colony and Dominion of Virginia, Planter, of one part and JOHN OLD
       of Province of PENSYLVANIA and JOHN WILKINSON of County aforesaid of other
part Witnesseth that for sum of Thirty pounds current money to him said BENJAMIN WHITE in hand paid by said OLD and WILKINSON before the sealing and delivery of these presents doth bargain and sell unto said JOHN OLD and JOHN WILKINSON their heirs a certain parcel of land lying and being in Albemarle aforesaid & beginning at Captain HUDSONs Corner two white Oaks and a Maple by a Branch, running thence on his lines North eight degrees West twenty poles to a red Oak marked fore and aft North three degrees East twenty eight poles to a white Oak marked Elbow, North twenty seven degrees East one hundred and twenty two poles to a white Oak saplin on HARDWARE RIVER, thence down the same according to its meanders in a strait line one hundred and seventy four poles to a red Oak on the River, thence into the Woods North seventy nine degrees West one hundred and forty eight poles to the first station together with all Improvements profits and appurtenances thereunto belonging Except two acres already sold to JOHN COLE and assigns which is always excepted In witness whereof said BENJAMIN WHITE hath hereunto set his hand and Seal the day and year above written Signed Sealed and Delivered in the presence of

JNO. FRY,   BENJAMIN his mark + WHITE
RICHARD GILLIAM,
AUTHER his mark + GILLIAM

 Memorandum that the day and year within mentioned Peaceable and Quiet possession of within tract of land with the appurtenances thereunto belonging was had of BENJA-MIN WHITE and by his delivered to JOHN OLD and JOHN WILKINSON their heirs and assigns according to the within mentioned Deed
Signed Sealed and Delivered in the presence of

JOHN FRY,   BENJAMIN his mark + WHITE
RICHARD GILLIAM,
AUTHER his mark V GILLIAM

Received of JOHN OLD and JOHN WILKINSON this Twentyeth day of February One thou.d
seven hundred and Sixty nine the sum of Thirty pounds current money in full the consideration of the within Deed p me
Test   JOHN FRY,   BENJAMIN his mark ✝ WHITE
        RICHARD GILLIAM,
        AUTHER his mark ✝ GILLIAM
  At Albemarle May Court 1769
This Indenture memorandum and Receipt were acknowledged by BENJA. WHITE party
thereto and ordered to be recorded

pp.   THIS INDENTURE made this ninth day of December in the ninth year of the
81-   Reign of our Sovereign Lord George the third by the grace of God of Great
83   Britain France & Ireland King Defender of the Faith &c. and in the year of our
       Lord One thousand seven hundred and Sixty eight Between WM. HAMNER of the
Parish of St. Anne County of Albemarle Colony & Dominion of Virginia, Planter, of one
part and SAMUEL HAMNER of the Parish and County aforesaid, Son of said WILLIAM, of
other part Witnesseth that said WILLIAM HAMNER for and in consideration of the
natural love and affection which he hath and beareth unto said SAMUEL HAMNER and
for the better maintenance and livelihood of him said SAMUEL HAMNER but more es-
pecily for sum of Five Shillings current money to said WILLIAM HAMNER in hand paid
by SAMUEL HAMNER before the sealing and delivery of these presents doth bargain
and sell unto SAMUEL HAMNER his heirs One hundred and forty eight acres of land
being the one half of a tract of land purchased of THOMAS FITZPATRICK by said WIL-
LIAM HAMNER and by said WILLIAM HAMNER devided by a Line agreable to both parties that moiety joining to JACOB MOON JUNR. to be hereby intended to the said SAMUEL
his heirs also one Negro wench named Jane and her Child named Philis, the said lands
and slaves in the tenure and occupation of said SAMUEL HAMNER and all houses profits
and appurtenances whatsoever to said lands belonging free and discharged of all Incumbrances whatsoever In Witness whereof said WILLIAM HAMNER hath hereunto set
his hand and Seal the day and year first above written
Signed Sealed and Delivered in the presence of
        WM. MOON,   WILLIAM HAMNER
        WM. WATSON, JEREMIAH HAMNER
  Memorandum the day and year within mentioned Livery and Seisen was delivered by
WILLIAM HAMNER unto said SAML. HAMNER of within mentioned tract of land with the
slaves within mentioned and all the appurtenances to hold to him said SAMUEL HAM-
NER his heirs and assigns forever according to the within mentioned Deed
                                                     WILLIAM HAMNER
  At Albemarle May Court 1769
This Indenture and memorandum were acknowledged by WILLIAM HAMNER party
thereto and ordered to be recorded

pp.   THIS INDENTURE made this ninth day of March One thousand seven hundred and
83-   Sixty nine Between JAMES GAMMELL of one part and ANDREW RAY of other Wit-
84   nesseth that said JAMES GAMMELL for sum of Eighty pounds Currt. money of
       Virginia by these presents for the consideration aforesaid doth bargain sell and
confirm unto said ANDREW RAY and his heirs a certain tract or parcel of land lying and
being in Albemarle County on MECHEAMS RIVER containing Two hundred and nine
acres and bounded Beginning at a Hickory on the bank of the North side of the River
and runing South twelve degrees West thirty four poles to a Pine, South twenty five

degrees West One hundred poles crossing a branch of said River to a Pine and pointers,
South fifty eight degrees East one hundred and seventy two poles crossing OWENS
BRANCH to pointers in ROBERT LEWIS's Line and with LEWIS's Line North fifty eight
and a half degrees East One hundred and ninety two poles crossing a branch to pointers, then new lines North sixty six and a half degrees West two hundred and eighty
poles crossing MEACHAMS RIVER to the first station; Also another tract of land con-
tining Two hundred & three acres lying and being in Albemarle County on the South
side of MEACHAMS RIVER on OWENS BRANCH and bounded Beginning at pointers in his
& ROBERT LEWIS's Line and running with his line North fifty eight degrees East one
hundred & seventy two poles crossing OWENS BRANCH to a Pine & pointers, then new
lines South forty three & a half degrees West two hundred and thirty four poles
crossing a branch to a Pine, South sixty one and a half degrees East forty two poles
pointers on ROBERT LEWIS's line and with his line the same course continued seventy
two poles, in all one hundred and twenty poles crossing the South Fork of OWENS
BRANCH to pointers North fifteen poles to a Pine, North fifty eight and a half degrees
East two hundred and thirty six poles to the first station To have and to hold the said
lands together with all houses orchards and all other improvements belonging unto
said ANDREW RAY and his heirs In Witness whereof the parties to these presents do
interchangably set their hands and affix their Seals the date above written
Signed Sealed & Deld. in presents of
    JOEL TERRELL,   JAMES GAMMELL
    RICHD. WOODS, SAML. TALIAFERRO
  Memorandum that Quiet & peaceable possession was had and taken of the said lands by
said JAMES GAMMELL & by him delivered up unto said ANDREW RAY
    JOEL TERRELL,   JAMES GAMMELL
    RICHD. WOODS, SAML. TALIAFERRO
  Received Eighty pounds of ANDREW RAY in consideration of the within
Test SAML. TALIAFERRO   JAMES GAMMELL
  At Albemarle May Court 1769
This Indenture memorandum & Receipt were proved by the Oath of JOEL TERRELL,
RICHARD WOODS & SAMUEL TALIAFERRO witnesses thereto and ordered to be recorded

pp.   THIS INDENTURE made the twelvth day of May in year of our Lord One thousand
84-   seven hundred and Sixty nine Between JAMES CARR of County of Albemarle &
85   SARAH his Wife of one part & HENRY RANDOL of same County of other part Wit-
       nesseth that said JAMES CARR and SARAH his Wife for sum of Thirty five pounds
current money of Virginia to them in hand paid by said HENRY RANDOL by these presents do bargain and sell unto HENRY RANDOL his heirs one certain tract of land containing by estimation Two hundred acres be the same more or less lying and being in
County of Albemarle it being part of Two thousand acres granted unto CHARLES HUDSON
and bounded Begining at a white Oak runing thence North thirty five degrees West two
hundred poles to a Stake among several marked trees, North fifty five degrees East one
hundred & sixty poles to a Stake in the Muster Feald Meadow, South thirty five degrees
East two hundred poles to a white Oak in the Pattent line and longe the same South fifty
five degrees West one hundred & sixty poles to the first station with all woods profits
and appurtenances whatsoever to said tract of land belonging To have & to hold said
tract of land with the appurtenances unto HENRY RANDOL his heirs and JAMES CARR
for himself his heirs will warrant & forever defend by these presents In Witness
whereof said JAMES CARR & SARAH his Wife have hereunto interchangably set their
hands & affixed their Seals the day & year first above written

Signed Sealed & Delivered in presence of
     (no witnesses shown)

                                             JAMES KERR
                                             SARAH KERR

At Albemarle May Court 1769
This Indenture was acknowledged by JAMES KERR & SARAH his Wife parties thereto and ordered to be recorded

pp.   THIS INDENTURE made this twelth day of May in year of our Lord One thouand
85-   seven hundred and Sixty nine Between JAMES KERR of County of Albemarle &
86   SARAH his Wife of one part and WILLIAM LANGFORD of same County of other
        part Witnesseth that said JAMES KERR and SARAH his Wife for sum of Thirty six
pounds current money of Virginia to them paid by these presents do bargain and sell
unto WILLIAM LANGFORD his heirs one certain tract or parcel of land containing by
estimation One hundred & thirty five acres be the same more or less lying and being in
County of Albemarle and bounded Begining at a Chesnut Oak runing South five degrees
East sixty six poles to a Hiccory, South seventeen degrees East sixty two poles to a red
Oak, South twelve degrees West forty poles to a black Oak, South sixty one degrees West
fifty six poles to a red Oak, North sixty two degrees West ninety two poles to pointers,
North eight degrees West fifty two poles to a red Oak, North sixty three degrees West
twenty six poles to a red Oak, North thirty three degrees West twenty poles to pointers,
North nineteen degrees East twenty six poles to a white Oak, East ninety six poles to
pointers, North sixty one degrres East fifty poles to a Chesnut and North one Degree East
forty poles to the beginning with all Commons profits advantages whatsoever belonging and JAMES KERR his heirs will warrant and forever defend by these presents
In Witness whereof said JAMES KERR & SARAH his Wife have hereunto interchangably set their hands & affixed their Seals the day and year first above written
Sealed & Delivered in the presents of
     (no witnesses shown)

                                             JAMES KERR
                                           SARAH KERR

At Albemarle May Court 1769
This Indenture was acknowledged by JAME KERR and SARAH his Wife parties thereto & ordered to be recorded

pp.   THIS INDENTURE made this ninth day of May One thousand seven hundred &
87-   Sixty nine Between JOHN GRILLS of County of Albemarle of one part and THO-
88   MAS WALKER of County aforesaid of other part Witnesseth that said JOHN
        GRILLS for sum of Fifty pounds current money of Virginia to him in hand paid
by these presents do bargain and sell unto THOMAS WALKER his heirs one certain tract
or parcel of land lying and being in County of Albemarle containing Four hundred
acres and bounded Beginning at a Pine at the head of a Branch of IVY CREEK running
thence new lines South ten degrees West three hundred & twenty poles to pointers,
South eighty degrees East two hundred poles to a black Oak, North ten degrees East three
hundred and twenty poles to a Pine and North eighty degrees West two hundred poles to
the first station together with all houses profits & hereditaments whatsoever to the
same belonging and JOHN GRILLS his heirs will warrant & defend the said land and premises with the appurtenances unto said THOMAS WALKER his heirs In Witness whereof
said JOHN GRILLS hath hereunto set his hand & Seal the day and year above written
Signed Sealed & Delivered in the presence of
     MICHAEL THOMAS,   JOHN GRILLS
     CHARLES IRVING, JOHN JONES,
     JOHN MARTIN, WILLIAM MOOR, WILLIAM COX

Memorandum that on the day & year within written Quiet and peaceable possession of
the land & premises within mentioned with the appurtenances thereunto belonging
was given by JOHN GRILLS to THOMAS WALKER according to the form & effect of the
within written Indenture
Witness MICHAEL THOMAS, JOHN MARTIN,   JOHN GRILLS
       JOHN JONES, CHARLES IRVING,
       WILLIAM MOORE, WILLIAM COX
Received of THOMAS WALKER the day and year aforesaid the sum of Fifty pounds
current money it being the consideration within mentioned
                                                        JOHN GRILLS

   At Albemarle May Court 1769
This Indenture memorandum & receipt were proved by the Oaths of JOHN MARTIN,
JOHN JONES & WILLIAM MOORE Witnesses thereto & ordered to be recorded

pp.   THIS INDENTURE made this fourth day of March in year of our Lord One thou-
88-   sand seven hundred and Sixty nine Between WILLIAM CREASEY JUNR. of
89   BUCKINGHAM COUNTY of one part & GEORGE THOMPSON of County of Albemarle
        of other part Witnesseth that said CREASEY for sum of Thirty pounds current
money to him in hand paid by GEORGE THOMPSON by these presents doth bargain and
sell unto said GEORGE THOMPSON one certain tract or parcel of land containing by estimation Two hundred acres of land be the same more or less lying and being in County
of Albemarle on both sides of CUNNINGHAMS CREEK joining the lands of WILLIAM
PRINCE, JOHN HADEN & JOSEPH THOMPSON deced, which said land was granted to EDWD
MOODY by Patent & by him conveyed to SAMUEL BIRKS which said land with the appurtenances thereunto belonging said WILLIAM CREASEY JUNR. doth hereby confirm unto
said GEORGE THOMPSON to hold said tract of land with the appurtenances unto said
GEORGE THOMPSON his heirs and said CREASEY will warrant and forever defend by these
presents In Witness whereof said CREASEY hath hereunto set his hand & Seal the day &
year first above written
Signed Sealed & Delivered in the presence of
       PATK. NAPIER,   WILLIAM CREASEY JUNR.
       JOHN WILLIAMSON,
       ROGER THOMPSON, THOS. NAPIER
 Memorandum that on the day of the within written Indenture Quiet & peaceable pos-
session & Seizin of the lands was taken by WM. CREASEY JUNR & by him given to GEORGE
THOMPSON according to the form & effect of the within Deed
In presence of PATK. NAPIER,   WILLIAM CREASEY JUNR.
       ROGER THOMPSON, JOHN WMSON.,
       THOS. NAPIER
 Reced on day of the date of within Indenture of GEORGE THOMPSON the sum of Thirty
pounds current money being the consideration money within expressed I say reced
       ROGER THOMPSON,   p me   WILLIAM CREASEY JUNR.
       JNO. WMSON., THOS. NAPIER
  At Albemarle May Court 1769
This Indenture & memorandum & Receipt were proved by the Oath of JOHN WILLIAM-
SON witness thereto & the same having been proved by two other witnesses were
ordered to be recorded

pp.   Albemarle Coty. Sct
89-   TO ALL TO WHOM these presents shall come Know ye that for and in considera-
90   tion of sum of Twenty three pounds Eleven Shillings & three pence to me in
        hand paid by ROBERT CLARK, WILLIAM HOWARD, Goldsmith, hath sold & deli-
vered unto ssid ROBERT CLARK the following goods & Chattels &c. One feather bed & furniture, one Gray Mare and Colt, one frying pann, one Seal skin trunk, two one Iron
morter, one Cow & Calf, one womans Saddle, one half acre of land or Lot in the Town of
CHARLOTTESVILLE adjacent to the Lotts of RICHARD WOODS (and bought of said WOODS)
and one Negro woman named Doll and being the same that was formerly the property
of GILES ALLEGRE which said feather bed &c. to said ROBERT CLARK and his heirs & the
said WILLIAM HOWARD for himself & his heirs will forever warrant & defend by these
presents In Witness whereof the said HOWARD hath hereunto set his hand & Seal this
30th day of December 1768
Test THOS. ANDERSON   WM. HOWARD
    At Albemarle May Court 1769
This Deed was acknowledged by WILLIAM HOWARD party thereto & ordered to be
recorded

p.   THIS INDENTURE made the (blank) day of (blank) one thousand seven hundred
90   & sixty nine Between JOHN CLARK & MARY his Wife of Albemarle County of one
        part and JOSIAH WOOD of said County of other part Witnesseth that said JOHN
CLARK and MARY his Wife for sum of Sixteen pounds current money of Virginia by
these presents for the consideration aforesaid doth bargain and sell unto said JOSIAH
WOOD and his heirs a certain tract or parcel of land lying and being in Albemarle County containing Two hundred acres and bounded Beginning at a red Oak in the said WOOD's
line, thence with the said line North fifty seven and a half degrees East one hundred &
sixty six poles to pointers, thence new lines South eight two degrees East one hundred
pole to pointers, thence South forty degrees East seventy poles to a red Oak, thence
South forty eight degrees West sixty poles to pointers, thence South seventy two degrees
West one hundred & sixty four poles to pointers, thence South eighty degrees East fifty
six poles to a red Oak, thence South seventy two degrees West fifty six poles to pointers,
thence North eighteen degrees West fifty six poles to pointers, thence North twenty &
three quarters degrees West eighty four poles to pointers, North seven degrees East ten
poles to the first station To have hold possess and enjoy the premises together with all
houses orchards gardens improvements unto same belonging unto said JOSIAH WOOD
and his heirs In Witness whereof the parties to these presents do interchangably set
their hands & affix their Seals the day already above written
Signed Sealed & delivered in presence of
        (no witnesses shown)   JOHN CLARK
                                                              MARY CLARK
    At Albemarle May Court 1769
This Indenture was acknowledged by JOHN CLARK & MARY his Wife parties thereto &
ordered to be recorded

pp.   THIS INDENTURE made the 5th day of April in year of our Lord Christ One thou-
91-   sand seven hundred Fifty & nine between JOHN CHISWELL Gent. in the Parish of
92   Saint Martin in County of HANOVER and Colony of Virginia of one part and JOHN
        ALLEN of Parish of Saint Anns in the County of Albemarle of other part Witnes-
seth that said JOHN CHISWELL for sum of Twenty pounds Currant money of Virginia to
him in hand paid by these presents doth bargain and sell unto JOHN ALLEN his heirs

one certain tract or parcel of land containing Two hundred acres lying & being in County of Albemarle near the BLUE MOUNTAINS & bounded Beginning at pointers in THOMAS BELLs line and with his line South twenty six degrees East two hundred poles to a Chesnut in Colo. JOHN CHISWELLs back line and with it North fifty three degrees East one hundred & six poles to a white Oak, new lines North twenty three degrees thirty minutes West two hundred poles crossing a Branch to pointers, & South fifty three degrees West One hundred & seventy poles to the first station being part of a larger tract belonging to said JOHN CHISWELL Gent. To have & to hold said tract of land containing Two hundred acres as above bounded with all houses profits whatsoever and JOHN CHIS- WELL his heirs the said tract of land with the appurtenances unto said JOHN ALLEN his heirs will warrent & forever defend by these presents In Witness whereof said JOHN CHISWELL hath hereunto set his hand affixed his Seal the day & year above written Signed Sealed & Delivered in presence of

JOHN HENDERSON JUNR.,   JNO. CHISWELL
DAVID CRAWFORD, MICAJAH CHILES

Memorandum that on the 5th day of April One thousand seven hundred & Fifty nine livery and Seizen of the within sold land & premises was made and done by JOHN CHIS- WELL to the said JOHN ALLEN within mentioned
Witness present JOHN HENDERSON, JUNR.   JNO. CHISWELL
DAVID CRAWFORD, MICAJAH CHILES

April the 5th 1769 Then received of JOHN ALLEN the consideration money within mentioned reced p me   JNO. CHISWELL
Witness present JOHN HENDERSON JUNR.,
DAVID CRAWFORD, MICAJAH CHILES

At Albemarle May Court 1769
This Indenture memorandum & receipt were proved by the Oath of MICAJAH CHILES & the same having been before proved by two other Wits. was ordered to be recd.

pp.   THIS INDENTURE made this first day of April in year of our Lord God One thou-
93-   sand seven hundred & Sixty nine Between DAVID LEWIS JUNR. of Parish of St.
94   Anne of County of Albemarle of one part and HENRY TILLEY of same County and
        Parish of other part Witnesseth that said DAVID LEWIS JUNR. for consideration
of thirty pounds to him in hand paid by these presents doth bargain & sell unto HENRY TILLEY his heirs one certain track of land one hundred and twenty nine acres & being in County of Albemarle on South Branch of MECHUMS RIVER and bounded Begining at a Corner white Oak of WILLIAM LITTLEs and with his line South fourteen degrees East sixty poles to a Pine saplin, North eighty degrees East ninety nine to a white Oak in JOHN WOODS line and with his line South thirteen degrees West Eighty poles to pointers South thirty degrees East eighty two poles crossing the South Branch of MECHUMS RIVER to corner red Oak & white Oak saplins in MATHEW MILLS's line & with his lines South sixty two degrees West ninety eight poles to a white Oak South twenty five de- grees West twenty eight poles to a Pine, thence on new lines North thirty seven degrees West twenty six poles to pointers in SAMUEL BLACKs line and with his lines North forty degrees East twenty poles to pointers, North eleven degrees East one hundred & four poles crossing the South Branch of MECHUMS RIVER to a Pine, North sixty two degrees West seventy two poles to pointers round a Rock, North forty five degrees West fifty six poles to a Pine a new line North thirty six degrees West fifty two poles to pointers in THOS. READ's line and with his line North Eighty one degrees East eight poles to the be- ginning To have and to hold the said tract of land with all houses prophits and whatsoever and DAVID LEWIS for himself his heirs to said HENRY TILLEY his heirs shall war-

rant and by these presents forever defend In Witness whereof said DAVID LEWIS hath
sett his hand & Seal the first day of April 1769

DAVID LEWIS JUNR.

Memorandum that on the first day of April One thousand seven hundred & sixty nine
Livery & Seisin of the above granted land & premises was given by DAVID LEWIS unto
HENRY TILLEY

DAVID LEWIS JUNR.

At a Court held for Albemarle County the 8th day of June 1769
This Indenture & memorandum was acknowledged by DAVID LEWIS JUNR. party thereto
and ordered to be recorded

pp.   THIS INDENTURE made this fifth day of June One thousand seven hundred Sixty
94-   nine Between SAMUEL STOCKTON of Parish of St. Anne County of Albemarle
95   Colony & Dominion of Virginia, Planter, of one part and JAMES GARLAND of the
         Parish and County aforesaid, Planter, of other part Witnesseth that SAMUEL
STOCKTON for sum of Thirty pounds current money to him in hand paid by said JAMES
GARLAND by these presents doth bargain & sell unto said JAMES GARLAND all that
messuage & tenement commonly called THE MILL & LOTT situate on STOCKTONS RUN
known by the name of STOCKTONS MILL the land bind upon PATRICK DAVIS's, JOHN
SHIELD, & said JAMES GARLAND containing Twenty eight acres and all houses woods and
all appurtenances which to said Mill & Lands do appertain To have and to hold the said
Tenement Mill Lands & premises abovementioned with the appurtenances unto said
JAMES GARLAND his Executors & assigns for and during the term of Four years Provided always & upon condition that if said SAMUEL STOCKTON his heirs do well & truly
pay or cause to be paid unto sd JAMES GARLAND his Executors or assigns the sum of
Thirty pounds current money with legal Interest for the same in & upon the first day of
June next ensuing the date hereof then these presents & every thing therein con-
tained shall cease determine & be void any thing herein contained to the contrary notwithstanding In Witness whereof the sd SAMUEL STOCKTON have to these presents sent
his hand & Seal the day & year first above written
Signed Sealed & Delivered in the presence of
         (no witnesses shown)   SAMUEL STOCKTON
  At Albemarle June Court 1769
This Indenture was acknowledged by SAMUEL STOCKTON party thereto and ordered to be
recorded

pp.   THIS INDENTURE made this (blank) day of (blank) One thousand seven hundred
95-   and Sixty nine Between MICHAEL WOODS of Parish of St. Anne, County of Albe-
97   marle Colony & Dominion of Virginia, Planter, of one part and WILLIAM WOODS
         of the Parish of Fredericksville, County & Colony aforesaid, Son of said MICHAEL,
of other part Witnesseth that in consideration of the love & good will & for the better
maintenance of him the said WILLIAM WOODS but more especially for the sum of Five
Shillings current money to him said MICHAEL WOODS in hand paid by sd WILLIAM by
these presents doth give bargain sell & confirm unto said WILLIAM WOODS his heirs a
certain tract or parcel of land containing Three hundred acres lying & being in County
of Albemarle on the Branches of IVY CREEK and bounded Beginning at a Pine on Colo.
ROBERT LEWIS line and with it North fifty six degrees East three hundred & eighty poles
to pointers, new line North sixty eight degrees West at ninety poles at a Marsh at one
hundred & ten poles another one hundred & thirty poles to pointers, West at fifty poles
one hundred and twenty four poles to pointers, South three degrees East sixty four

poles to pointers, South sixty six degrees West at seventy eight poles a branch eighty six poles to a white Oak, South fifty poles to pointers, South fifty one degrees East forty four poles to pointers, South Eleven degrees West forty poles to pointers and South fifty five poles to the first station Together with all houses orchards profits and appurtenances thereunto belonging free and discharged or otherwise sufficiently kept harmless and Indemnified from all Incumbrances whatsoever In Witness whereof said MICHAEL WOODS hath set his hand & Seal to these presents the day & year first above written Sign'd Seal'd & Deliver'd in the presence of

(no witnesses shown)   MICHAEL WOODS

Memorandum that on the day & year within written peaceable possession of the within tract of land was had of MICHAEL WOODS and by him delivered to WILLIAM WOODS to be enjoyed by him his heirs & assigns forever according to the within Deed Signed Sealed & Delivered in presence of

(no witnesses shown)   MICHAEL WOODS

At Albemarle June Court 1769
This Indenture & memorandum was acknowledged by MICHAEL WOODS party thereto & ordered to be recorded. ANN the Wife of the said MICHAEL personally appeared in Court and being first privately examined as the Law directs voluntarily relinquished her right of Dower in the Estate conveyed by her sd Husband

pp.   THIS INDENTURE made the Eighth day of June One thousand seven hundred and
97-   Sixty nine Between ANDREW RAY and MARY his Wife of Albemarle County in
98   the one part and WILLIAM MICHIE of said County of other part Witnesseth that
         ANDREW RAY and MARY his Wife for and in consideration of one Negro man
slave named Bristol by these presents doth bargain sell and confirm unto WILLIAM MICHIE his heirs a certain tract of land containing by Estimation One hundred & fifty acres lying and being in Albemarle County in the Parish of Fredericksville on MEA-CHAMS RIVER and is part of the land purchased by said RAY of JAMES GAMMELL and bounded Beginning at a Hickory on the bank of the North side of said River & running South twelve degrees West thirty four poles to a Pine, South twenty five degrees West down to the said River, thence down with the River about fifty poles, thence across the said River to a Beech on the other side, thence along the Main Ridge which divides this land principal branches in the said late purchased land to ROBERT LEWIS's line, thence with said line North fifty eight and a half degrees East about two hundred poles crossing a branch to pointers, thence a new line North forty six and an half degrees West two hundred & eighty six poles crossing MEACHAMS RIVER to the first Station To have and to hold said One hundred & fifty acres of land within the said bounds be the same more or less with all Improvements to the same belonging unto WILLIAM MICHIE and his heirs and ANDREW RAY doth for himself his heirs warrant the said One hundred & fifty acres of land unto WILLIAM MICHIE his heirs In Witness whereof said ANDREW RAY & MARY his Wife doth hereunto set their hands & Seals the day & year first above written
Signed Sealed & Delivered in presence of

(no witnesses shown)   ANDREW RAY
                                                         MARY RAY

At Albemarle June County 1769
This Indenture was acknowledged by ANDREW RAY & MARY his Wife parties thereto & ordered to be recorded

p.   KNOW ALL MEN by these presents that I HUGH DOUGHERTY of Albemarle County
98   in Virginia for and in consideration of sum of Three hundred and fifty two
        pounds current money to me in hand by GEORGE BLANE of said County before
the sealing and delivery of these presents doth bargain and sell in open market unto sd
GEORGE BLANE his heirs seven slaves with all the goods Cattle Hogs and Plantation Tools
& utensils with two Mares & one Colt with every other necessaries to me belonging except the Wheat, Corn & other Grain & Tobo. at said Plantation already made and other
things by me already accepted to be the property from henceforth of said GEORGE
BLANE & his heirs and will warrant & forever defend Given under my hand & Seal this
30th day of January Anno Domini 1769
Signed Sealed & Delivered in presence of
        CHAS. LAMBERT,   HUGH his mark ─✝─ DOUGHERTY
        GEORGE LAMBERT, DAVID LAMBERT
  At Albemarle June Court 1769
This Deed was acknowledged by HUGH DOUGHERTY party thereto & ordered to be re-
corded

pp.   THIS INDENTURE made this twelfth day of April in year of our Lord God One
98-   thousand seven hundred & sixty nine Between HUGH DOUGHERTY of County of
100   Albemarle of ye one part & GEORGE BLANE of same County of other part & both
        of Colony of Virginia. Whereas by one Pattent under the Great Seal of the
Colony & Dominion of Virginia bearing date the fifth day of August One thousand seven
hundred & Thirty seven & in the Eleventh year of the Reign of our Sovereign Lord
King George the second by the grace of God of Great Britain France & Ireland, King Defender of the Faith &c. there was granted unto HUGH DOUGHERTY one certain tract or
parcel of land containing Four hundred acres lying & being in County of Albemarle on
both sides of BISKET RUN a Branch of MOORES CREK by virtue of said Pattent remaining
of record in the Secretaries Office of this Colony relation thereunto being had may
more fully appear Now This Indenture Witnesseth that ye said HUGH DOUGHERTY for the
sum of Eighty pounds current money of Virginia to me in hand paid by GEORGE BLANE
by these presents doth bargain & sell unto said GEORGE BLANE his heirs two hundred
acres of land a part of the aforesaid tract of four hundred Beginning at two white Oaks
running thence South forty eight degrees East Seventy one poles to pointers, thence
South forty two Degrees West & upon that line to extend until it includes two hundred
and by or Deviding between that part of above tract already granted to MICHAEL
DOUGHERTY deced as by the records may more fully appear with all houses orchards
mines minerals swamps profits & hereditament whatsoever belonging To have & to hold
the said tract of land unto said GEORGE BLANE his heirs and HUGH DOUGHERTY his heirs
will warrant and forever defend by these presents In Witness whereof I do hereby set
my hand & Seal the day & year above written
Signed Sealed and Delivered in presence of
        CHARLES GOLDSBY,   HUGH his mark ⸺ DOUGHERTY
        DAVID LAMBERT, CHAS. LAMBERT
  Memorandum that this day & year within mentioned Quiet & peaceable possession of
the within mentioned tract of land with the apprentices thereof was had of HUGH
DOUGHERTY & by him delivered to GEORGE BLANE to be by him his heirs forever enjoyed
acording to the within mentioned Deed
Signed Sealed & Delivered in the presence of
        CHARLES GOLDSBY,   HUGH his mark ⸺ DOUGHERTY
        DAVID LAMBERT, CHARLES LAMBERT

Received this twelfth day of April One thousand seven hundred & sixty nine the sum of
eighty pounds current money being in consideration of the within parcel of land
Test CHAS. LAMBERT &c. &c.   p me   HUGH his mark   DOUGHERTY
    At Albemarle June Court 1769
This Indenture memorandum & receipt was acknowledged by HUGH DOUGHERTY party
thereto & ordered to be recorded

pp.   GEORGE the Third by the grace of God of Great Britain, France & Ireland, King
100-   Defender of the faith &c. To HENRY GILBERT & GARLAND ANDERSON Gent.
101   Greeting. Whereas BEN BROWN & SUSAN his Wife by their Indenture of Feoff-
        ment bearing date the Xth day of March 1767 have conveyed the Fee simple
Estate of Eight hundred & fifty acres of land lying & being in County of Albemarle unto
JOHN WINSTON And Whereas the said SUSAN cannot conveniently travel to our County
Court of Albemarle to make acknowledgment of said conveyance, Therefore we do give
unto you power to receive the acknowledgment which the said SUSAN shall be willing
to make before you of the conveyance aforesaid contained in the said Indenture hereunto annexed and when you have received her acknowledgment and Examined her as
aforesaid that you distinctly & openly certify our Justices thereof in our said County
Court under your Seals sending then there this Writ. Witness JOHN NICHOLAS Clk. of our
said Court the XVth day of March 1769 in the Eighth year of our Reign
                                        HENRY FRY DC
    The Execution of this Writ appears in a certain Schedule hereunto annexed

HANOVER COURT By Virtue of the Commission hereto annexed, we the Subscribers do
on the 25th day of March in the 9th year of the Reign of our Sovereign Lord George the
Third and in the year of our Lord Christ 1768 go to said SUSAN and examined her
privately (return of the Execution of the privy Examinmation of SUSAN, Wife of BEN BROWN)
Witness our hands & Seals this 25th day of March 1769   HENRY GILBERT
                                                          GARL. ANDERSON
    At Albemarle August Court 1769
This Relinquishment was returned to Court and ordered to be recorded

pp.   GEORGE the Third by the grace of God of Great Britain France & Ireland King De-
101-   fender of the Faith &c. to HENRY GILBERT and GARLAND ANDERSON Gent.
102   Greeting. Whereas BEN BROWN and SUSAN his Wife by their Indenture bearing
        date the XIth day of December 1767 have conveyed the fee simple Estate of Five
hundred & sixty three acres of land lying & being in County of Albemarle unto WIL-
LIAM OVERTON WINSTON And Whereas the said SUSAN cannot conveniently travel to
our said Court of Albemarle to make acknowledgment of said conveyance therefore we
do give unto you power to receive the acknowledgment which the said SUSAN shall be
willing to make before you of the conveyance aforesaid and when you have received
her acknowledgment and examined her as aforesaid that you distinctly & openly certify
our Justices thereof under your Seals sending then there this Indenture and this Writ
Witness JOHN NICHOLAS Clk. of our sd Court the XVIth day of March in the Eighth year
of our Reign   HENRY FRY DC
    The Execution of this Writ apprears in a certain schedule hereunto annexed

HANOVER COUNTY
    By virtue of the Commission hereunto annexed (the return of the Execution of the privy
Examination of SUSAN, the Wife of BEN BROWN) Witness our hands and Seals this 25th day of

March 1769   HENRY GILBERT
                                                      GARL. ANDERSON

At Albemarle August Court 1769
This Relinquishment was returned to Court and ordered to be recorded

pp.   GEORGE the third by the grace of God of Great Britain, France & Ireland King
102-   Defender of the faith &c. to HENRY GILBERT & GARLAND ANDERSON Gentlemen
103   Greeting. Whereas BEN BROWN & SUSAN his Wife by their Indenture of Feoff-
         ment bearing date the XXIVth day of December 1767 have conveyed the fee
simple Estate of eight hundred and twenty six acres of land lying and being in the
County of Albemarle unto ANTHONY WINSTON And Whereas the said SUSAN cannot conveniently travel to our County Court of Albemarle to make acknowledgment of the said
Conveyance Therefore we do give unto you power to receive the acknowledgment the
said SUSAN shall be willing to make before you and when you have received her acknowledgment that you distinctly & openly certify our Justices thereof in our County
Court under your Seals sending then there this Indenture & this Writ Witness JOHN
NICHOLAS Clk. of our said Court the XVIth day of March in the eighth year of our Reign
                                                      HENRY FRY DC
    The Exection of this Commission appears in a certain schedule hereunto annexed

HANOVER to wit
  By virtue of the Commission hereunto annexed we the Subscribers did on the 25th day
of March in the 9th year of the Reign of our Sovereign Lord George the third and in
the year of our Lord Christ 1769 go to the said SUSAN (return of the Execution of the privy
Examination of SUSAN, the Wife of BEN BROWN) Witness our hands & Seals this 25th day of
March 1769   HENRY GILBERT
                                                      GARL. ANDERSON

  At Albemarle August Court 1769
This Relinquishment was returned to Court and ordered to be recorded

pp.   GEORGE the Third by the grace of God of Great Britain, France & Ireland, King
103-   Defender of the faith &c. to WILLIAM MICHELL, WILLIAM HARRISON Gent.
104   Greeting Whereas ROBERT LEWIS & JANE his Wife by their Indenture of Feoff-
         ment bearing date the Ninth day of February One thousand Seven hundred &
Sixty nine have conveyed the fee simple Estate of Eight hundred acres of land lying and
being in County of Albemarle unto SAMUEL MARTIN & Whereas the said JANE cannot
conveniently travel to our said County Court of Albemarle to make acknowledgment of
the said conveyance, Therefore we do give unto you power to receive the acknowledgment which the said JANE shall be willing to make before you of the conveyance
aforesaid and when you have received her acknowledgment and Examined her as
aforesaid that you distinctly & openly certify our said Justices thereof in our County
Court of Albemarle under your Seals sending then there this Writ Witness JOHN
NICHOLAS Clk. of our said Court the 13th day of June 1769 in the ninth year of our
Reign   TUCK. WOODSON Dy. Clk.

GOODCHLANDCOUNTY
  We WILLIAM MITCHEL & WILLIAM HARRISON two of his Majesties Justices of the peace
for the County aforesaid have personally & apart from her Husband examined the
within named JANE LEWIS who freely & willingly relinquishes her right of Dower to

the within mentioned tract of land & premises Certified under our hand this first day
of July 1769   WIL. MICHELL
                                                               WM. HARRISON

At Albemarle August Court 1769
This Acknowledgment was returned to Court & ordered to be recorded

pp.   THIS INDENTURE made this twenty fourth day of May One thousand seven hun-
104-   dred & Sixty nine Between ROBERT ADAMS of County of Albemarle of one part
105   and JAMES & ROBERT DONALDS & CO. of the other part Witnesseth that said
           ROBERT ADAMS for sum of Six hundred & four pounds One Shillings & Five pence
current money of Virginia to him in hand paid by these presents doth bargain & sell
unto JAMES & ROBERT DONALDS & CO. two tracts of land (to wit) One tract containing
Eleven hundred acres whereon I now live, another tract on MECHUNK CREEK containing Eight hundred acres, as also one case knife which said land and case knife are
now in the possession of said JAMES & ROBERT DONALDS & CO. the said lands & case knife
above mentioned have bargained & sold unto said JAMES & ROBERT DONALDS & CO. their
heirs Provided Always & upon condition that if said ROBERT ADAMS his heirs do pay or
cause to be paid unto said JAMES & ROBERT DONALDS & CO. their heirs the full sum of Six
hundred & four pounds One Shillings & Five pence with lawfull Interest thereon from
this date til the twenty fourth day of May One thousand seven hundred & seventy two
that then these presents and everything herein contained shall cease determine & be
void anything herein to the contrary notwithstanding In Witness whereof said ROBERT
ADAMS hath hereunto set his hand & Seal the day & year above written
Signed Sealed & Delivered in the presence of
           TUCK. WOODSON JR.,   ROBT. ADAMS
           JOEL TERRELL, PETER DAVIE
   Received this day & year within written of JAMES & ROBERT DONALDS & CO. Six hun-
dred & four pounds One Shillings and Five pence the within consideration
Test   TUCK. WOODSON JUNR.   ROBT. ADAMS
           JOEL TERRELL, PETER DAVIE
   At Albemarle August Court 1769
This Indenture was proved by the Oath of TUCKER WOODSON JUNR., JOEL TERRELL &
PETER DAVIE Witnesses thereto & together with the Receipt thereon endorsed ordered to
be recorded

p.   KNOW ALL MEN by these presents that we EDWARD CARTER & PETERFIELD TRENT
105   both of Albemarle County Colony & Dominion of Virginia are held & firmly
           bound unto JOHN GILLUM of County & Colony aforesaid in the sum of One thou-
sand pounds Sterling to be paid unto said JOHN GILLUM his heirs and for the perfor-
mance of this bond we bind ourselves jointly & severally Sealed with our seals and
dated this seventh day of July One thousand seven hundred & Sixty nine
   The Condition of the above obligation is such that whereas the above named JOHN
GILLUM purchased a certain Negro wench from the above EDWARD CARTER for the sum
of Seventy five pounds current money Now know ye that if the above EDWARD CARTER
and PETERFIELD TRENT for themselves their heirs will forever warrant and maintain
the right & property of ye above Negro wench and her increase if any to sd JOHN
GILLUM his heirs freed & sufficiently saved & kept harmless of and from all former Incumbrances whatsoever which the said Negro might be subject to before the above
purchase then the above obligation to be void otherwise to remain in full force &
virtue

Signed Sealed & Delivered in the presence of
    JAMES TURNER,   EDWD. CARTER
    WM. WATSON, JOHN SWANN   PETRFIELD TRENT
  At Albemrle August Court 1769
This Bond was proved by JAMES TURNER, WM. WATSON & JOHN SWANN witnesses thereto
& ordered to be recorded

pp.   THIS INDENTURE made the Tenth day of August in year of our Lord One thousand
106-   seven hundred & sixty nine Between ELISHA LYON of Albemarle County of one
107   part and CHARLES MARTIN of the same County of other part Witnesseth that
       said ELISHA LYON for sum of One hundred pounds current money of Virginia to
him in hand paid by CHARLES MARTIN by these presents doth bargain & sell unto
CHARLES MARTIN and to his heirs one certain tract of land containing One hundred
acres by estimation be the same more or less it being the land whereon I now live part
of the said land being in Albemarle & part in AMHERST joyning JOHN LYON, NICHOLAS
LYON, PETER LYON & WEBB KIDDs lines together with all houses orchards and every of
their appurtenances To have and to hold the said hundred acres of land & other the
premises hereby granted unto CHARLES MARTIN his heirs In Witness whereof the said
ELISHA LYON hath hereunto set his hand & Seal the day & year above written
                                ELISHA his mark   LYON

  Memorandum that the day & year within mentioned Quiet & peaceable possession of
the within tract of land was delivered to CHARLES MARTIN according to the within
mentioned Deed
                                ELISHA his mark   LYON
  Received of CHARLES MARTIN the sum of One hundred pounds current money it being
in full consideration of the within tract of land
                                ELISHA his mark   LYON

  At Albemarle August Court 1769
This Indenture Memorandum & Receipt were acknowledged by ELISHA LYON party
thereto & ordered to be recorded. MARY the Wife of the said ELISHA appeared in Court
& having been first privately Examined as the Law directs relinquished her right of
Dower in the land conveyed by her said Husband

pp.   THIS INDENTURE made the twenty first day of June in year of our Lord One thou-
107-   sand seven hundred and Sixty nine Between GILBERT MARSHALL of AUGUSTA
108   COUNTY of one part and ABRAHAM MUSICK of Albemarle County of other part
       Witnesseth that GILBERT MARSHALL for sum of Thirty pounds current money of
Virginia to him in hand paid by these presents do bargain sell and confirm unto ABRA-
HAM MUSICK his heirs one certain tract of land containing three hundred and thirty
acres lying and being in County of Albemarle on LICKENHOLE CREEK beginning at a
white Oak of HENRY KERRs four poles to a point of Rocks JOHN COWENS Corner and with
COWENS lines North eighty two degrees East seventy eight poles to pointers, then with
new lines North seventeen degrees West one hundred & twelve poles to a Pine and
North forty nine Degrees West One hundred & thirty two poles to pointers in DAVID
MILLS line and with his line South fifty degrees West one hundred and thirty six poles
to pointers and North seventy two degrees West one hundred and sixty poles to pointers
in ANDREW McWILLIAMS line & with it South thirteen degrees East two hundred & forty
poles to pointers in HENRY KERRs line & with his lines North thirty three degrees East
one hundred poles to pointers and South eighty five degrees East two hundred & ten

poles to the beginning To have & to hold the said Track of land and all houses profits &
whatever as Witness my hand & Seal this twenty first day of June 1769
Signed Sealed & delivered in presence of
  HENRY CARR,   GILBERT MARSHAL
  SAMUEL CARR, TERRELL MUSICK
 Memorandum that on the twenty first day of June in year of God One thousand seven
hundred & sixty nine peaceable & Quiet possession and Seisen of the land & premises
within mentioned was had and taken by within named GILBERT MARSHAL and his heirs
forever
Test HENRY CARR,   GILBERT MARSHAL
  SAMUEL CARR, TERRELL MUSICK
 At Albemarle August Court 1769
This Indenture & memorandum was proved by the Oath of HENRY CARR, SAMUEL CARR
& TERRELL MUSICK witnesses thereto & ordered to be recorded

p. (On margin: Exad. and taken out by the said)
109 TO ALL TO WHOM these presents shall come I ABEL HAZELRIGG send Greeting.
  Know ye that for and in consideration of the natural love & affection I bear to
my Daughter, SALLY, do give her one Negro wench named Mill & my best feather bed &
furniture to her and her heirs forever reserving to me said Negro and said Bed untill
such time my Daughter shall arrive to age and after a moderate rent for my support
paid me yearly during my life and my Wife. Item for same cause me thereunto moving I
do give to my beloved Son, RICHARD, one Negro child named Jenny now about 10
months old as also a Cow & Calf to him the said RICHARD and his heirs to be subject o the
same provisoe as the Negro wench given to his Sister. Item and next and for the same
cause I do give to my Son in Law JOSEPH PYE a Sorrel Mare branded on the near buttock
N & a good cow & calf to him the said JOSEPH & his heirs but under the same limitations
with my Daughter, SALLY, and my Son, RICHARD, and to my Son in Law JOSEPH PYE I do
freely warrant & make good as Witness my hand this 10th day of August 1769
       ABEL his mark A HAZELRIGG
 At Albemarle August Court 1769
This Deed was acknowledged by ABEL HAZELRIGG party thereto and ordered to be recorded

pp. THIS INDENTURE made this (blank) day of (blank) in year of our Lord One thou-
109- sand seven hundred & Sixty eight Between JOHN KINKEAD, Farmer, of County of
110 Albemarle of one part & ABNER WOOD of sd County of other part Witnesseth that
  JOHN KINKEAD for sum of Thirty six pounds current money of Virginia to him
paid by ye sd ABNER WOOD by these presents doth bargain & sell unto ABNER WOOD & his
heirs one certain tract or parcel of land containing One hundred acres more or less
being part of a Tract of land conveyed by WILLIAM GRAYSON to sd JOHN KINKEAD this
said One hundred acres being part of five hundred & twenty acres which was conveyed
by Mr. JOHN ROBINSON Esqr. to ye sd GRAYSON and bounded Begining at HUGHES Corner
stone & pointers, thence North thirty degrees West thirty eight poles to pointers,
thence South fifty four Deg. West fifty eight poles to pointers in JOHN ALLENs Line,
thence North seventy two degrees West twenty two poles to a new corner red Oak sapling, thence on new lines One hundred & ten poles to pointers, thence North sixty two
Deg. East on a strait line that runs to SAMUEL JENKINS corner white Oak the said line
being two hundred & five poles long and the line to run so far as the Line as ANDREW &
JOHN KINKEAD hath agreed the other part of the line belonging to sd ANDREW KINKEAD

and from that course of their making to ye beginning HUGHES Corner Stone & pointers
Together with all houses & advantages whatsoever to sd land belonging To have & to
hold the sd land & premises with ye appurtenances unto ABNER WOOD his heirs and
JOHN KINKEAD his heirs and all other persons will warrant & forever defend by these
presents In Witness whereof the sd JOHN KINKEAD hath hereunto set his Seal
Sealed & delivered in presence of
  (no witnesses shown)   JOHN KINKEAD
 Then received of ABNER WOOD the sum of thirty six pounds being the consideration
within mentioned   JOHN KINKEAD
 At Albemarle August Court 1769
This Indenture & receipt were acknowledged by JOHN KINKEAD party thereto and
ordered to be recorded

pp. THIS INDENTURE made this seventh day of August in year of our Lord One thou-
110- sand seven hundred & Sixty nine Between RICHARD MELTON of County of Albe-
111 marle of one part and JAMES COOPER of said County of other part Witnesseth
  that said RICHARD MELTON for sum of Ten pounds current money of Virginia to
him in hand paid by said JOHN COOPER by these presents doth bargain and sell unto
JAMES COOPER his heirs one certain tract or parcel of land lying & being in County of
Albemarle and bounded on the Branches of RACOON & CUNNINGHAM CREEKS to witt
Beginning at a Pine running thence new lines South twenty three degrees West two
hundred and Sixty three poles crossing a Branch to a Pine, North sixty seven degrees
West One hundred & seventy five poles and a half to the Deviding Line and being laid of
by a line of markt trees crossing a tract of land and being the lower part of the said
tract of land of four Hundred acres granted unto JOHN WEBB by Patent bearing date the
tenth day of June One thousand seven hundred & Sixty and conveid to said RICHARD
MELTON and containing by estimation Two hundred acres be the same more or less with
the appurtenances To have & to hold said tract of land with the appurtenances unto
said JAMES COOPER his heirs and RICHARD MELTON his heirs &c. will warrant & forever
defend by these presents In Witness whereof said RICHARD MELTON to these presents
hath set his hand and Seal the day & year above written
Signed & Delivered in presence of
  DELMUS JOHNSON,   RICHARD MELTON
  JOHN HANDCOCK, JOHN COOPER
 Memorandum that on the day of the date of the within written Indenture full & peaceable seisen and possession of the within mentioned premises with the appurtenances
was had and taken by me the within said RICHARD MELTON & by me given & delivered
unto JAMES COOPER Witness my hand
Witness DELMUS JOHNSON,   RICHARD MELTON
  JOHN HANDCOCK, JOHN COOPER
 Received on the day of the date of within written Indenture of JAMES COOPER the sum
of Ten pounds current money being the consideration money within mentioned Reced
p me   RICHARD MELTON
 At Albemarle August Court 1769
This Indenture memorandum & receipt were acknowledged by RICHARD MELTON party
thereto & ordered to be recorded

pp. THIS INDENTURE made this seventh day of August in year of our Lord One thou-
112- sand seven hundred & Sixty nine Between RICHARD MELTON of County of Albe-
113 bemarle of one part and WILLIAM WHITE of sd County of other part Witnesseth
  that RICHARD MELTON for the sum of Ten pounds current money of Virginia to

him in hand paid by said WILLIAM WHITE by these presents doth bargain & sell unto
WILLIAM WHITE his heirs one certain tract or parcel of land lying & being in County
of Albemarle and bounded on the Branches of RACOON & CUNNINGHAM CREEKS to wit
Beginning at a (   ) line in said land running one hundred & twenty two poles & a
half crossing a small branch to pointers, North twenty three degrees East two hundred
& Sixty three poles crossing two branches to pointers & South sixty seven degrees East
two hundred & forty five poles crossing a branch to the first station it being part of the
land sold to JAMES COOPER, the upper part of the tract the said RICHARD MELTON had of
JOHN WEBB was granted unto JOHN WEBB by Patent bearing date the tenth day of June
One thousand seven hundred & Sixty containing two hundred acres by Estimation be
the same more or less To have & to hold the said tract of land with the appurtenances
unto WILLIAM WHITE his heirs and RICHARD MELTON his heirs will warrant & forever
defend by these presents In Witness whereof said RICHARD MELTON to these presents
hath set his hand & affixed his Seal the day & year above written
Signed & Delvered in the presence of
    JOHN HANDCOCK,   RICHARD MELTON
    DELMUS JOHNSON, JOHN COOPER
  Memorandum that on the day of the date of the within written Indenture full & peaceable Seisen and possession of the within mentioned premises with the appurtenances
was had & taken by me the within named RICHARD MELTON and by me given and deli-
vered unto the within named WILLIAM WHITE Witness my hand
Witness JOHN HANDCOCK,   RICHARD MELTON
    DELMUS JOHNSON, JOHN COOPER
 Received on the day of the date within written Indenture of the within named WIL-
LIAM WHITE the sum of Ten pounds current money it being the consideration money
within mentioned Reced p me   RICHARD MELTON
  At Albemarle August Court 1769
This Indenture memorandum & receipt were acknowledged by RICHARD MELTON party
thereto and ordered to be recorded

pp.   THIS INDENTURE made this January ye 30th day in the year of our Lord One
113-   thousand seven hundred & Sixty nine Between AMBROSE DOWELL of Parish of
114   Fredericksville in County of Albemarle, Planter, of one part and WILLIAM HEN-
      SON of Parish aforesaid of other part Witnesseth that said AMBROSE DOWELL for
and in consideration of one Horse vallue Five pounds current money of Virginia to him
in hand paid by DAVID DOLTON by these presents doth bargain and sell unto WILLIAM
HENSON his heirs all that the said AMBROSE DOWELL his parcell or tract of land containing One hundred & fifty acres more or less in the Parish & County aforesaid and is
bounded beginning at a Pine in ANDREW JONSONs line runing thence along a line of
new markt trees to Mr. DICKSONs line, thence along DICSONs line unto ANDREW JOHN-
SONs line thence along the said line to the beginning which said land is part of a tract
granted to JOHN DOWELL with all houses profits and appurtenances theretunto belonging To have & to hold said tract of land with the appurtenances to said WILLIAM
HENSON his heirs and shall warrant & forever defend by these presents freed and discharged of and from all Incumbrances whatsoever the Quit rents from hence forth to
grow due to our Sovereign Lord the King his heirs only excepted & foreprized In
Witness whereof said AMBROSE DOWELL hath Interchangeably set his hand & affixed
his Seal the day & year first above written
Signed Sealed & Delivered in the presence of
    SAMUEL MUNDAY,   AMBROSE his mark ✗ DOWELL
    THOMAS DOWEL, WILLIAM HEREN

Memorandum that on the day & year within written peaceable & Quiet possession of the within mentioned land & its appurtenances was given by AMBROSE DOWEL to WILLIAM HENSON according to the true intent and meaning of these presents

AMBROSE his mark X DOWEL

January 20th 1769 Received of the within named WILLIAM HENSON the within mentioned consideration of Five pounds & I do hereby acquit him & his heirs of every part thereto
Witness SAMUEL MUNDAY,   AMBROSE his mark X DOWEL
      THOMAS DOWEL, WILLIAM HEREN
  At Albemarle August Court 1769
This Indenture memorandum & receipt was acknowledged by AMBROSE DOWEL party thereto & ordered to be recorded

pp.   THIS INDENTURE made on the Eight day of June in year of our Lord One thousand
115-   seven hundred & Sixty (blank) Between CHARLES HUDSON of County of Albe-
116   marle of one part and WILLIAM BURRASS of the same County of other part Witnesseth that Whereas the said WILLIAM at his special request and for the debt of sd WILLIAM by one Obligation dated on the six day of February in year of our Lord One thousand seven hundred & sixty eight did become jointly & severally bound unto DAVID NOWLIN in the sum of Sixty pounds for the paiment of Thirty pounds on or before the first day of June which shall be in the year of our Lord One thousand seven hundred & sixty nine & by one other Obligation bearing date the same six day of February in the year first mentioned did become jointly & severally bound unto said DAVID in one other sum of Thirty pounds for the paiment of Fifteen pounds on or before the first day of June which shall be in the year of our Lord One thousand seven hundred & Seventy & by one other Obligation bearing date the same six day of Feby. in the year first mentioned did become jointly & severally bounded unto the sd DAVID NOWLIN in one other sum of Thirty pounds for the paiment of Fifteen pounds on or before the first day of June which shall be in the year of our Lord One thousand seven hundred & Seventy one and Whereas also the said WILLIAM hath undertaken to indemnify and save harmless the said CHARLES HUDSON of and for all the premises now the said WILLIAM to the end & in consideration that the said CHARLES his heirs shall be indemnified and kept harmless of & for all the bonds and sureteships aforementioned doth bargain & sell said CHARLES HUDSON a certain parcel of land in the County aforesaid containing by estimation One hundred & ninety five acres lying & being on the Branches of TAYLORS CREEK and being the same purchased by said WILLIAM of DAVID NOWLIN aforesaid together with all its appurtenances To have & to hold sd parcel of land with its appurtenances unto said CHARLES his heirs and the sd WILLIAM will warrant & defend Provided that if the sd WILLIAM his heirs shall save harmless sd CHARLES his heirs for the bonds & sureteships aforesaid that then this bargained & sold lands with their appurtenances shall be utterly void In Witness whereof sd WILLIAM hath hereunto subscribed his name & affixed his Seal on the day & year first above written
Signed Sealed & delivered in presence of
    PETER GILLUM,   WILLIAM his mark MB BURRASS
    JEREMIAH WHITE, JOHN MARTIN,
    COLEMAN his mark N NELSON,
    WM. GRAYSON
  At Albemarle August Court 1769
This Indenture was acknowledged by WILLIAM BURRASS party thereto & ordered to be recorded

pp.   THIS INDENTURE made this first day of February in year of our Lord One thou-
116-   sand seven hundred & Sixty nine Between DAVID STAPLES of County of Albe-
117   marle of one part and JOHN MARTIN of same County of other part Witnesseth
that said DAVID STAPLES for sum of Seventeen pounds current money of Virginia to him in hand paid by said JOHN MARTIN doth by these presents bargain & sell
unto JOHN MARTIN & to his heirs one certain tract or parcel of land containing four
hundred acres lying & being in County of Albemarle on both sides of CARYS CREEK the
Middle Fork and bounded beginning at JOHN MARTINs Corner Pine on BENJAMIN
WOODSONs line, then on MARTINs line South sixty eight degrees East forty poles crossing the Creek to pointers, then South eighty eight & half degrees East Eighteen poles to
pointers, then down the said Creek as it meanders to pointers, then North sixty degrees
East forty eight poles to pointers, then South forty one degrees East twelve poles to
pointers, then on GEORGE ANDERSONs line North sixty nine degrees East forty three
poles to a Pine, then new lines South thirteen degrees East one hundred & six poles to a
Pine, then South sixty degrees West two hundred & forty poles to a Pine, then North
sixty six degrees West two hundred & sixty four poles to pointers on the said WOODSONs
line, then on his line North forty six degrees East two hundred & forty poles to the first
station and all the Reversions and Remainders thereof with the rents & issues thereof
To have & to hold the sd tract or parcel of land with the appurtenances thereunto belonging unto said JOHN MARTIN his heirs and DAVID STAPLES & his heirs will warrant
& forever defend by these presents In Witness whereof said DAVID STAPLES hath set
his hand & affixed his Seal the day & year first above written
Signed Sealed & Delivered in presence of us
         THOMAS APPLEBURY,   DAVID STAPLES
         WILLIAM APPLEBURY, JAMES MARTIN   CHRISTIAN STAPLES
   Memorandum that on the day & year within written peaceable & Quiet possession &
Seizen was had & taken by said JOHN MARTIN which was granted by DAVID STAPLES In
Witness whereof said DAVID STAPLES hath hereunto set his hand & Seal this first day of
February 1769
Witness THOMAS APPLEBURY   DAVID STAPLES
         WILLIAM APPLEBURY, JAMES MARTIN   CHRISTIAN STAPLES
   February the first 1769 Then received of JOHN MARTIN the sum of Seventeen pounds
Currt. money it being in full satisfaction of the within   DAVID STAPLES
                                                              CHRISTIAN STAPLES

At Albemarle August Court 1769
This Indenture memorandum & receipt were acknowledged by DAVID STAPLES party
thereto & ordered to be recorded

pp.   THIS INDENTURE made the twenty seventh day of July One thousand seven hun-
118-   dred and Sixty nine Between SAMUEL BROCKMAN & REBECCA his Wife of ORANGE
119   COUNTY of one part and WILLIAM BROCKMAN of said County of other part Witnesseth that whereas SAMUEL BROCKMAN the Older of said County of ORANGE did
by his last Will & Testament bearing date the third day of November Anno Domini
MDCCLXII devise unto his two Sons, the said SAMUEL & WILLIAM, the tract of land
which he had in Albemarle County containing about three hundred and fifty acres to
them and their heirs to be devided as they themselves should think proper recourse
being had to the said Will recorded in ORANGE COURT may more fully appear, & whereas
the said SAMUEL BROCKMAN the Devisee & REBECCA his Wife for sum of Ten pounds
current money of Virginia by said WILLIAM BROCKMAN the other Devisee to said
SAMUEL BROCKMAN in hand paid by these presents do bargain sell & confirm unto

WILLIAM BROCKMAN his heirs all their right title dower and demand to and in the one moiety of said tract of land devised to said SAMUEL BROCKMAN by his Father in his last Will and Testament as aforesaid situate & lying in County of Albemarle To have & to hold said moiety of land together with all houses orchrds profits and appurtenances whatsoever to the same belonging unto WILLIAM BROCKMAN his heirs and SAMUEL BROCKMAN & REBECCA his Wife their heirs shall warrant & forever defend by these presents In Witness whereof said SAMUEL BROCKMAN & REBECCA his Wife have hereunto set their hands & Seals the day & year first above written
Signed Sealed & Delivered in the presence of
    MARY WILLSON,   SAML. his mark   BROCKMAN
    RICHARD WILSON, JOHN WALKER,
    DANIEL FARGASON
 At Albemarle August Court 1769
This Indenture was proved by the Oath of MARY WILSON, RICHARD WILSON & DANIEL FARGASON wits. thereto & ordered to be recorded

pp.   THIS INDENTURE made the tenth day of August in year of our Lord One thousand
119-   seven hundred & Sixty nine Between JOHN WOODS of Albemarle County & LETTIS
120   his Wife of one part and JAMES COLEMAN of County of LOUISA of other part Wit-
        nesseth that said JOHN WOODS for sum of Ninety five pounds to him in hand paid
by said JAMES COLEMAN by these presents doth bargain & sell unto JAMES COLEMAN his heirs one certain tract or parcel of land containing by estimation Two hundred & fifty acres be the same more or less lying & being in County of Albemarle and bounded Beginning at JOHN GREERs Corner Chesnut Oak on the top of GRANNIES HILL running a new line South eighty degrees East sixty poles to a Pine & South forty poles to pointers in CHARLES HUDSONs line, thence on his line South fifty five degrees West eighty poles to a red Oak & North thirty six degrees East twenty six poles to a white Oak & Pine in HUDSONs line, thence new lines South Eleven degrees East forty four poles to a Pine in DAVID STOCKTONs line, thence on the same South eighty three degrees West One hundred & thirty poles to a red Oak saplin by a Hickory Stump thence continued the same One hundred poles to pointers, North fifty four degrees West one hundred & ten poles to a white Oak saplin, North twenty nine poles to two white Oak saplins, North thirty five degrees East fifty four poles to pointers, North fifty nine degrees East sixty poles to a black Oak saplin, North seventy degrees East twenty poles to pointers in GRANNIES HILL East forty poles to pointers in JOHN GREERs line, then on his line South forty degrees East four poles to a white Oak Saplin, thence South thirty degrees East one hundred & one poles to the beginning with all woods, profits and appurtenances whatsoever to the parcel of land belonging and JOHN WOODS & LETTIS his Wife for him & his heirs will warrant & forever defend by these presents In Witness whereof JOHN WOODS & LETTIS his Wife have hereunto interchangably set their hands & affixed their Seals the day & year first above written
Sealed & Delivered in the presence of
    JOHN WOODSON,   JOHN WOODS
    ARCHIBALD WOODS, HUGH ALEXANDER   LETTAS WOODS
 Received the day & date of the within written Deed of JAMES COLEMAN the sum of Ninety five pounds current money of Virginia being the full consideration of the within mentioned land & Tenements   JOHN WOODS
 At Albemarle August Court 1769
This Indenture & Receipt were acknowledged by JOHN WOODS & LETTAS his Wife parties thereto & ordered to be recorded

p.   THIS INDENTURE made this tenth day of August in year of our Lord One thousand
121   seven hundred & Sixty nine Between JACOB MOON of the Parish of Saint Anns &
        County of Albemarle of one part and EDWARD CARTER & PETERFIELD TRENT of
the same County and Parish of other part Witnesseth that JACOB MOON for sum of Sixty
pounds current money of Virginia to him in hand paid by sd CARTER & TRENT by these
presents doth bargain sell & confirm unto said CARTER & TRENT one certain tract or
parcel of land containing One hundred acres lying in Albemarle County on the Waters
of JUMP.G BRANCH on both sides FITZPATRICKS ROAD & bounded Begining at a white Oak
and pointers in JOSEPH FITZPATRICKs line, thence No. 40 1/2 d. W. 162 poles to pointers,
then with the said line So. 80 d. W. 80 poles crossing a branch and a Road to pointers,
thence So. 23 d. West 10 poles NELSONs Corner, thence along NELSONs line the same
course continued 59 poles in all 69 poles crossing a road to pointers in a Branch, thence
& new line So. 67 1/2 d. E. 212 poles to a red Oak in FITZPATRICKs line, thence with the
said FITZPATRICKs line N. 32 E. 32 poles to the begining with all houses and other advantages thereunto belonging In Witness whereof sd JACOB MOON hath hereunto set his
hand & affixed his Seal the day & year first above written
Signed Seald & Delivered in the presence of us
        MATTHEW NIGHTINGALE,   JACOB MOON
        WILLIAM HENDERSON, JOHN SWANN
   1769 August 10th Received the within sum of Sixty pounds current money of Virginia
Test   JOHN SWANN,   JACOB MOON
        WM. HENDERSON, MATTHEW NIGHTINGALE
   At Albemarle August Court 1769
This Indenture & Receipt were proved by the Oath of JOHN SWANN, WM. HENDERSON &
MATTHEW NIGHTINGALE Wits. thereto & ordered to be recorded

pp.   THIS INDENTURE made this fifth day of July One thousand seven hundred & Sixty
122-   nine Between ABRAHAM ALLEN of AUGUSTA COUNTY of one part and JOHN
123   DOWEL of County of Albemarle of other part Witnesseth that said ABRAHAM
        ALLEN for sum of Thirty pounds current money of Virginia to him in hand paid
by these presents doth bargain sell & confirm unto JOHN DOWEL his heirs one certain
tract or parcel of land containing by estimation One hundred and Eighty acres lying &
being in Albemarle County at the foot of PINEY MOUNTAIN it being the land the said
ALLEN lived on beginning at a Pine & white Oak corner of RICHARD ALLEN, thence
North twenty five degrees East two hundred & eight poles to several Pines pointers,
thence North fifty four degrees West one hundred & sixty nine poles to a large Pine on
PINEY MOUNTAIN, thence South twenty five degrees West one hundred and twenty nine
poles to a markt white Oak, thence South thirty two degrees East two hundred poles to
the first station together with all houses orchards and water courses thereunto belonging and the said ABRAHAM for himself and his heirs the said lands with the appurtenances to said JOHN DOWEL his heirs will warrant & forever defend by these presents
freely and clearly discharged of all Incumbrances whatsoever In Witness whereof said
ABRAHAM ALLEN hath hereunto set his hand & Seal the day & year above written
Test   WM. DOLTON,   ABRAHAM his mark   ALLEN
        EDWARD COFFEY, JACOB WATTS
   At Albemarle August Court 1769
This Indenture was proved by the Oath of WILLIAM DOLTON., EDWARD COFFEY & JACOB
WATTS Wits. thereto & ordered to be recorded

p.   THIS INDENTURE made this twenty eight day of July in year of our Lord One
123   thousand seven hundred & Sixty nine Between JOHN PRINCE of County of Albe-
        marle of one part & JOHN SWANN of same County of other part Witnesseth that
sd JOHN PRINCE for sum of Forty five pounds Curt. money of Virga. to him in hand paid
by sd SWANN by these presents doth bargain sell & confirm unto said SWANN his heirs
one certain tract or parcel of land lying on the Waters of GREEN CREEK in Albemarle
County containing Two hundred & ten acres bounded by the lines of WILLIAM HENDER-
SON, JNO. SOUTHARD, TERISHA TURNER it being the same land he purchased of GEORGE
BLANE with all houses orchards & other advantages whatsoever to sd land belonging To
have & to hold the said land with the appurtenances unto said JOHN SWANN his heirs &
JOHN PRINCE his heirs will warrant & forever defend by these presents In Witness
whereof sd JOHN PRINCE hath hereunto set his hand & affixed his Seal the day & year
above written
Signed Sealed & Delivered in the presence of us
     MATTHEW ANDERSON,   JOHN PRINCE
     THOMAS COLLINS, FRANCIS WEATHERRED
 At Albemarle August Court 1769
This Indenture was acknowledged by JOHN PRINCE party thereto & ordered to be re-
corded

pp.   THIS INDENTURE made the Eighth day of August in year of our Lord One thou-
124-   sand seven hundred & Sixty nine Between WILLIAM HAMNER of Albemarle
125   County of one part and the Revd. Mr. SAMUEL LEAK of the same County of other
       part Witnesseth that said HAMNER for and in consideration of One hundred &
thirty pounds Virginia Currency to him in hand paid by these presents doth give grant
& confirm unto said LEAK his heirs one certain tract or parcel of land lying and being
in County of Albemarle on the branches of HARDWAY containing by computation Two
hundred & forty eight acres & a half being part of a tract of land which said HAMNER
purchased of THOMAS FITZPATRICK adjoining to & lying between SAMUEL HAMNER who
now posseth the other part of the tract, WILLIAM MELTON & WILLIAM HORRALL with
all woods houses orchards & hereditaments whatsoever belonging To have and to hold
the said parcel of land & premises which land said HAMNER acknowledgeth to be free
from all incumbrances whatsoever and warrant & forever defend In Witness whereof
he hath set his hand and affixed his Seal the day & date above written
Signed Sealed & Delivered in presence of
     MARK LEAK,   WILLIAM HAMNER
     SAMUEL HAMNER, JOHN WHARTON
 Memorandum that on the eighth day of August A. D. One thousand seven hundred &
sixty nine quiet & peaceable possession of within premises was had by WILLIAM HAM-
NER & by his delivered to SAMUEL LEAK
Testes MARK LEAK,
     SAML. HAMNER, JOHN WHARTON
Received of the Reverend SAML. LEAK the full & just sum of One hundred & thirty
pounds currt. money of Virginia being the consideration money of the within men-
tioned land & premises this day & date within written
Testes SAML. HAMNER,   WILLIAM HAMNER
     JOHN WHARTON, MARK LEAK
 At Albemarle September Court 1769
This Indenture & Receipt were acknowledged by WILLIAM HAMNER party thereto and
ordered to be recorded. ELIZABETH the Wife of said WILLIAM personally appeared in

Court and being first privately examined as the Law directs, voluntarily relinquished her right of Dower in the Estate conveyed by her said Husband

p. THIS INDENTURE made the fourteenth day of September in year of our Lord One
125 thousand seven hundred & Sixty nine Between JACOB TIREE of AMHERST COUNTY
    and MARY his Wife and WEB KIDD of Albemarle County Witensseth that said
JACOB TIREE & MARY his Wife for sum of Twenty pounds to him in hand paid doth bargain & sell to WEB KIDD his heirs one parcel of land in County of Albemarle in the RICH
COVE containing by estimation One hundred & ninety two acres and bounded Begining
at a red Oak runing thence South forty two degrees East one hundred & eight poles to a
red Oak, South ten degrees East One hundred & forty poles to a Chesnut Oak, South thirty
eight degrees West Seventy poles to pointers, thence South sixty seven degrees West One
hundred & fifty poles to pointers in Colo. LEWIS line, thence North twenty seven degrees East one hundred & ninety six poles to a red Oak, thence North seventy nine degrees West seventy two poles to a Hickory, thence North twenty three degrees East one
hundred & sixty four poles along LEWIS's line to the beginning with all appurtenances
To have and to hold said parcel of land with the appurtenances to WEB KIDD his heirs
and said JACOB TIREE and MARY his Wife and their heirs said land with its appurtenances to said WEB KIDD and his heirs will warrant & defend In Witness whereof said
JACOB TIREE and MARY his Wife hath hereto subscribed their named and affixed their
Seals the day & year above written

In presence of PETER DAVIE,   JACOB TYREE
        CHAS. HUDSON, CHAS. LAMBERT,   MARY TYREE
        CHAS. LEWIS

  Memorandum that on the day & year within written livery of seisen of within lands
was made to WEB KIDD by JACOB TIREE and MARY his Wife
In presence of PETER DAVIE, CHAS. HUDSON,   JACOB TYREE
        CHAS. LAMBERT, CHAS. LEWIS   MARY TYREE

  Received of within named WEB KIDD on the day and year within written the sum of
twenty pounds currant money
Test CHAS. LEWIS   JACOB TYREE

  At Albemarle September Court 1769
This Indenture memorandum & receipt were acknowledged by JACOB TYREE & MARY his
Wife parties thereto & ordered to be recorded

p. THIS INDENTURE made the thirteenth day of Sept. One thousand seven hundred
126 & Sixty nine Between JOHN MECHIE of Albemarle County of one part and WIL-
    LIAM FERGUSON of other Witnesseth that JOHN MECHIE for divers good causes
and considerations him hereunto moving but more especially for and in consideration
of the special regard and friendship that he has unto said FERGUSON by these presents
doth give grant & confirm unto WILLIAM FERGUSON his heirs a certain tract of land
lying on MEACHUMS RIVER on the North side of the said River and running thence on
new lines North twenty five degrees West sixteen poles to a Corner white Oak, thence
North seventy degrees West to a corner Pine, thence South seventy four degrees West
fifty two poles a Corner Pine, thence South ten degrees West ninety poles to a corner
Pine on the North side of MOREMANS RIVER, thence down the same to MEACHUMS
RIVER and down by the meanders to the first station To have & to hold the said One
hundred acres of land together with all its several appurtenances to said WILLIAM
FERGUSON & his heirs In Witness whereof said JOHN MECHIE doth hereunto set his hand
and Seal the date above written

Signed Sealed & Delivered in presence of
    WILL. MECHIE,
    ROBERT MECHIE, JOSIAH WOOD
  At Albemarle September Court 1769

JOHN his mark /M/ MECHIE

This Indenture was proved by the Oath of WILLIAM MECHIE, ROBERT MECHIE & JOSIAH
WOOD Wits. thereto & ordered to be recorded

pp.   TO ALL TO WHOME these presents shall come Know ye that I JOHN FORD of Albe-
126-   marle County and Parish of Fredericksville for sum of Nine pounds current
127   money of Virginia to me paid have bargained sold and made over unto PETER
        BERNARD of Parish & County aforesaid & to his heirs all my two hundred & fore
acres of land lying and being in the Parish & County aforesaid on the Branches of
MECHUNK CREEK which said five hundred & five acres of land was taken up by me the
said JOHN FORD and pattented bearing date the sisteenth day of August in year of our
Lord One thousand seven hundred & Fifty six and is bounded Beginning at two Pines in
JNO. FORSIEs line and runing new lines North 57 & an half degrees East one hundred &
six poles to pointers, North twenty three degrees East one hundred poles to the County
Line and with it South eighteen degrees East twenty two poles and South fifty nine degrees East one hundred & forty five poles to a Pine, thence new lines South twenty & an
half degrees West one hundred and forty poles to pointers, South eighty two degrees
West sixty poles to pointers, West sixty nine poles to pointers in JNO. FORSIEs line and
with it North forty five degrees West one hundred & sixteen poles crossing the Creek to
the beginning And all the Estate right title and claim of me the said JOHN FORD my heirs
unto the premises To have and to hold the said two hundred & fore acres of land be the
same more or less according to the bounds aforesaid and said JOHN FORD and my heirs
will warrant & forever defend by virtue of these presents In Witness whereof I have
hereunto set my hand & Seal this thirteenth day of April in year of our Lord One thousand seven hundred & Sixty nine
Signed Sealed & Delivered in the presence of
    JOHN FORSIE JUNR. ABNER BERNARD,   JOHN FORD
    BENJAMIN FORSIE, JAMES BOYD
  Memorandum that peaceable and quiet possession of the premises given by JOHN FORD
TO PETER BERNARD with Livery and Seizen as Witness my hand & Seal the day & year
within written
Signed Sealed & Delivered in presence of
    JOHN FORSIE JUNR., ABNER BERNARD,   JOHN FORD
    BENJAMIN FORSIE, JAMES BOYD
  Received of PETER BERNARD the day and year within written the sum of nine pounds
Virginia currency being the consideration money mentioned In Witness whereof I
have hereunto put my hand
    JOHN FORSIE JUNR. THOMAS BOYD   JOHN FORD
    ABNER BERNARD, BENJAMIN FORSIE
  At Albemarle September Court 1769
This Indenture memorandum & receipt was acknowledged by JOHN FORD party thereto &
ordered to be recorded

pp.   THIS INDENTURE made this twenty fourth day of August in year of our Lord One
128-   thousand seven hundred & Sixty nine Between WILLIAM MOON of County of
129   Albemarle of one part and JACOB MOON, his Son, of County aforesaid, of other
        part Witnesseth that for and in consideration of sum of Five Shillings cash in

hand paid by him the said JACOB MOON to him the sd WILLIAM MOON, his Father, by
these presents doth give bargain & sell unto JACOB MOON one tract or parcel of land
lying & being in County of Albemarle on the Branches of HARDWARE RIVER containing Two hundred & forty five acres granted by Letter Patent to WILLIAM LEE in the
year of our Lord One thousand seven hundred and Forty six and bounded Begining at a
Hiccory saplin on MILDRED MERRIWETHERs line runing thence a new line South fifty
three degrees East forty three poles to THOMAS FITZPATRICKs Corner pointers, thence
on his line South forty six degrees East two hundred & sixty six poles his corner pointers, thence on new lines South forty six degrees East twenty poles to a Hiccory, North
forty five degrees East fifty eight poles to a red Oak and North twenty two degrees West
at fifteen a branch in all forty poles to MILDRED MERRIWETHERs red Oak, thence on her
line West three hundred & twenty two poles to the beginning with all the rights title
and demand whatsoever of him the sd WILLIAM MOON his heirs and all houses orchards
profits and hereditaments to said land belonging free and clear of all Incumbrances
whatsoever and will warrant & forever defend by these presents In Witness whereof
said WILLIAM MOON hath hereunto set his hand and Seal the day & year above written
Signed Sealed & Delivered in present of

      JOHN WHARTON,   WILLIAM MOON
      SAML. HAMNER, GEORGE LOVALL
 August the twenty fourth Received of JACOB MOON the within consideration in full I
say reced p me
Test JOHN WHARTON,   WILLIAM MOON
      SAML. HAMNER, GEORGE LOVALL
 At Albemarle September Court 1769
This Indenture was acknowledged by WILLIAM MOON party thereto & together with the
Receipt therein endorsed were ordered to be recorded

     (The remainder of page 129, about half the page, has been darkened and nothing appears.
The top half of pge 130 is blank; the lower portion darkened and nothing appears.)

pp.   THIS INDENTURE made this twenty fifth day of May in year of our Lord God One
131- thousand seven hundred and Sixty nine Between MATTHEW MULLINS & MARY
132   his Wife of Albemarle County and Parish of Fredericksville of one part and
      CLIFTON RODES of County of LOUISA of other part Witnesseth that said MATTHEW
MULLINS for sum of One hundred & Twenty pounds current money of Virginia to him
in hand paid by said CLIFTON RODES by these presents doth bargain sell and confirm
unto said RODES one certain tract or parcel of land lying and being in County of Albemarle containing Two hundred & twenty three acres on the Branches of MOREMANS
RIVER on the sides of the Mountain bounded Begining at a Hiccory WILLIAM McCORDs
corner on a spurr of the Mountain, runing thence in his line South fifteen degrees
West two poles to a Hiccory saplin, thence new lines South fifty three degrees East fifty
two poles to pointers on the side of a Mountain, North seventy five degrees East one
hundred & four poles to a Chesnut Oak, North fifty degrees East seventy poles to a Chesnut Oak, North twenty five degrees East seventy six poles to pointers, North five degrees West sixty one poles crossing a branch of MOREMANS RIVER to a Chesnut, West
One hundred & twenty four poles to pointers, South sixty five degrees West One hundred & thirty poles to pointers on WILLIAM McCORDs line, and on the same South forty
degrees East sixty six poles to the first station together with all houses orchards and
improvements whatsoever To have & to hold sd land with every of their appurtenances
to him said CLIFTON RODES his heirs and MATTHEW MULLINS his heirs will warrant and

forever defend by these presents In Witness whereof the parties to these presents his
hand & Seal have set the day & year first above written
      MOSIAS JONES,   MATTHEW MULLINS
      CHRISTOPHER HARRISS, THOS. GRUBBS
  At Albemarle September Court 1769
This Indenture was acknowledged by MATTHEW MULLINS party thereto & ordered to be
recorded

pp.   THIS INDENTURE made the 21st day of November in year of our Lord One thou-
132-   sand seven hundred and Sixty Eight Between CHRISTOPHER HARRISS of Albe-
133   marle County of one part and THOMAS GRUBBS of the aforesaid County of other
       part Witnesseth that said CHRISTOPHER HARRISS for sum of Twenty pounds cur-
rent money to him in hand paid by said THOS. GRUBBS do bargain & sell to said GRUBBS
& his heirs one tract of land lying in aforesaid County on both sides of MOREMANS
RIVER containing Seventy seven acres and bounded Beginning at a forked Chesnut by
a branch in the said THOMAS GRUBBS line running thence with the said GRUBBS line
North twelve degrees West eight two poles to a white Oak, thence North fifty five degrees East one hundred & twenty four poles crossing MOREMANS RIVER to a white Oak,
then South twenty degrees East thirty poles to pointers, thence South forty five degrees East seventy six poles to pointers, thence a new line South seventy one degrees
West twenty two poles to the mouth of a Branch according to the meanders thereof to
the Beginning together with the appurtenances thereunto belonging To have and to
hold the said tract of land with its appurtenances to said THOMAS GRUBBS & his heirs &
said CHRISTOPHER HARRISS & his heirs will warrant & defend In Witness whereof said
CHRISTOPHER HARRISS hath hereunto subscribed his name & affixed his Seal the day &
year first above written
Signed Sealed & Delivered in the presence of
      MOSIAS JONES, HIGGASON GRUBBS,   CHRISTOPHER HARRISS SENR.
      TYREE HARRISS, ROBT. HARRISS
  Memorandum that on the day & year within written peaceable & quiet possession was
given by CHRISTOPHER HARRISS to THOMAS GRUBBS of the within land & premises according to the true intent and meaning of these presents Witness my hand this 21st day
of Novemb. 1768
      MOSIAS JONES, HIGGASON GRUBBS,   CHRISTOPHER HARRISS
      TYREE HARRISS, ROBT. HARRISS
  At Albemarle September Court 1769
This Indenture & memorandum were acknowledged by CHRISTOPHER HARRISS party
thereto & ordered to be recorded. AGNES the wife of said CHRISTOPHER appeared in
Court and being first privily examined as the Law directs, voluntarily relinquished her
right of dower in the lands conveyed by her said Husband

pp.   THIS INDENTURE made this 14th day of Sept. in year of our Lord One thousand
133-   seven hundred & Sixty nine Between JOHN ALLEN of County of Albemarle and
134   MARY ALLEN his Wife of their parts and THOMAS SMITH of said County of other
       part Witnesseth that JOHN ALLEN and MARY his Wife for sum of Seventy pounds
current money of Virginia to him paid by THOMAS SMITH by these presents doth bargain & sell unto THOMAS SMITH his heirs a certain tract or parcel of land containing
Two hundred acres lying & being in County aforesaid near the BLUE MOUNTAINS and
bounded Beginning at pointers in THOS. BELLs line and with his line South twenty six
degrees East two hundred poles to a Chesnut in Colo. JOHN CHISWELLs back line, & with

it North fifty three degrees East One hundred & sixty poles to a white Oak, new line
North twenty three degrees & thirty minutes West two hundred poles crossing a branch
to pointers & South fifty three degrees West One hundred & seventy poles to the first
station being part of a larger tract belonging to the said CHISWELL Gent. & now in possession of the sd THOS. SMITH with all houses & advantages whatsoever to sd land belonging To have & to hold the said premises with the appurtenances unto THOS. SMITH
his heirs and JOHN ALLEN & MARY his Wife & their heirs will warrant & forever defend
by these presents In Witness whereof sd JOHN ALLEN & MARY his Wife hath hereunto
set their hands & affixed their Seals the day & year above written
In the presence of us ABNER WOOD,   JOHN ALLEN
      BRADLEY BERREY, WILLIAM WOOD   MARY her mark ᚺ ALLEN
   Sept. (blank) day Recd. of THOMAS SMITH the sum of Seventy pounds current money it
being the consideration within mentioned p
In presence of us ABNER WOOD,   JOHN ALLEN
      BRADLEY BERREY, WILLIAM WOOD   MARY her mark ᚺ ALLEN
   At Albemarle September Court 1769
This Indenture was acknowledged by JOHN ALLEN & MARY his Wife parties thereto and
together with the Receipt thereon endorsed were ordered to be recorded

p.   KNOW ALL MEN by these presents that I SOLOMON NELSON of Albemarle County
134   & St. Ann's Parish for sum of Seventy nine pounds thirteen Shillings and nine
        pence currt. money of Virginia which I owe unto RICHARD WOODS & MICAJAH
CHILES of said County bargain & sell unto RICHARD WOODS & MICAJAH CHILES their
heirs one Negro man slave named Cesar & one Negro woman named Filless and one
horn comb and SOLOMON NELSON for himself his heirs will warrant & forever defend
by these presents In Witness whereof I have hereunto set my hand & Seal this
Eleventh day of May One thousand Seven hundred & Sixty nine
   The Condition of the above obligation is such that if SOLOMON NELSON his heirs shall
pay or cause to be paid unto RICHARD WOODS & MICAJAH CHILES their heirs the just &
full sum of Seventy nine pounds thirteen Shillings and nine pence current money of
Virginia on or before the tenth day of December next ensuing that then this Obligation
to be void and of none effect otherwise to be and remain in full force & virtue in Law
Signed Sealed & Delivered in presence of
      CLAUDIUS BUSTER,   SOLOMON his mark ᚺ NELSON
      MICHAEL McNEELY
   At Albemarle September Court 1769
This Deed was acknowledged by SOLOMON NELSON party thereto & ordered to be recorded

pp.   THIS INDENTURE made this fourteenth day of November in year of our Lord One
135-   thousand seven hundred and Sixty eight Between JOHN GILLUM and ELIZABETH
136   his Wife of Parish of St. Anns and County of Albemarle of one part and
        NATHANIEL GILES, JOHN LEE WEBSTER and JOHN WILKINSON of BALTIMORE
COUNTY and Province of MARYLAND of the other part Witnesseth that Whereas on the
twenty seventh day of November in the year of our Lord One thousand seven hundred &
Sixty seven said JOHN WILKINSON did agree with the said JOHN GILLUM for the purchase
of ten acres of land lying part of the tract whereon said JOHN GILLUM now lives and
bounded as is hereafter expressed on which sd Ten acres of land it was promised and
supposed that there was a quantity of Iron Oar for the price of Twenty pounds Currt.
money of Virginia And Whereas said JOHN WILKINSON did at the time of makeing the
agreemt. stile himself partner and joint adventurer with said NATHANIEL GILES & JOHN

LEE WEBSTER and for and on behalf of the said NATHANIEL GILES and JOHN LEE WEBSTER and himself did make the agreement aforesaid for the said Ten acres of land & for their common benefit and advantage and for the advantage and benefit of none other person or persons whatsoever. Now in pursuance of the true intent and meaning of the said agreement and that the same may be fully answered & complied with on the part of said JOHN GILLUM, This Indenture Witnesseth that JOHN GILLUM & ELIZABETH his Wife for sum of Twenty pounds current money of Virginia to them in hand paid by said NATHANIEL GILES, JOHN LEE WEBSTER & JOHN WILKINSON doth bargain & sell (them) and their heirs all that parcel of land containing by Estimation Ten acres be the same more or less lying and being in the County of Albemarle being that part of said GIL-LUMs tract where he holes or dug for Iron mine and beginning for the same near a hollow at three marked trees and thence running Northerly twenty eight poles to two small Hickory pointers thence running to two small Chesnut pointers eighteen poles thence altering the Course a little Southardly inclosing & running up the Hill a Wester-ly Course thirty six poles to two Chesnuts & a Locust pointers for a Corner, thence Southardly sixteen poles to a Rock Stone and a Hickory pointers for a Corner, thence on Easterly to the begining mark'd trees to include Ten acres of land be the same more or less To have & to hold the said tract of land as aforesaid contained by estimation Ten acres be the same more or less with the appurtenances unto NATHANIEL GILES, JOHN LEE WEBSTER & JOHN WILKINSON their heirs and JOHN GILLUM his heirs will warrant and forever defend by these presents In Witness whereof the parties to these presents their hands & Seals interchangably have set and affixed the day & year above written Signed Sealed & Delivered in presents of
CHRIS. LAMBERT, JACOB MOON,   JOHN GILLUM
CHS. MARTIN, JAS. TURNER,   ELIZABETH her mark —+— GILLUM
WM. WATSON
Received Nov. 14th 1768 of NATHANIEL GILES, JOHN LEE WEBSTER & JOHN WILKINSON the sum of Twenty pounds Currt. money of Virginia as a full and ample satisfaction for the within mentioned bargained land & premises as fully expressed within
                                     JOHN GILLUM
Memorandum that on the day & year within written full possession was had & taken of the land & premises within granted by JOHN GILLUM and by him delivered to the with-in named NATHANIEL GILES, JOHN LEE WEBSTER & JOHN WILKINSON to hold to them their heirs &c. according to the contents & true meaning of the within written Indenture In presence of
CHAS. LAMBERT, CHAS. MARTIN,   JOHN GILLUM
JACOB MOON, WM. WATSON,
JAMES TURNER
At Albemarle September Court 1769
This Indenture memorandum & Receipt were proved by the Oath of CHARLES MARTIN a Wits. thereto & the same having been before proved by two other Wits. were ordered to be recorded

p.   THIS INDENTURE made this Tenth day of November in year of our Lord Christ
137   One thousand seven hundred & Sixty nine Between GEORGE LOVALL of Parish of
      St. Anns & County of Alblemarle of one part & WILLIAM GOLDSBY of same County
and Parish of other part Witnesseth that GEORGE LOVALL for sum of Twenty seven pounds Ten Shillings Currt. money of Virginia to him in hand paid by sd GOLDSBY by these presents doth bargain & sell unto sd WM. GOLDSBY his heirs one certain tract or parcel of land lying on the waters of HARDWARE in Albemarle County contain.g One

hundred & twenty acres & bounded by the lines of WM. SOUTHARD, THOS. MARTIN &
JOHN WHARTON it being the same lands he the sd LOVALL bought of WM. HORRELL & the
same he now lives on with all houses orchards & other advantages whatsoever to sd
land belonging To have & to hold said land with all the appurtenances unto the sd
GOLDSBY his heirs and GEO. LOVALL his heirs shall warrant & forever defend by these
presents In Witness whereof sd GEO. LOVALL hath hereunto set his hand & affixed his
Seal the day & year first above written
Signed Sealed & delivered in presence of
          WM. CABELL, HENRY MARTIN,   GEORGE LOVALL
          JACOB MOON, JOHN SWANN
     Memorandum that the Tenth day of November in year of our Lord One thousand seven
hundred & Sixty nine peaceable & quiet possession & seisen of the within land & pre-
mises with the appurtenances was delivered by GEO: LOVALL unto WILLIAM GOLSBY
accord.g to the purport true intent & meaning of the within Deed
In the presence of WM. CABELL,   GEORGE LOVALL
          HENRY MARTIN, JACOB MOON,
          JOHN SWANN
     At Albemarle November Court 1769
This Indenture & memorandum was proved by the Oath of HENRY MARTIN, JACOB MOON
& JOHN SWANN witnesses thereto & ordered to be recorded

pp.   THIS INDENTURE made this fourth day of October in year of our Lord One thou-
138-   sand seven hundred & Sixty nine Between SARAH MORAN likewise JOHN SMITH
139   of Parish of St. Anne County of Albemarle, Colony & Dominion of Virginia,
           Planter, & BETTY his Wife of one part & WM. SMITH of aforesaid Parish, County,
Colony & Dominion of Virginia, Planter, of other part Witnesseth that for sum of Forty
pounds current money to them in hand paid said SARAH MORAN, JOHN SMITH & BETTY
his Wife by these presents doth bargain & sell unto WILLIAM SMITH & his heirs a certain tract of land lying and being in Albemarle County on the head of the Western Fork
of WHITESIDES CREEK being the Southern branch of STOCKTONS MILL CREEK and is part
of MECHUMS RIVER containing One hundred & forty acres more or less being the South
East end of a certain tract of land containing Two hundred & eighty two acres granted
to JOHN MORAN, Husband to the within named SARAH MORAN, by Patent bearing date at
WILLIAMSBURG the tenth day of August One thousand seven hundred & Fifty nine, the
North end of the said tract was granted to NICHOLAS MORAN by the said JOHN MORAN as
by record may appear the dividing line between them by them agreed as by record will
appear to the Proprietors Processioners of Possessors of said premises, Together with all
the houses orchards profits and appurtenances whatsoever to said tenement belonging
and the said JOHN SMITH & BETTY his Wife by the acknowledgmt. of JOHN MORAN
bearing date the tenth of October in year of our Lord One thousand seven hundred and
Sixty six as by record will appear and SARAH MORAN her transferring voluntary her
right of Dower of sd Land without any incumbrances In Witness whereof the said
SARAH MORAN, JOHN SMITH & BETTY his Wife hath to these presents set their hands &
Seals the day & year above written
Signed Sealed & Delivered in presence of
          WILLIAM WOOD,   SARAH her mark ✝ MORAN
          SAMUEL his mark ɕ FENCHER,   JOHN SMITH
          FRANCIS FENCHER   BETTY SMITH
     Memorandum As SARAH MORAN Wife of the within mentioned JOHN MORAN never
acknowledged any of the within premises in a Legal way to JOHN SMITH and not

through obstinacy in her it was required by WM. SMITH that SARAH MORAN should join
in this acknowledgment as receipt as well as in the proceeding Indenture Vizt. that the
day & year within written Quiet & peaceable possession of the within tract of land with
all the appurtenances thereunto belonging was had of SARAH MORAN, JOHN SMITH &
BETTY his Wife & by them delivered to WM. SMITH to be by him & his heirs enjoyed and
also that the said SARAH MORAN, JOHN SMITH & BETTY his Wife have received October
fourth day MDCCLIX of WILLIAM SMITH the sum of Forty pounds currt. money of Virginia being in full consideration for tract of land as Witness our hands & Seals the day
& year above written
Signed Sealed & Delivered in presence of

WILLIAM WOOD,   SARAH her mark + MORAN
JAMES FENCHER,   JOHN SMITH
SAMUEL his mark ∫ FENCHER   BETTY SMITH

At Albemarle May Cout 1770
This Indenture & memorandum were proved by the Oath of FRANCIS FENCHER a Wits.
thereto the same having been proved by two other Wits. were ordered to be recorded

p.   THIS INDENTURE made the (blank) day of (blank) One thousand seven hundred
140   & Sixty nine Between SAMUEL RAY & JANE his Wife of one part and FRANCIS
        GRIMES of other Witnesseth that said SAMUEL RAY & JANE his Wife for sum of
(blank) pounds Currt. money of Virginia by these presents doth bargain & sell unto
FRANCIS GRIMES & his heirs tract of land lying the South side of the South Branch of
the North Fork of JAMES RIVER in Albemarle County contain.g forty nine acres
bounded Beginning on the Bank of the said River at a red Oak in said GAINES line
runing thence on his line South Eighty degrees West at twenty four poles a white Oak
and a Dogwood, South six degrees West thirty six & a half poles to pointers, thence North
Sixty degrees East one hundred & forty eight poles the River thence up the River by the
meanders one hundred twenty eight poles on a straight line to the first Station, To have
and to hold said land & premises to said GRIMES & his heirs forever In Witness whereof
the said parties to these presents do set their hands & Seals the date above written
Signed Sealed & Delivered in presence of
        (no witnesses shown)   SAMUEL RAY
                                                     JANE RAY

At Albemarle November Court 1769
This Indenture was acknowledged by SAMUEL RAY & JANE his Wife, parties thereto, &
ordered to be recorded

p.   TO ALL TO WHOM these presents shall come Know ye that I DANIEL MAUPIN of
141   Albemarle County for & in consideration of Eighty pounds of Sterling money to
        me paid by these presents do for the aforesaid consideration bargain sell & make
over unto WILLIAM VICE JUNR. of ye County aforesaid & unto his heirs all my One hundred acres of land lying & being in the County of Albemarle & bounded Begining at a
red Oake on ye North side of ye RIVANNA in HANOVER COUNTY line by the river side
runing thence up the river to its meanders two hundred & forty two poles to a white
Oake, thence crossing ye River to the mouth of IVY CREEK & up IVY CREEK thirty poles
to two Maples, thence North seven degrees West ninety two poles to pointers in HAN-
OVER COUNTY LINE, thence on HANOVERs line South sixty four degrees East two hundred & eighteen poles crossing the River to the beginning and all the premises and
every of the appurtenances To have and to hold the Hundred acres of land according to
ye bounds unto WILLIAM VICE JUNR. his heirs and ye sd DANIEL MAUPIN for myself

my heirs will warrant forever & defend by these presents In Witness whereof I have
hereunto set my hand & Seal this (blank) day of (blank) One thousand seven hundred &
Sixty nine
Signed Sealed & Delivered in the presene of us
        JOHN LANCASTER,   DANIEL MAUPIN
        MATT. MULLINS, JAS. BOWERS
    At Albemarle November Court 1769
This Indenture was acknowledged by DANIEL MAUPIN party thereto & ordered to be
recorded

p.   THIS INDENTURE made this ninth day of November One thousand seven hundred
142   & Sixty nine Between JOHN CANNON, Atto. for EDWARD BLACKBURN of one part
        & JOHN SPENCER of other part Witnesseth that JOHN CANNON for EDWARD
BLACKBURN for sum of Twenty five pounds Ten Shillings Virginia Curry. have bargained sold and delivered unto JOHN SPENCER one certain tract or parcel of land containing by Estimation One hundred & forty acres & bounded by the lands of HENRY
TILLEY, JOHN GRILLS & MAURY deceased, which said tract of land said JOHN CANNON for
EDWARD BLACKBURN doth forever warrant & defend To have & to hold said parcel of
land with the appurtenances unto JOHN SPENCER & his heirs In Witness whereof said
JOHN CANNON for EDWARD BLACKBURN have hereunto subscribed his name & affixed
his Seal the day & year above written
Sign'd Seal'd & Delivered in presence of
        (no witnesses shown)   JOHN CANNON
    At Albemarle November Court 1769
This Indenture was acknowledged by JOHN CANNON party thereto & ordered to be re-
corded

pp.   THIS INDENTURE made on the twelfth day of October in year of our Lord One
142-   thousand seven hundred & Sixty nine Between THOS. WALKER of Albemarle
143   County of one part and JOHN SHIFLET of same County of other part Witnesseth
        that said THOS. WALKER for sum of Fourteen pounds current money to him in
hand paid by said JOHN SHIFLET doth bargain & sell said JOHN SHIFLET & his heirs one
tract of land containing by estimation One hundred acres be the same more or less
lying in Albemarle County & bounded Beginning at a Shrubby Oak in LEATHERDALEs
line, thence a strait line to a Pine in MILLS's line, from thence to a white Oak on MILLS
line, from thence along LEATHERDALEs line to the Beginning, together with the appurtenances thereunto belonging To have & to hold said tract of land with the appurtenances thereto belonging unto JOHN SHIFLET & his heirs & THOS. WALKER will forever
warrant & defend In Witness whereof said THOS. WALKER hath hereunto subscribed his
name & affixed his Seal the day & year first above written
Signed Sealed & Delivered in the presence of
        THOS. SMITH, DANL. SMITH,   THOMAS WALKER
        NICHS. MERIWETHER, WILLIAM LEWIS
    At Albemarle November Court 1769
This Indenture was proved by the Oath of DANL. SMITH, NICHS. MERIWETHER & WIL-
LIAM LEWIS Wits. thereto & ordered to be recorded

pp.   THIS INDENTURE made this Seventh day of September in year of our Lord One
143-   thousand seven hundred & Sixty nine Between ROBERT THOMPSON of Parish of
144   Fredericksville and County of Albemarle, Planter, of one part & THOMAS LANG-
        FORD of County & Parish aforesaid of other part Witnesseth that said ROBERT

THOMPSON for sum of Five Shillings to him in hand paid by said THOS. LANGFORD by these presents doth bargain & sell unto THOS. LANGFORD one certain tract or parcell of land contain.g Thirty five acres more or less lying & being in County aforesd. on the West side of KIDS BRANCH bounded begining at a white Oak on the bank of KIDS BRANCH from thence runing North seventy seven poles to a white Oak on the bank the aforesd. Branch which is JOHN OGGs Corner and from thence West fifteen poles on OGGs line to a Poplar, from thence runing South fifty three poles to a red Oak, from thence runing seventeen poles South East to a Spanish red Oak, from thence runing East thirteen poles to the begining with all houses plantations profits & advantages whatsoever to the same belonging To have & to hold said Thirty five acres of land bounded as aforesaid with the appurtenances unto said THOS. LANGFORD his Exrs. & assigns from the day before the date hereof for & during the term of one whole year paying the yearly rent of one grain of Indian Corn at the Feast of St. Michael the Arch Angel only if the same demanded to the intent that by virtue of these presents & the Statute for transferring uses into possession & be enabled to accept a grant of the Reversions to him & his heirs forever In Witness whereof the parties to these presents Interchangably have put their hands & Seals the day of the month & year first above written
Signed Sealed & Delivered in the presence of
    RICHD. BRUCE, JAMES EPPERSON,   ROBT. THOMSON
    CATY BRUCE, BARTLET DAVIS
Memorandum that full & peaceable possession & seizen was this day delivered by ROBT. THOMPSON to THOS. LANGFORD of the land & premises within mentioned in the presents of us whose names are subscribed as witness whereof the said ROBERT THOMPSON hath hereunto set his hand & seal the day & year within mentioned
    (no witnesses shown)   ROBT. THOMSON
At Albemarle November Court
This Indenture & memorandum were proved by the Oath of RICHARD BRUCE, JAMES EPPERSON & CATY BRUCE Wits. thereto & ordered to be recorded

pp. 144-145   THIS INDENTURE made this ninth day of November in year of our Lord One thousand seven hundred & Sixty nine Between FRANCIS JERDONE of County of LOUISA, Mercht., of one part and WADDY THOMPSON of same County of other part Witnesseth that for sum of Eighty seven pounds Ten the said FRANCIS hath bargained & sold unto said WADDDY THOMPSON one certain tract of land lying in Coty. of Albemarle on IVY CREEK and its branches containing Two hundred and fifty acres more or less and bounded Beginning at a Hickory in a Branch in the Dividing Line between CHARLES STATHAM & WADDY THOMPSON & down the said Branch 293 po. to IVY CREEK, thence down the Creek 40 po. to a Hickory, thence S. 85 Et. 61 po. to pointers, thence So. 36 E. 23 po. to a Pine along COCKRANs line, thence So. 45 E. 73 po. to a red Oak, thence S. 67 E. 62 po. to a white Oak, thence S. 21 E. 29 po. to a red Oak, thence S. 55 1/2 E. 83 po. to a red Oak & pointers, Corner of CHARLES STATHAMs and in the Dividing Line between the said STATHAM and said THOMPSON, thence S. 62 W. 121 po. to a forked Spanish Oak saplin in the said Dividing Line and so along the same according to the Surveyors Plott (making several little variations) to the first Station, To have & to hold the said Two hundred & fifty acres of land with the appurtenances thereunto belonging to said WADDY THOMPSON his heirs and FRANCIS JERDONE for himself & his heirs doth by these presents forever warrant & defend the sd Two hundred & fifty acres of land against the claim of any person In Witness whereof said FRANCIS JERDONE hath hereunto set & affixed his hand & Seal the day & year above written
Signed Sealed & Delivered in presence of

(no witnesses shown)   FRANCIS JERDONE
Memorandum that on the day & year within written full possession & Seisen was had &
taken by FRANCIS JERDONE & by him delivered over to WADDY THOMSON to hold to him
the said WADDY THOMSON his heirs according to the true meaning of the within written
Indenture   FRANCIS JERDONE
Reced of WADDY THOMSON Eighty seven pounds & Ten Shillings Currt. the considera-
tion money for the within bargained land & premises   FRANCIS JERDONE
At Albemarle November Court 1769
This Indenture memorandum & receipt were acknowledged by FRANCIS JERDONE party
thereto & ordered to be recorded

p.   THIS INDENTURE made this ninth day of November One thousand seven hundred
146   & Sixty nine Between FRANCIS JERDONE of one part & CHARLES STATHAM of
         other part Witnesseth that FRANCIS JERDONE for sum of One hundred & fifteen
pounds currt. money have bargained & sold unto CHAS. STATHAM one certain tract of
land lying in County of Albemarle on the waters of IVY CREEK containing Two hundred
& fifty acres and bounded Beginning at a Maple in a branch, thence down the Branch
to a Hickory 120 po., thence No. 67 E. 97 po. to a Pine, thence along the Dividing Line
between the said STATHAM & ROBERT (   ) to a red Oak in COCKRANs line, thence
along COCKRANs line S. 51 E. to a Chesnut, thence S. 167 Et. to a white Oak corner tree,
thence S. 87 W. 134 po. along ROBERT FRYs line to pointers, thence So. 16 1/2 W. 169 po.
to a Corner Spanish Oak stump, thence N. 69 1/2 W. 184 po. to the first station To have &
to hold said Two hundred & fifty acres of land with all the appurtenances thereunto belonging unto said CHARLES STATHAM his heirs the said FRANCIS JERDONE doth forever
& by these presents warrant & defend the said Two hundred & fifty acres of land unto
said CHARLE STATHAM his heirs In Witness whereof said FRANCIS JERDONE hath hereunto set & affixed his hand & Seal the day & year above written
Signed Sealed & Delivered in presence of us
(no witnesses shown)   FRANCIS JERDONE
Memo. that on the day & year within written full possession & seisin was had & taken
by FRANCIS JERDONE & by him made over to CHARLES STATEM to hold to him his heirs
&c. according to the intent & true meaning of the within written Indenture in
presence of
(no witnesses shown)   FRANCIS JERDONE
Reced of CHARLES STATEM One hundred & fifteen pound the consideration for the
within bargained premises   FRANCIS JERDONE
At Albemarle November Court 1769
This Indenture memorandum & receipt were acknowledgedby FRANCIS JERDONE party
thereto & ordered to be recorded

p.   THIS INDENTURE made the 9 day of 8ber One thousand seven hundred & Sixty
147   nine Between SAMUEL RAY & JANE his Wife of one part & ROBERT MECHIE of
         other part Witnesseth that SAMUEL RAY & JANE his Wife for sum of Eighty
pounds current money of Virginia by these presents doth bargain sell & confirm unto
ROBERT MECHIE & his heirs a tract of land lying on both sides of the South Branch of
the North Fork of JAMES RIVER in County of Albemarle and bounded Beginning at a red
Oak in BALLARDs line on the North side of the said River & runing thence South
seventy degrees West at sixty four poles West at one hundred & twenty poles a red Oak,
South eighty two poles to JOHN MECHIE Corner four black Gums and a red Oak thence
over the River South sixty seven degrees East one hundred & twenty poles to pointers,

North ten degrees East forty six poles to pointers, North thirty one degrees East forty &
an half poles over a branch to a Pine on a Ridge, North ten degrees West sixty four
poles to the River thence along the same by the meanders to the first Station To have &
to hold said land by Estimation one hundred & forty acres be the same more or less unto
said ROBERT MECHIE & his heirs In Witness whereof the parties to these presents do set
their hands & seals the date above written
Sign'd Seal'd & d'l'd in pres.ce of
    MOSIAS JONES,   SAMUEL RAY
    WILLIAM WATSON, PAT. MECHIE   JANE RAY
  At Albemarle November Court 1769
This Indenture was acknowledged by SAML. RAY & JANE his Wife parties thereto &
ordered to be recorded

pp.   THIS INDENTURE made the 18th day of January 1770 Between ABNER WITT of the
148-   Parish of St. Ann & County of Albemarle of one part and WILLIAM PAYNE of the
149   same Parish & County of other part Witnesseth that said ABNER WITT for sum of
        One hundred pounds Virginia Currency to said ABNER WITT by said WILLIAM
PAYNE in hand paid by these presents doth bargain sell & make over unto said WIL-
LIAM PAYNE & to his heirs one certain tract of land lying in County of Albemarle containing One hundred & Sixty acres & bounded Beginning at a Sycamore at the mouth of
HENSLEYS CREEK at the said PAYNEs Corner, thence down the same to a Hickory, thence
down the River against the Falls to the mouth of a Gut to a Sycamore thence from the
River side the woods to the back line to a corner red Oak, thence up the back line to a
Scrub Oak to Mr. PAYNEs back corner, from thence down that line to the beginning,
with all houses gardens and all other appurtenances to the same belonging, To have &
to hold said land according to the bounds aforesaid unto WILLIAM PAYNE & his heirs
and ABNER WITT his heirs will warrant & forever defend by virtue of these presents In
Witness whereof I have hereunto set my hand & seal the day & year above written
Sealed Signed & Delivered in presence of
    JOHN MARTIN, HENRY MARTIN,   ABNER WITT
    PHILIP MAC RAE, HUDSON MARTIN
  Memorandum that Quiet possession & Seizen of the lands was made and given by
ABNER WITT unto WILLIAM PAYNE according to the true form & intention of the within
writing In presence of
    JOHN MARTIN, HENRY MARTIN,   ABNER WITT
    PHILIP MAC RAE, HUDSON MARTIN
  January 18th 1770 Reced of WILLIAM PAYNE One hundred pounds current money of
Virginia being the consideration money within mentioned as witness my hand the day
& year above written   ABNER WITT
  At Albemarle January Court 1770
This Indenture memorandum & receipt were acknowledged by ABNER WITT party
thereto and ordered to be recorded. ANN, Wife of said ABNER, personally appeared in
Court & being first privately examined as the Law directs, voluntarily relinquished her
right of Dower in the lands conveyed by the said Indenture

pp.   THIS INDENTURE made the ninth day of March One thousand seven hundred &
149-   Seventy in year of our Lord Christ Between WILLIAM SUMTER of Albemarle
150   County of one part & JOSEPH POINDEXTER of AUGSTY COUNTY of other part Wit-
        nesseth that said JOSEPH POINDEXTER for sum of Five pounds current money of
Virginia to him in hand paid hath bargained and sold unto WILLIAM SUMTER one cer-

tain tract or parcel of land containing Two hundred & seventy five acres be the same more or less lying & being in County abovesaid lying & being on the North Fork of JAMES RIVER of which bounded Begining at an Ash & Sassafras near a run at the foot of the PINEY MOUNTAIN, North thirty six degrees West sixty poles to corner red Oak, thence South seaventy five degrees West two hundred & thirty two poles to a corner black Gum on the West side of the MARSH RUN thence North forty degrees West eighteen poles to a small white Oak in place of the old Corner which was burnt down on the River bank, thence along down the said Run to three Hickories on the River bank, thence up a line of new markt trees two hundred & sixty eight poles to a Persimmon tree, thence North fifteen degrees East ninety poles to the beginning with all the appurtenances thereto belonging the Quit rents to the King excepted To have and to hold the said tract of land with appurtenances unto said WILLIAM SUMTER In Witness whereof we have hereunto set our hand & the day & year first above written
Sighn'd Seal'd & Delivered in the presence of
          (no witnesses shown)   JOSEPH POINDEXTER
   The sd WM. SUMTER his heirs & assigns against the said JOSEPH POINDEXTER him his heirs against the claim of every person whatsoever & that WILLIAM SUMTER his heirs shall at all times hereafter peaceably & quietly have hold & possess the land with the appurtenances clearly & freely from all Incumbrances In Witness whereof the parties to these presents have hereunto set their hand & Seals the day & year first above Riten
Signed Sealed & Delivered in the presence of us
The Sum of Thirty five pounds Currt. money being first paid
     JAMES KENNERLY,   JOSEPH POINDEXTER
     WM. DAVIS, CLEAVLAND COFFEY
   At Albemarle March Court 1770
This Indenture was ackd. by JOSEPH POINDEXTER party thereto & ordered to be recorded

pp.   THIS INDENTURE made the Eighth day of March in year of our Lord One thousand
151-   seven hundred Seventy between JOHN BURROWS of County of Albemarle of one
152   part & WILLIAM GOOCH JUNR. of the same County of other part Witnesseth that
         JOHN BURROWS for consideration of Sixty six pounds of Lawfull money of Virginia by him said WILLIAM GOOCH JUNR. to him said JOHN BURROWS in hand pd. by these presents doth bargain & sell unto WILLIAM GOOCH JUNR. his heirs one certain tract or parcel of land containing Two hundred & Ninety acres lying & being in County of Albemarle on the Branches of MOORES CREEK being part of the land that JOHN BURROWS obtained a Patent bearing date the tenth day of September One thouand seven hundred & Fifty four for Four hundred acres, Also being the land JOHN BURROWS formerly lived on joining the other part of the land mentioned in the sd Pattent sold to HENRY WOOD by the said JOHN BURROWS To have & to hold the said plantation & tract of land with the appurtenances unto WILLIAM GOOCH JUNR. his heirs and JOHN BURROWS his heirs will warrant & forever defend by these presents free & discharged from all Incumbrances whatsoever In Witness whereof I have hereunto set my hand & Seal the day & year above written
Sign'd Seal'd & Deliver'd before us
     JOHN HENDERSON JUNR.   JOHN his mark   BURROWS
     CHARLES WINGFIELD,
     NATHAN his mark X WHITLOCK
   Memorandum That on the day & year within written full possession & seisin was had & taken of the land granted by JOHN BURROW & by him delivered unto WILLIAM GOOCH JUNR. to hold to him his heirs according to the contents & true meaning of the within

Indenture In presence of
    JNO. HENDERSON JUNR.
    CHARLES WINGFIELD,
    NATHL. his mark X WHITLOCK   JOHN his mark J BURROWS
 At Albemarle March Court 1770
This Indenture memorandum were acknowledged by JOHN BURROWS party thereto &
ordered to be recorded

pp.   TO ALL TO WHOM these presents shall come Greeting. Know ye that I ROBERT
152-   SHARP SENR. of County of Albemarle and the of Fredericksville for & in con-
153   sideration of sum of Forty five pounds current money of Virginia to me in hand
        paid by these presents for me & my heirs do give bargain sell & make over unto
SAMUEL HUCKSTEP of County of Albemarle & Fredericksville Parish & to his heirs one
track or parcel of land lying in the said County on the head of the PLUMTREE BRANCH
containing One hundred acres more or less and is bounded Beginning at a Corner Maple
on the South side of the PLUMBTREE BRANCH on WILLIAM BARTONs line, & thence
along a new line to a corner red Oak on the East side of the THREE CHOPT ROAD, thence
running down the said Road to a red Oak on the old line, thence along the said line to a
Corner Pine on BENJAMIN BENGERs line & thence along said BENJAMIN BENGERs line to
a corner Oak and thence along the said WILLIAM BARTONs line to the Maple begun at
with all houses gardens orchards Estate right & title of said RICHARD SHARP SENR. To
have & to hold said parcel of land according to the bounds aforesaid & every of their
appurtenances unto SAMUEL HUCKSTEP and to his heirs and ROBERT SHARP SENR. doth
covenant that he will warrant said land unto SAMEUL HUCKSTEP & his heirs & forever
defend by these presents In Witness whereof I have hereunto set my hand & Seal this
Eighth day of March One thousand seven hundred & Seventy
Signed Sealed & delivered in presence of
    (no witnesses shown)   ROBERT his mark R SHARP
 Memorandum that on the 8th day of March 1770, Quiet & peaceable possession & seisin
was given with Livery Seisen of the lands by ROBERT SHARP SENR. unto SAMUEL
HUCKSTEP according to the true form effect of the within writing as witness the said
ROBERT SHARPs hand and Seal
Signed Sealed & Delivered in presence
    (no witnesses shown)   ROBERT his mark R SHARP
 Then received the sum of Forty five pounds current money the consideration money
within mentioned of the said SAML. HUCKSTEP as Witness my hand
                                               ROBERT his mark R SHARP
    At Albemarle March Court 1770
This Indenture memorandum & receipt were acknowledged by ROBERT SHARP party
thereto & ordered to be recorded. SUSANNAH, the Wife of the said ROBERT, personally
appeared in Court & being first privately examined as the Law directs voluntarily relinquished her right of Dower in the lands conveyed by this Indenture

pp.   THIS INDENTURE made this Eighth day of March in year of our Lord One thou-
154-   sand seven hundred & Seventy Between WILLIAM GEORGE of County of Albe-
155   marle & Parish of St. Ann of one part and SAMUEL BENGE of said County of other
        part Witnesseth that WILLIAM GEORGE for sum of Twenty five pounds current
money of Virginia in hand paid by said SAMUEL BENGE by these presents do bargain &
sell unto SAMUEL BENGE his heirs one certain tract or parcel of land in County of Albemarle on the North side of the North Fork of HARDWARE RIVER and bounded Beginning
at a Beach on the North side of HARDWARE thence a new line to JOHN WINKFIELDs cor-

ner, thence on JOHN WINGFIELDs corner line fourteen degrees East ninety poles to a
Spanish Oak, thence new line North thirty nine degrees West one hundred & 6 poles
crossing a branch to a white Oak and black Oak, thence on the sd line to HARDWARE
RIVER, thence down the River according to its meanders to the first station To have & to
hold unto said SAMUEL BENGE his heirs free & discharged from all Incumbrances whatsoever and WILLIAM GOUGE the above mentioned land and appurteances will forever
warrant & defend In Witness whereof said WILLIAM GOUGE hath hereunto set his hand
& affixed his Seal the day & year above written
Sealed & delivered in presence of
        JNO. HENDERSON JUNR.,   WILLIAM GOOCH
        CHAS. WINGFIELD, PHILIP THURMAN
  Memo. that full & peaceable possession was had & taken by the within WILLIAM GOUGE
of the land & premises & by him delivered to SAMUEL BENGE in the name of the Livery
& Seisen of all the land within granted to hold to him said SAMUEL BENGE his heirs ac-
cording to the purport & true intent & meaning of the within Deed
In presence of JNO. HENDERSON JUNR.,   WILLIAM GOOCH
        CHARLES WINGFIELD, PHILIP THURMOND
  Reced this eighth day of March One thousand seven hundred & Seventy of SAMUEL
BENGE the sum of Twenty five pounds Currt. money being the consideration of the
money within mentioned
Test JNO. HENDERSON JUNR.,   WILLIAM GOOCH
        CHARLES WINGFIELD, PHILIP THURMAND
  At Albemarle March Court 1770
This Indenture memorandum & Receipt were acknowledged by WILLIAM GOOCH party
thereto & ordered to be recorded

pp.   THIS INDENTURE made this Eighth day of March in year of our Lord One thou-
155- sand seven hundred & Seventy Between ELIJAH MORAN of Albemarle County of
156   one part and WILLIAM MORAN of same County of other part Witnesseth that
        ELIJAH MORAN for the consideration of Fifteen pounds Currt. money of Virginia
to him in hand paid by WILLIAM MORAN by these presents doth bargain sell & confirm
unto WILLIAM MORAN and his heirs a certain tract of land containing twenty acres be
the same more or less in Albemarle County on one of the Branches of SOUTH HARDWAY
called the ELM BRANCH which Branch is agreed on for the line to divide this track from
the said tract of land from the said ELIJAH MORANs land as it is part of the sd ELIJAH
MORANs tract Together with all the houses orchards & every of the appurtenances to
said tract of land whatsoever the said tract of land bounded Joining JOHN DIVERS line
on South side and also JOHN MORANs on the North side followin JOHN GILMONs old line
to the said ELM BRANCH To have & to hold said twenty acres of land unto WILLIAM
MORAN him and his heirs In Witness whereof said ELIJAH MORAN hath set his hand &
Seal the day & year above written
Signed Sealed & Delivered in presence of
    (no witnesses shown)   ELIJAH MORAN
  Memorandum that the day & year within written Quiet & peaceable possession of with-
in tract of land was had by ELIJAH MORAN & by him delivered to WILLIAM MORAN to be
by said WILLIAM MORAN his heirs according to the within mentioned Deed Enjoyed
Signed & Sealed in presence of us
    (no witness shown)   ELIJAH MORAN
  Received of WILLIAM MORAN the sum of fifteen pounds Currt. money it being in full
consideration of the within tract of land
                p me   ELIJAH MORAN

At Albemarle March Court 1770
This Indenture memorandum & Receipt was acknowledged by ELIJAH MORAN party
thereto & ordered to be recorded

p.   THIS INDENTURE made this twenty sixth day of February One thousand seven
157   hundred & Seventy Between WILLIAM McGEHEE of Albemarle County & JAMES
        & ROBERT DONALDS & CO., Merchants in GLASGOW, Witnesseth that said WIL-
LIAM McGEHEE for sum of Twenty seven pounds current money of Virginia to him in
hand paid by said JAMES & ROBERT DONALDS &c., by these presents doth bargain sell &
confirm unto said DONALDS & CO. their heirs one certain tract or parcel of land lying &
being in County of Albemarle on the Branches of HENDERSONS CREEK & bounded by the
line of THOS. JEFFERSON & EDWD. CARTER the same whereon he now lives containing
One hundred & Ninety three acres more or less with all orchards Houses & other appurtenances thereunto belonging To have and to hold the said One hundred & ninety three
acres of land unto JAMES & ROBERT DONALDS their heirs and WILLIAM McGEHEE doth
covenant & agree with said DONALDS & CO. the above sold land & premises to warrant &
defend from the claim of any person whatsoever In Witness whereof he has hereunto
set his hand & Seal the day & year above written
Sealed & Delivered in the presence of
        DAVID SHEPHERD,   WM. McGEHEE
        GEO: THOMPSON, PETER DAVIE
    Feby. 26th 1770, Reced the within mentioned consideration
                                                            WM. McGEHEE

    At Albemarle March Court 1770
This Indenture was proved by the Oth of DAVID SHEPHERD, & PETER DAVIE Wits. thereto & together with the receipt thereon endorsed ordered to be recorded

pp.   THIS INDENTURE made the first day of March in year of our Lord One thousand
158-   seven hundred & Seventy Between CHARLES LEWIS JUNR. of County of Albe-
159   marle of one part & CHARLES LILBURN LEWIS, Son of said CHARLES, of same
        County of Albemarle of other part Witnesseth that said CHARLES LEWIS JUNR.
for & in consideration of the Love & parentall affection which he hath & beareth unto
said CHARLES LILBURN LEWIS & for his advancement in the World by these presents
doth give & confirm unto his said Son, CHARLES LILBURN LEWIS, & to his heirs a certain tract of land containing Three hundred & fifty acres be the same more or less
lying in County of Albemarle on South side of RIVANNA RIVER & bounded Begining at
the mouth of BUCK ISLAND CREEK on South side of said River, thence up the said Creek
according to its meanders One hundred & sixty six poles to three corner Hickories
standing by the Creek side, thence North nineteen degrees West one hundred & seventy
poles to a corner Pine, thence North thirty seven degrees East to a new corner Pine
standing by an Old Road, thence new line near an East Course to a corner Poplar on a
gut side, thence down the said gut according to its meanders to the River, thence down
the said River according to its meanders to the place began at and all houses orchards
and every part thereof belonging and also Eleven Negro slaves together with the issue
of the aforenamed Female slaves and all Deeds evidences & writing touching the same
To have & to hold the said tract of land & the slaves unto said CHARLES LILBURN LEWIS
his heirs free clear and discharged from all Incumbrances whatsoever the Quit rents &
Taxes after to grow due & payable to our Lord the King his heirs & Successors only excepted & foreprized and CHARLES LEWIS JUNR. & his heirs shall warrant & forever
defend by these presents In Witness whereof CHARLES LEWIS JUNR. hereunto set his

hand & Seale the day & year first above written
Test CHARLES HUDSON,   CHAS. LEWIS
     THOS. GARTH, BENNETT HENDERSON
   Memorandum That on the day & year first within written peaceable & Quiet possession
and Seisin of the within lands & premises was delivered by CHARLES LEWIS JUNR. to
CHARLES LILBURN LEWIS in presence of
     CHAS. HUDSON,   CHAS. LEWIS JUNR.
     THOS. GARTH, BENNETT HENDERSON
  At Albemarle March Court 1770
This Indenture & memorandum were proved by the Oath of CHAS. HUDSON, THOS. GARTH
& BENNETT HENDERSON, Wits. thereto, & ordered to be recorded

pp.   THIS INDENTURE made this third day of November One thousand seven hundred
159-   & Sixty nine Between ANDREW HARRISON of County of GOOCHLAND & Colony of
161   Virginia, Planter, & SAMUEL MARTIN of WHITEHAVEN & of the Kingdom of Great
         Britain of other part Witnesseth that ANDREW HARRISON for sum of One hun-
dred & Twenty pounds current money of Virginia to him in hand paid by these presents doth bargain sell & confirm unto said SAMUEL MARTIN his heirs a certain tract of
land caled PETER FIELDS containing One hundred & Eighty acres lying & being in
County of Albemarle on the lower side of the North Fork of JAMES RIVER being bounded
by the lines of JOHN HENSON, PHILIP THURMAN & SAMUEL MARTINs own line and
SOLOMON BRYANT & the said North Run it being the land said ANDREW HARRISON purchased & had of HENRY CRUMPTON MARTIN with all houses woods water courses thereon standing growing together with all profits commodities & hereditaments thereunto
belonging To have & to hold the said tract of land with the appurtenances unto said
SAMUEL MARTIN his heirs and ANDREW HARRISON for himself & his heirs doth warrant & defend the said land with the appurtenances unto SAMUEL MARTIN & his heirs
against the claim of every person whatsoever In Witness whereof said ANDREW HAR-
RISON hath hereunto set his hand & affixed his seal the day & year first above written
Signed Sealed & Delivered in presence of
     WM. HARRISON, JOHN his mark + HENSON,   ANDREW HARRISON
     JNO. MARTIN, JOHN WARE,
     HENRY his mark + COPELAND,
     BENJ. HARRISON, THOMAS HARRISON
  Memo. That on the day of the date within written Indenture full & peaceable possession & seisen of the within land & premises was had by ANDREW HARRISON & by him
delivered & given unto SAMUEL MARTIN according to the within Indenture & agreable
to the true Intent & meaning thereof Witness my hand
     WM. HARRISON, THOS. HARRISON,   ANDREW HARRISON
     JNO. MARTIN, JOHN his mark + HENSON,
     JOHN WARE, BENJ. HARRISON,
     HENRY his mark + COPELAND
  Reced by ANDREW HARRISON of the within named SAMUEL MARTIN the just & full sum
of One hundred & twenty pounds Currt. money Virginia being the consideration money
for the within mentioned land & premises which I acknowledge to be in full for the
same
Test WM. HARRISON, THOS. HARRISON   ANDREW HARRISON
     JNO. MARTIN, JOHN his mark + HENSON,
     JOHN WARE, BENJAMIN HARRISON,
     HENRY his mark + COPELAND

At Albemarle March Court 1770
This Indenture memorandum & receipt were proved by the Oath of WILLIAM HARRISON, JOHN WARE & HENRY COPELAND Wits. thereto & ordered to be recorded

pp.
161-
162

THIS INDENTURE made the (blank) day of March One thousand seven hundred & Seventy years Between BARBARA RAMSAY of St. Anns Parish, Albemarle County of one part and ABRAHAM EADES of ye Parish & County of AMHERST of the other part Witnesseth that BARBARA RAMSAY for sum of Twenty four pounds Currt. money of Virginia to him in hand paid by said ABRAHAM EADES JUNER by these presents doth bargain sell & confirm unto said ABRAHAM EADES & to his heirs one certain tract or parcel of land containing Three hundred acres which said tract of Three hundred acres JOHN RAMSAY purchased of JACOB EADES whom had purchased the same of WM. SUDARTH situate lying & being in County of Albemarle on both sides of the South Fork of TOTIER CREEK & bounded beginning at BOLLING CLARKs corner pointers in Mr. STITHs line running thence on his line South Eighty seven degrees West one hundred & one poles to a white Oak, South twenty seven degrees West One hundred & twenty four poles to his Corner Chesnut Oak, thence on new line North fifty five degrees West eight eight poles to a Shrubby white Oak, North twenty five degrees East seventy four a branch at One hundred & Sixty, One hundred & Eighty, & Two hundred & thirty three more branches at two hundred & ninety six, the South Fork of TOTIER CREEK in all their branches hundred & forty seven poles to pointers & South Eighty six degrees East One hundred & fifty two poles to pointers in BOLLING CLARKs line, thence along the said CLARKs lines South thirty six degrees West One hundred & fifteen poles to Hiccory saplin & South twenty six the South Fork of TOTIER CREEK in all One hundred & forty poles to the Beginning, together with all woods water courses & all other appurtenances to the same belonging and BARBARA RAMSAY unto the said ABRAHAM EADES his heirs against the claim of her & against all persons whatsoever shall warrant by these presents & forever defend In Witness whereof said BARBARA RAMSAY hath hereunto set her hand & seal the day & year above written
Signed Sealed & Delivered in presence of
THOMAS RICHARDS   BARBREE RAMSAY
JOHN WILKINSON, RICHARD his mark WILBURN
At Albemarle March Court 1770
This Indenture was acknowledged by BARBARA RAMSAY party thereto & ordered to be recorded

p.
163

THIS INDENTURE made this 11 day of February One thousand seven hundred & Seventy Between JOHN DOLTON JUNR. of PITTSYLVANIA COUNTY of one part & THOMAS TERRY of Albemarle County of other part Witnesseth that JOHN DOLTON for sum of Three pounds Fifteen Shillings to him in hand paid by said THOMAS TERRY by these presents bargain sell & make over to said TERRY his heirs one certain tract or parcell of land lying & being in County of Albemarle containing by Estimation One hundred acres be the same more or less (being one moiety of two hundred acres that was gave by JOHN KEY to MARY DOLTON, the Mother of said JOHN DOLTON) lying & being in County of Albemarle on the head branches of KEYS MILL RUN on the North side of the SOUTH WEST MOUNTAIN and bounded by the lands of WM. GILLUM, WM. RAGLAND, MARTIN KEY & McKENZIEs Entry & a new line run for THOMAS CARR who bought the other moiety of the said DOLTONs land, beginning at a Chesnut Sprout on WM. GILLUMs line & ending at a Spanish Oak in MARTIN KEYs line & the Reversion, title, property of said hundred acres of land more or less in fee simple to said TERRY & his heirs the said

DOLTON against himself his heirs will warrant & defend by these presents as witness
the hand & Seal of the said DOLTON the day & year above written
Signed Sealed & Delivered in presence of
    JNO. MOORE, ROBT. ANDERSON,   JOHN DOLTON
    GILES ALLEGRE JUNR., JNO. MOORE JUNR.,
    THOMAS CARR
  Memo. That on the day & year within written full possession & Seisen was had & taken
of the within One hundred acres of land by JOHN DOLTON & by him made over & deli-
vered to THOS. TERRY to hold to him the said TERRY & his heirs according to the
contents & true meaning of the within written Indenture
In Presence of JNO. MOORE,   JOHN DOLTON
    ROBT. ANDERSON, GILES ALLEGRE JUNR.
    JNO. MOORE JUNR., THOMAS CARR
  At Albemarle March Court 1770
This Indenture & memorandum were proved by the Oath of JOHN MOORE, JOHN MOORE
JUNR. & ROBT. ANDERSON, Wits. thereto & ordered to be recorded

p. 164 THIS INDENTURE made this fourteenth day of July One thousand seven hundred
& Sixty nine Between THOMAS ANDERSON of one part & JOHN WALKER Gent. of
other part Witnesseth that THOMAS ANDERSON for sum of Sixteen pounds Eighteen Shillings & five pence farthing as also the costs of a Suit that hath accrued on an
action against the said ANDERSON, to him in hand paid by these presents doth bargain &
sell unto JOHN WALKER his heirs one feather bed bedstead & furniture, two chaf beds
bedsteads & furnitre, one mans Saddle, one womans Saddle, seven chairs & two tables,
one trunk, one Box, on doz. plates & three pewter dishes, two Iron potts, a Tea Kettle, two
sets China ware, two pewter teapots, one pewter tankard together with all the other
personal Estate that I am now possessed of upon Condition that if said THOMAS ANDER-
SON shall pay unto JOHN WALKER his heirs the aforesaid sum with Interest thereon
from the date hereof together with the costs aforesaid before the fourteenth day of July
One thousand seven hundred & seventy then the above bargained premises to be re-
leased to said THOMAS ANDERSON In Witness whereof he hath hereunto set his hand &
Seal the day & year first above written
Signed Sealed & Delivered in presence of
    TUCKER WOODSON JUNR.,   THOS. ANDERSON
    JNO. HARVIE, SAML. WOODS
  Memo. It is agreed by JOHN HARVIE that if it appears that THOS. ANDERSON hath paid
any part of the money within mentioned to JOHN WALKER that the same with the
Interest calculated therein shall be deducted
Test TUCKER WOODSON JUNR.,   JOHN HARVIE
    SAML. WOODS
  At Albemarle March Court 1770
This Indenture was proved by the Oath of JOHN HAVIE & TUCKER WOODSON JUNR. & the
memorandum likewise proved by said TUCKER & ordered to be recorded

pp. 165-166 THIS INDENTURE made the Eight day of March in year of our Lord One thousand
seven hundred & Seventy Between JOHN McCONNALL of Parish of St. Anns in
County of Albemarle of one part & WILLIAM TERRELL LEWIS of the other part of
the Parish & county aforesaid Witnesseth that said JOHN McCONNALL for sum of
Thirty pounds current money of Virginia to him in hand paid by WILLIAM TERRELL
LEWIS by these presents doth bargain sell & confirm unto WILLIAM TERRELL LEWIS

and to his heirs one certain tract or parcell of land lying & being in the Parish & County aforesaid containing Two hundred & fifty acres & bounded by OBEDIAH (B   ) lines, WILLIAM TERRELL LEWIS lines, JOHN KINGs lines, STEPHEN HUGHES line & JAMES DAVENPORTs line & RICHARD RENNOLDs line member & appurtenances and all houses orchards profits hereditaments whatsoever to the tract of land belonging and all Deeds evidences & writings touching the same To have & to hold the said tract of land & every of their appurtenances unto WILLIAM TERRELL LEWIS & to his heirs and JOHN McCONNALL & his heirs will warrant & forever defend by these presents In Witness whereof sd JOHN McCONNALL hath hereunto set his hand & Seal the day & year above written Signed Sealed & Delivered in presence of
          (no witnesses shown)   JOHN McCONNALL
   Memorandum That on the Eight day of March One thousand seven hundred & seventy quiet & peaceable possession and Seisen of within land was delivered by JOHN McCONNALL to WILLIAM TERRELL LEWIS and his heirs &c. according to the true meaning of the within Indenture   JOHN McCONNALL

   At Albemarle March Courth 1770
This Indenture & memorandum were ackd. by JOHN McCONNALL party thereto & ordered to be recorded. ANNE, Wife of sd JOHN, personally appeared in Court & being first privately examined as the Law directs, voluntarily relinquished her right of Dower in the lands conveyed by this Indenture

pp.   THIS INDENTURE made the Tenth day of May in year of our Lord One thousand
166-   seven hundred & Seventy between WILLIAM SHELTON & LUCY his Wife of one
167   part of County of Albemarle & Parish of Fredericksville and JOHN RODES of the
        same County & Parish of other part Witnesseth that WILLIAM SHELTON & LUCY
his Wife for sum of One hundred pounds Currt. money of Virginia to them in hand paid by JOHN RODES by these presents doth bargain sell & confirm unto JOHN RODES three tracts of land joining each other lying & being in County of Albemarle on both sides of MOOREMANS RIVER containing Four hundred & twenty four acres and bounded Beginning at a Chesnut on the Mountain near a Spring House on new lines South seventy five degrees East forty one poles to a Chesnut as will more fully appear in two Patents of WILLIAM SHELTONs land bearing date the Thirtieth day of August One thousand seven hundred & Sixty three signed by FRAN: FAUQUIER, the other bearing date the 14th day of July One thousand seven hundred & Sixty nine signed by BOTETOURT & one Patent of DAVID GLASS bearing date the Seventh day of May One thousand seven hundred & Fifty nine signed by FRAN: FAUQUIER together with all houses orchards gardens and all other Improvements whatsoever To have & to hold the said land & premises with every of their appurtenances unto said JOHN RODES his heirs and WILLIAM SHELTON & LUCY his Wife & their heirs shall warrant & forever defend by these presents In Witness whereof the parties to these presents their hands & Seals have set the day & year first above written
Signed Sealed & Delivered in presence of
          (no witnesses shown)   WM. SHELTON
                                                           LUCY SHELTON
   Memorandum that Quiet & peaceable possession of the within granted land was given by WILLIAM SHELTON & LUCY his Wife to JOHN RODES by delivery of Turf & Twig of the same as simbols of Livery and Seisin In Witness whereof we have hereunto set our hand & Seals this 10th day of May 1770   WM. SHELTON
                                                           LUCY SHELTON

At Albemarle May Court 1770
This Indenture and Memorandum were acknowledged by WILLIAM SHELTON & LUCY his
Wife parties thereto & ordered to be recorded

pp.   THIS INDENTURE made this (blank) day of (blank) One thousand seven hundred
168-   & Seventy Between WILLIAM KEATON and MARGARET his Wife of County of
169   Albemarle of one part and MICHAEL AHART of County of CULPEPER of other part
         Witnesseth that WILLIAM KEATON and MARGARET his Wife for sum of Sixteen
pounds Current money of Virginia to them in hand paid by MICHAEL AHART by these
presents do bargain sell and confirm unto MICHAEL AHART his heirs one certain tract
or parcel of land containing One hundred acres more or less lying & being in Albemarle County on ROCKEY CREEK and bounded beginning at three Hickorys in a bunch
on the low grounds of the Creek runing thence South forty degrees West one hundred &
thirteen poles to a small Pine and white Oak bush thence South sixty degrees East fifty
six poles to two white Oaks on the side of a Hill, thence East One hundred & forty four
poles to three Pines, thence North seventy four poles to a white Oak and Pine, thence
North twenty nine Degrees West thirty poles to two white Oaks and red Oak, thence
North Eighty and a half degrees West ninety six poles to a white Oak and Hickory saplin
thence South sixty degrees West twelve poles to the beginning together with all houses
gardens & water courses thereunto belonging To have & to hold said land and appurtenances whatsoever to the same belonging unto said MICHAEL AHART his heirs freely &
clearly discharged of all Incumbrances In Witness whereof said WILLIAM KEATON &
MARGARET his Wife have hereunto set their hands & Seals the day & year above written
Signed Sealed & delivered in presence of
         (no witnesses shown)   WILLIAM his mark XX KEATON
                                          MARGARET her mark M KEATON

   At Albemarle May Court 1770
This Indenture was acknowledged by WILLIAM KEATON & MARGARET his Wife parties
thereto & ordered to be recorded

pp.   THIS INDENTURE made this 22d day of November in year of our Lord One thou-
169-   sand seven hundred & Sixty nine Between JOHN MULLINS JUNR. of Albemarle
170   County of one part and BEN BROWN of HANOVER COUNTY of other part Witnes-
         seth that JOHN MULLINS for sum of Twenty pounds Virginia Currency to him in
hand paid by these presents do bargain sell & confirm unto BEN BROWN his heirs one
tract of land containing by estimation Sixty six acres be the same more or less lying &
being in Albemarle County on both sides of DOYLES RIVER and bounded Begining at a
Hickory on a Piny nole of the Mountain, runing thence North eighty five degrees West
One hundred and thirty four poles to a red Oak saplin on EAGLEs line, thence due South
Sixty two poles to a chesnut Oake, thence South seventy four & a half degrees East one
hundred & fifty six poles to PHILLIPS Old Line in said MULLINs Land on the Mountain,
thence along the said line Eighty four poles to the Hickory saplin at the beginning
with all houses and the Improvements and appurtenances to the tract of land belonging To have & to hold the said tract of land the improvements & appurtenances
belonging unto said BEN BROWN his heirs and JOHN MULLINS do covenant & agree the
said BEN BROWN his heirs he will at all times defend a good perfect & absolute Estate of
Inheritance in fee simple in the said tract of Sixty six acres of land In Witness whereof
said JOHN MULLINS hath hereunto set his hand & Seal the day & year above written
Signed Sealed & Delivered in presence of
         BERNARD BROWN,   JOHN MULLINS
         BERNICE BROWN, BENAJAH BROWN

Memorandum that on the day & year first within written peaceable & Quiet possession
& Seisen of within land was had & taken by JOHN MULLINS and by him delivered to BEN
BROWN according to the purport and true intent & meaning of the within Indenture
Test BENAJAH BROWN,   JOHN MULLINS
     BERNARD BROWN, BERNICE BROWN
  Received of the withn mentioned BEN BROWN the consideration money in full for the
land within mentioned 22d day of November 1769
     BENAJAH BROWN,   JOHN MULLINS
     BERNARD BROWN, BERNICE BROWN
  At Albemarle May Court 1770
This Indenture memorandum & receipt was proved by the Oath of BERNARD BROWN,
BERNICE BROWN & BENAJAH BROWN Wits. thereto & ordered to be recorded

pp.   THIS INDENTURE made this nineteenth day of September in the year of the
171-   Reign of our Sovereign Lord George the Third by the Grace of God of Great
172   Britain, France & Ireland, King defender of the faith &c. and in the year of our
       Lord God One thousand Seven hundred & Sixty nine Between WILLIAM WHITE-
SIDES of County of AMHERST of one part and ADAM DEAN of County of Albemarle of
other part Witnesseth that WILLIAM WHITESIDES & ELIZABETH WHITESIDES for sum of
Fifty pounds current money of Virginia to them in hand paid by these presents doth
bargain sell & confirm unto ADAM DEAN his heirs all that devidend track or parcel of
land lying & being in County of Albemarle & Parish of St. Ann containing One hundred
& eighty one acres more or less lying & being on both sides of STOCKTONS MILL CREEK
and bounded Begining at MOSES AGERs Corner Hickory on his own line, runing thence
on said AGERs line South forty five degrees West Fifty nine poles crossing the Creek to a
red Oak, then new lines North forty six degrees West fifty five poles to pointers, then on
JOHN CAMPBELLs line North fifty two degrees East eighty four poles to a white Oak
North one and a half degrees East two hundred & fifty four poles to pointers, thence
North thirty two degrees West seventy four poles to pointers, new lines South Eighty
three degrees East one hundred & thirty four poles to pointers, thence South forty nine
degrees East one hundred & thirty poles to pointers, thence on his own line South
seventy seven degrees West one hundred & seventy poles to a Pine, thence South
twenty five degrees West one hundred poles to two Hickories, thence South five degrees
East One hundred & seventy two poles to the first Station together with all timber water
commodities whatsoever to the same belonging To have & to hold the said parcel of land
to ADAM DEAN his heirs and WM WHITESIDES & ELIZABETH WHITESIDES the said dividend
or parcel of land to said ADAM DEAN his heirs will warrant & defend In Witness
whereof said WILLIAM WHITESIDES & ELIZABETH WHITESIDES doth hereunto set their
hands & affix their seals the day & year above written
Signed Sealed & delivered in presence of
     SAMUEL STOCKTON,   WILLIAM his mark C WHITESIDES
     JOHN DAVIS, JAMES WALKER,   ELIZABETH her mark W WHITESIDES
     PRUDENCE her mark U STOCKTON
  At Albemarle May Court 1770
This Indenture was proved by the Oath of JOHN DAVIS & PRUDENCE STOCKTON Wits.
thereto & the same having been before proved by one other Wits. was ordered to be
recorded

pp.   THIS INDENTURE made the 8th day of May One thousand seven hundred & Seven-
172-   ty Between SAMUEL KERR of County of Albemarle of one part and JOHN BURK of
173   County of AUGUSTA of other part Witnesseth that SAMUEL KERR for sum of

Fifty pounds current money of Virginia to him in hand paid by the said WM. CRAW-FORD by these presents doth bargain sell & confirm unto said JOHN BURK one certain tract or parcel of land containing Three hundred and Thirty one acres lying & being in County of Albemarle on both sides of South Fork of ROCKEY CREEK and bounded Beginning at HENRY BUNCHes corner of two white Oaks, thence on his line North sixty degrees West fifty one poles to MOSIAS JONES's Corner of several marked trees in BUNCHes line, thence on JONES's line North eighty four degrees West one hundred & thirty poles to his Corner Pine, thence on his line South nineteen degrees West eighty two poles ROCKEY CREEK continued twenty poles to the Corner Pine, thence South thirteen degrees West one hundred & forty four poles to a corner white Oak by the side of a Branch, thence South seventy degrees East one hundred & twenty four poles to a shrubby white Oak, thence North sixty five degrees East One hundred & seventy four poles crossing the Creek to a white Oak in the line of HENRY BUNCH, thence on his lines North twenty nine degrees West eighty eight poles to his corner Pine, thence on his line North ten degrees East ninety seven poles to the Beginning together with all houses orchards & all other Improvements whatsoever and SAMUEL KERR the said land & premises before bargained & sold with every of their appurtenances to said JOHN BURK his heirs shall warrant & defend by these presents In Witness whereof the parties to these presents have put their hands & Seals the day of year above written Signed Sealed & delivered in presence of

(no witnesses shown)   SAM: KERR

At Albemarle May Court 1770
This Indenture was acknowledged by SAMUEL KERR party thereto & ordered to be recorded

pp.   THIS INDENTURE made the 10th day of May One thousand seven hundred & Sixty
174-   nine Between WILLIAM MARTIN & SUSANNAH his Wife of Parish & County of
175   AMHERST of one part & RICHARD WILBURN of Parish of St. Anns & County of
          Albemarle of other part Witnesseth that WILLIAM MARTIN & SUSANNAH his
Wife for sum of Twenty pounds current money of Virginia to him in hand paid by said
RICHARD WILBURN by these presents doth bargain & sell unto RICHD. WILBURN & to his
heirs one certain tract or parcell of land containing One hundred & Sixty two acres (be
the same more or less) which said tract of One hundred & Sixty two acres of land is part
of a tract of Three hundred & twenty four acres which WILLIAM MARTIN bought of
MATTHIAS JORDAN whose Deed bears date the ninth day of Oct. One thousand seven
hundred & Fifty seven lying & being in County of Albemarle & bounded Beginning at
JAMES TULEYs corner pointers by a branch of TOTIER & running South thirty nine
degrees West three hundred eighty poles to a white Oak, North fifty one degrees West
crossing a Branch of BALLENGERS CREEK sixty two poles to a red Oak & joining ABRA-
HAM EADES & JAMES TULEYs to the beginning together with all woods water courses
and all appurtenances to the same belonging To have & to hold said one hundred & Sixty
two acres of land with every of their appurtenances to him sd RICHARD WILBURN his
heirs & WM. MARTIN & SUSANNAH his Wife their heirs will by these presents warrant
& forever defend In Witness whereof sd WILLIAM MARTIN & SUSANNAH his Wife hath
hereunto set their hands & Seals the day & year above written
Signed Sealed & Delivered in presence of
      JNO. GRAYHAM,
      JOHN LYON   WILLIAM his mark X MARTIN
At Albemarle May Court 1770
This Indenture & memorandum were acknowledged by WM. MARTIN party thereto &

ordered to be recorded. SUSANNAH, Wife of sd WM., personally appeared in Court & being first privately Examined as the Law directs, voluntarily relinquished her right of Dower in the land conveyed by this Indenture

pp. THIS INDENTURE made this 22d day of November in year of our Lord One thou-
175- sand seven hundred & Sixty nine Between JOHN MULLINS JUNR. of Fredericks-
176 ville Parish & Albemarle County of one part and BEN BROWN of St. Martins
Parish in HANOVER COUNTY of other part Witnesseth that said BEN BOWN for sum of Twenty pounds Current money of Virginia to him in hand paid by said JOHN MULLINS JUNR. by these presents do bargain sell & confirm unto said JOHN MULLINS JUNR. his heirs one certain tract of land lying & being in Fredericksville Parish & Albemarle County on the North side of DOYLES RIVER containing by Estimation Ninety acres be the same more or less & bounded Begining on the North side of DOYLES RIVER runing thence North sixty six degrees East fifteen poles to a Maple, thence North sixty seven & a half degrees One hundred & sixty two poles to a corner white Oak on a branch thence North thirty two & a half degrees West thirty one poles to a Hickory & pointers on a hill side, thence North sixty seven West One hundred & thirty six poles to the River thence down the River by the meanders thereof to the Begining and all houses woods water courses & all the appurtenances belonging unto him the said JOHN MULLINS JUNR. his heirs In Witness whereof said BEN BROWN hath hereunto set his hand & Seal the day & year above written
Sign'd Seal'd & Deliverd in presence of
BERNARD BROWN,   BEN BROWN
BERNICE BROWN, BENAJAH BROWN
Memorandum that on the day & year within written peaceable & Quiet possession & seizen of the within granted land was had and taken by BEN BROWN & by him delivered unto JOHN MULLINS his heirs according to the true meaning of the within Indenture
Test   BENAJAH BROWN,   BEN BROWN
BERNARD BROWN, BERNICE BROWN
Received of JOHN MULLINS the consideration within mentioned for ninety acres of land 22d Novr. 1769
Test   BENAJAH BROWN,   BEN BROWN
BERNARD BROWN, BERNICE BROWN
At Albemarle May Court 1770
This Indenture memorandum & receipt were proved by the Oath of BENAJAH BROWN, BERNARD BROWN & BERNICE BROWN Wits. thereto & ordered to be recorded

pp. THIS INDENTURE made ye fourteenth day of March One thousand seven hundred
177- & Seventy Between THOMAS McCULLOCK & ISABELLA his Wife of ye Parish of
178 St. Ann in County of Albemarle of ye one part and ROBERT TERRELL of ye Parish
of St. Thomas in the County of ORANGE of ye other part Witnesseth that ye said THOS. McCULLOCK & ISABEL his Wife for ye sum of One hundred & twenty two Seventeen Shillings & six pence current money of Virginia to them in hand paid by ye said ROBERT TERRELL by these presents doth bargain sell and confirm unto ROBERT TER-RELL his heirs one certain tract or parcel of land lying in County of Albemarle and bounded Begining at a red Oak corner of CHISWELL and runing thence North eighty seven degrees East sixty six poles to pointers at a large Rock, corner to WM. WINSTON, thence North fourteen degrees East thirty one poles to a Gum another Corner of ye sd WINSTON thence down the said Branch to pointers corner to WILLIAM WINSTON th. South ten degrees West eighteen poles to a saplin, thence North seventeen degrees West

one hundred & forty poles to a Pine, corner to WM. WINSTON, then South sixty degrees West one hundred & seventy six poles to pointers, corner to JOHN RODES, thence South eleven degrees East two hundred & ninety four poles to a Chesnut, thence North forty six degrees East two hundred & twenty two poles to ye Beginning the said tract of land doth contain Three hundred & fifty four acres together with all houses gardens and appurtenances whatsoever to ye tract of land belonging and THOMAS McCULLOCK the aforesaid tract of Three hundred & Fifty four acres of land to him the said ROBERT TERRELL his heirs will warrant & forever defend by these presents In Witness whereof said THOMAS McCULLOCK & ISABEL his Wife have hereunto set their hands & affixed their Seals the day & year above written

Sealed & Delivered in presence of

REUBEN TERRELL, PRES. DOLLINS,   THOS. McCULLOCK
RICHD. DOLLINS, WILLIAM WOOD, JUNR.   ISABEL her mark ⨍ McCULLOCK
WM. DOLLINS, ISAAC WOOD, JNO. DOLLINS,
WILLIAM WOOD, JNO. WOOD

Received of ROBT. TERRELL the consideration money within mentioned this fourteenth day of March 1770

Test REUBEN TERRELL,   THOS. McCULLOCK
RICHD. DOLLINS, WILLIAM WOOD

At Albemarle May Court 1770

This Indenture was proved by the Oath of REUBEN TERRELL, JOHN DOLLINS & JOHN WOODS Wits. thereto & ordered to be recorded

pp.   THIS INDENTURE made the twenty sixth day of Octr. in year of our Lord One
178-   thousand seven hundred & Sixty nine Between JAMES MARTIN & ANN his Wife
179   of Albemarle County of one part and WILSON MILES CARY of ELIZABETH CITY
             COUNTY of other part Witnesseth that JAMES MARTIN & ANN his Wife for sum of
One hundred & ten pounds current money of Virginia to them in hand paid by these presents doth bargain sell and confirm unto said WILSON MILES CARY his heirs a parcel of land lying & being in County of Albemarle on the North side of RIVANNA RIVER, the land the said JAMES now lives on, bequeathed to him by his Father in his last Will & Testament, begining at a Beach on the river bank & runing by a line of mark'd trees between him and his Brother, BENJAMIN MARTIN, and corner in the above said WILSON MILES CARY line thence up his line to a Gum on the River bank, thence down the River its several meanders to the begining containing One hundred & twenty eight acres be the same more or less together with all houses orchards and all the conveniences and appurtenances whatsoever to said land belonging To have & to hold the land with all its appurtenances whatsoever to him the said WILSON MILES CARY his heirs free and clear of all Incumbrances saving the Quit rents which shall become due to our Sovereign Lord the King his heirs & Successors In Witness whereof said JAMES MARTIN & ANN his Wife hath hereunto set their hands & Seals the day & year first above written

Signed Sealed & Delivered in presence of

WILLIAM TUCKER,   JAMES MARTIN
ELIAS WILLS, WILLIAM HARRISON   ANN MARTIN

Octr. 26th One thousand seven hundred & sixty nine Then received of WILSON MILES CARY the sum of One hundred & ten pounds current money of Virginia being the consideration money within mentioned I say reced p me

Witness WILLIAM TUCKER,   JAMES MARTIN
ELIAS WILLS, WILLIAM HARRISON

At Albemarle May Court 1770
This Indenture was proved by the Oath of WILLIAM HARRISON, & the same having been
before proved by two other Wits. together with the Receipt was ordered to be recorded

pp.   THIS INDENTURE made the tenth day of March One thousand seven hundred &
180-   Seventy Between ABRAHAM ALLEN of County of AUGUSTA of one part & JACOB
181   WATTS of County of Albemarle of other part Witnesseth that ABRAHAM ALLEN
        for sum of Eight pounds current money of Virginia to him in hand paid by said
JACOB WATTS by these presents do bargain sell and confirm unto JACOB WATTS his heirs
one certain tract or parcel of land containing by estimation One hundred acres be the
same more or less lying and being in Albemarle County and joining the land of said
JACOB WATTS and bounded Begining at a Pine corner of JACOB WATTS and running
thence South thirty degrees West One hundred & twenty eight poles to several Pines &
red Oak saplin pointers, thence South thirty two degrees East One hundred & twenty
eight poles to a Maple and persemand on a branch, thence North thirty degrees East
One hundred & twenty eight poles to a red Oak and a Pine together in WILLIAM SUMP-
TERs line, thence North thirty two degrees West one hundred & twenty eight poles to
the first station together with all houses gardens & water courses thereunto belonging
with all appurtenances whatsoever To have and to hold the said land unto said JACOB
WATTS his heirs In Witness whereof said ABRAHAM ALLEN hath hereunto set his hand
& Seal the day & year above written
Signed Sealed & Delivered in presence of
        W. BELL,   ABRAHAM his mark   ALLEN
        JOHN BELL, CLEAVLAND COFFEY
    Received of Mr. JACOB WATTS the just sum of Eight pounds current money of Virginia
it being the consideration mentioned in the within written Deed in the day & year
within written   reced p me
In presence of W. BELL,   ABRAHAM his mark ALLEN
        JOHN BELL, CLEAVLAND COFFEY
    At Albemarle May Court 1770
This Indenture was proved by the Oath of WM. BELL, JOHN BELL & CLEAVLAND COFFEY,
Wits. thereto, & together with a receipt thereon endorsed were ordered to be recorded

pp.   THIS INDENTURE made this Tenth day of May in year of our Lord One thousand
181-   seven hundred & Seventy between ROBERT HARRISS & LUCREASIA his Wife of
182   County of Albemarle of one part and WILLIAM COX of County of ORANGE of other
        part Witnesseth that ROBT. HARRISS & LUCREASIA his Wife for sum of Ninety
pounds current money of Virginia to them in hand paid by WILLIAM COX by these presents do bargain sell and confirm unto WILLIAM COX his heirs one certain tract or parcel of land containing by supposition three hundred & Seventy seven acres more or
less lying and being in Albemarle County on the GREAT MOUNTAIN and bounded begining at a large Chesnut Oak on the West side of a branch of DOYLES RIVER a new corner, thence North thirty two Degrees West Eighty poles to several Chesnuts, thence
North sixty four degrees West forty pole to a Chesnut, thence twenty nine degrees West
sixty six pole to a Chesnut, thence North eighty five degrees West thirty two poles to a
red Oak, thence South sixty one degrees East eighty two poles to pointers, thence South
twenty nine degrees West Sixty nine poles to pointers, thence North seventy degrees
West forty six poles to a Hickory saplin, thence South seventy two degrees West eighty
two poles to a white Oak, thence West sixty six poles to a Chesnut, thence South sixty
eight degrees West thirty poles to a white Oak, thence North fifty degrees West thirteen

poles to a white Oak, thence South seventy degrees West seventy six poles to a Chesnut &
red Oak on South Fork of DOYLES RIVER thence North eighty four degrees West eight
four poles to a Chesnut and red Oak, thence North fifty poles to a Chesnut, thence North
seventy degrees East One hundred & sixty six poles to a Chesnut red Oak, thence North
ninety nine pole to a Chesnut, thence North seventy two degrees East forty poles to
pointers, thence East eighty poles to a Dogwood, thence North fifty five degrees East One
hundred & thirty poles to a Chesnut red Oak, thence South eighty three degrees East one
hundred & twenty five poles to several marked trees on a branch of DOYLES RIVER
thence down the branch South twenty seven degrees West one hundred & twenty eight
poles to the Begining together with all houses orchards & waters courses thereunto belonging To have & to hold said lands & premises with the appurtenances whatsoever to
him the said WILLIAM COX his heirs clearly discharged of all former sales Dower and all
other rights & Estates whatseover thereunto belonging In Witness whereof said ROBT.
HARRISS & LUCREASIA his Wife hath hereunto set their hands & Seals the day & year
above written
Signed Sealed & Delivered in presence of
        (no witnesses shown)   ROBERT HARRISS
  Received of WILLIAM COX the just sum of Ninety pounds Currt. money of Virginia in
full satisfaction of the consideration mentioned in the within written Deed on the day &
year within written   Reced p me   ROBERT HARRISS
  At Albemarle May Court 1770
This Indenture was ackd. by ROBERT HARRISS party thereto & ordered to be recorded.
LUCREASIA, Wife of said ROBERT, personally apeared in Court & being first privately
examined as the Law directs, voluntarily relinquished her right of Dower in the lands
conveyed by this Indenture

p.   THIS INDENTURE made on the 8th day of May in year of our Lord One thousand
183   seven hundred and Seventy Between WILLIAM GARROT of LOUISA COUNTY of
          one part and JOHN JONES of Albemarle County of other part Witnesseth that
WILLIAM GARROT for sum of Thirteen pounds eight Shillings Currt. money to him in
hand paid by said JOHN JONES doth bargain & sell unto JOHN JONES and his heirs a tract
of land containing One hundred & thirty four acres lying in Albemarle County on the
branches of the North Fork of the HARDWARE RIVER and bounded Begining at a
branch called the GREAT BRANCH where the line of the land the said JONES bought formerly of said GARROT crosses it, running thence up the said branch according to its
meanders to the mouth of the MAPLE BRANCH, thence up MAPLE BRANCH and its Western Fork to a white Oak at the head thereof, thence a new line South eighty degrees
West thirty six poles to pointers a Ridge, South forty eight degrees West twelve poles to a
red Oak in sd JONES's line, thence with said JONES's line along the top of the Ridge South
seventy three degrees East twelve poles to a red Oak, South sixty seven degrees East
twenty three poles to a red Oak saplin, South eighty six degrees & a half East forty four
poles to pointers, thence South sixty eight degrees East two hundred & fifty poles to the
beginning together with all appurtenances to the same belonging To have & to hold
said land with its appurtenances unto JOHN JONES & his heirs and WILLIAM GARROT &
his heirs will forever warrant & defend In Witness whereof WILLIAM GARROT hath
hereunto subscribed his name & affixed his Seal the day & year first above written
Signed Sealed & Delivered in presence of
        (no witnesses shown)   WM. GARROTT
  At Albemarle May Court 1770
This Indenture was ackd. by WILLIAM GARROTT party thereto & ordered to be recorded

p.   THIS INDENTURE made on the tenth day of May in year of our Lord One thousand
184   seven hundred & Seventy Between WILLIAM GARROT of LOUISA COUNTY of one
        part & CHARLES LEWIS of Albemarle County of other part Witnesseth that WIL-
LIAM GARROT for sum of Twenty one pounds Fifteen Shillings & three pence current
money to him in hand paid by CHARLES LEWIS doth bargain & sell to said CHARLES
LEWIS & his heirs a tract of land containing by estimation fifty nine and a half acres
lying in Albemarle County on the Branchs of the North Fork of HARDWARE RIVER and
bounded begining at a black Oak in the said LEWIS's line & corner of said GARROTs land,
running thence along the line which was GARROTs North eighty five & a half degrees
West fifty five poles to the place his line crosses BAKERS BRANCH, thence down BAKERS
BRNCH according to its meanders to its confluence with the GREAT BRANCH & down the
GREAT BRANCH to the place where JOHN JONES's line crosses it, thence with said JONES's
line South seventy six degrees East twenty two poles to pointers in the said LEWIS's old
line and with it North fourteen degrees East two hundred & thirty four poles crossing
the MIRY BRANCH to the beginning together with the appurtenances thereunto belonging To have & to hold said land with the appurtenances unto CHARLES LEWIS & his
heirs and WILLIAM GARROT & his heirs the said tract of land with its appurtenances
unto said CHARLES LEWIS & his heirs will forever warrant & defend In Witness
whereof WILLIAM GARROT hath hereunto subscribed his name & affixed his Seal the
day & year above written
Signed Sealed & delivered in presence of
        (no witnesses shown)   WM. GARROTT
  At Albemarle May Court 1770
This Indenture was ackd. by WILLIAM GARROTT party thereto & ordered to be recorded

pp.   THIS INDENTURE made this twelvth day of October in year of our Lord One thou-
185-   sand seven hundred & Sixty nine Between HEZEKIAH INMON of County of Albe-
186   marle and ROBERT PAGE of County of AMHERST Witnesseth that HEZEKIAH IN-
        MON for sum of Fifty seven pounds current money of Virginia to him in hand
paid by ROBERT PAGE by these presents doth bargain sell and confirm unto said ROBERT
PAGE and to his heirs one certain tract or parcel of land lying and being in County of
Albemarle on a branch of ROCFISH lying on both sides of TAYLORS CREEK & joining to
the lands of WILLIAM AUSTIN & ROGER CAREY and bounded as by Patent granted to
HEZEKIAH INMON containing Three hundred & ninety eight acres be the same more or
less and conveyed to said INMON by Patent Begining at a Poplar thence North thirty
seven degrees West thirty five poles to a red Oak, North thirty five degrees East Sixty
poles to pointers, due North one hundred & four poles to a Chesnut tree, North Seventy
degrees West thirty poles to a Dogwood tree, due West fifty nine poles to a Chesnut Oak,
South fifty degrees West ninety one poles to pointers, South eighty degrees West eighty
five poles to a HIckory, South forty degrees East fifty four poles to pointers, South
fifteen degrees East one hundred & two poles to a Chesnut Oak, South fifty seven degrees
East one hundred & twenty poles to pointers, South sixty degrees West one hundred &
twenty poles to pointers, due South eighty three poles to a white Oak, South sixty three
degrees East eight poles to pointers North fifty eight degrees East seventy two poles to a
Spanish Oak, North ten degrees West one hundred & thirty poles to a Hickory, North
twenty four degrees East thirty poles to a Poplar, together with all houses profits &
other appurtenanances to the same belonging To have & to hold said Three hundred &
ninety eight acres of land with every of their appurtenances unto ROBERT PAGE his
heirs and HEZEKIAH INMON his heirs against all other persons whatsoever will forever
warrant & defend the same by these presents In Witness whereof said HEZEKIAH IN-

MON hath set his hand & Seal the day & year of our Lord above written
Signed Sealed & Delivered in presence of
      MICAJAH CHILES,   HEZEKIAH INMON
      WM. TERRELL LEWIS, ALEXANDER MOSS   JANE INMON

Memorandum That on the twelvth day of Octr. in year of our Lord One thousand seven hundred & Sixty nine Quiet & peaceable possession & seizin of the land & Tenements was had & taken by HEZEKIAH INMON in his proper person and by him delivered over unto ROBERT PAGE according to the form and Effect of the within Deed
In presence of MICAJAH CHILES,   HEZEKIAH INMON
      WM. TERRELL LEWIS, ALEXR. MOSS   JANE INMON

Then received of ROBERT PAGE the sum of Fifty seven pounds current money of Virginia being the consideration money within mentioned I say reced by me
                              HEZEKIAH INMON

    At Albemarle May Court 1770
This Indenture memorandum & Receipt were proved by the Oath of ALEXANDER MOSS a Wits. thereto & the same having been before proved by two other Wits. was ordered to be recorded

pp.   THIS INDENTURE made this Tenth day of May in year of our Lord One thousand
186-   seven hundred & Seventy Between DAVID NOWLIN & WILLIAM BURRASS of
187   County of Albemarle of one part and JOHN TOOL of the same County of other part
         Witnesseth that DAVID NOWLIN & WILLIAM BURRASS for sum of Sixty two
pounds Currt. money of Virginia to them in hand paid by sd JOHN TOOL by these presents doth bargain sell & confirm unto JOHN TOOL & his heirs one certain tract or parcel of land contain.g by estimation One hundred & Ninety seven acres lying & being in County of Albemarle in the Coves of one of the RAGGED MOUNTAINS at the head of TAYLORS CREEK, ninety seven acres being part thereof was Pattented to DAVID NOWLIN bearing date the Tenth day of Sept. One thousand seven hundred xixty seven, the other hundred acres was Deeded to DAVID NOWLIN by RICHARD LUDWELL formerly belonging to CHARLES WINGFIELD and bounded by the lines of NATHANIAL HAGGARD and the lands formerly belonging to HEZEKIAH INMON now ROBERT PAGE it being the same land that was bargained & sold by DAVID NOWLIN to said WILLIAM BURRASS & EDWARD BENBY now lives on with all houses orchards with all the appurtenances unto said JOHN TOOL & his heirs and DAVID NOWLIN & WILLIAM BURRASS their heirs will warrt. & forever defend by these presents Sealed the day & year above written
Signed Sealed and Delivered in presence of
    (no witnesses shown)   DAVID NOWLIN
                          WM. his mark /M\ BURRUSS

    At Albemarle May Court 1770
This Indenture was ackd. by DAVID NOWLIN & WM. BURRASS parties thereto & ordered to be recorded

pp.   GEORGE ye 3d &c. To MOSIAS JONES, ISAAC DAVIS & DAVID RODES Gent. Greeting
187-   Whereas SAMUEL KERR of County of Albemarle by his Indenture of Bargain &
188   Sale bearing date the Eighth day of May 1770 have conveyed the fee simple
         Estate of 331 acres of land lying & being in said County unto one JOHN BURK &
Whereas MARGARET KERR, Wife of said SAMUEL cannot conveniently tracel to our said County Court of Albemarle to make acknowledgment of the said conveyance, We Therefore give you or any two of you power to receive the acknowledgment which the said MARGARET shall be willing to make before you of the conveyance aforesaid contained

and when you have examined her as aforesaid that you distinctly & openly certify our
Justices thereof in our County Court under your Seals & this Writ Witness JOHN
NICHOLAS Clk, of our said Court the XIIth day of May in the Xth year of our Reign
   The Execution of this Writ appears in a certain Schedule hereunto annexed
   By virtue of the Writ to us directed, we have privily & apart examined the within
MARGARET KERR, Wife of said SAMUEL KERR, who declared that she did acknowledge all
her right & Title to the within land & that she did it freely without any force or com-
pulsion Witness our hands & Seals the 22d day of May 1770   MOSIAS JONES
                                                                    DAVID RODES

   At Albemarle June Court 1770
This acknowledgment was returned to Court & ordered to be recorded

pp.   THIS INDENTURE made this (blank) day of (blank) in year of our Lord One thou-
188-   sand seven hundred & Seventy Between WILLIAM MECHIE of Parish of
189   Fredericksville and County of Albemarle of one part & WILLIAM HARRISS of the
           Parish & County abovesaid of other part Witnesseth that WILLIAM MECHIE for
sum of Sixty pounds current money of Virginia to him in hand paid by WILLIAM HAR-
RISS by these presents do bargain sell & confirm unto WM. HARRISS his heirs one certain tract or parcel of land lying & being in Parish of Fredericksville & County of Albemarle containing One hundred & fifty acres be the same more or less & bounded Begining at a Hickory on the bank of the North side of MECHAMS RIVER and running
South twelve degrees West thirty four poles to a Pine, South twenty four degrees West
down the sd River, thence down with the said River about fifty poles, thence crossing
the said River to a Beach on the other side, thence along the main which divides the
two principal Branches on the said late purchased land to ROBERT LEWIS's line, thence
with the said line North fifty eight & a half degrees East about two hundred poles crossing a branch to pointers, thence a new line North sixty six and a half degrees West two
hundred & eighty six poles to a Pine on MEACHAMS RIVER to the first station with all
houses orchards and appurtenances thereunto belonging To have & to hold said land &
premises with the appurtenances unto WILLIAM HARRISS his heirs free & clear of all
Incumbrances whatsoever and WILLIAM MECHIE his heirs will warrant & forever defend against all persons whatsoever In Witness whereof WILLIAM MECHIE hath hereunto set his hand & Seal the day & year above written
Signed Sealed & Delivered in presence of
       (no witnesses shown)   WILLIAM MECHIE
   Memorandum That on ye day & year first written within peaceable & Quiet possession
& Seizen of the within granted land was had & taken by WILLIAM MECHIE & by him
delivered over unto said WILLIAM HARRISS his heirs according to the true meaning of
the within Indenture   WILLIAM MECHIE
   Received this day of (blank) 1770. WILLIAM HARRISS the sum of Sixty pounds current
money of Virginia being the consideration money for the within granted & sold land &
premises   WILLIAM MECHIE
   At Albemarle June Court 1770
This Indenture memorandum & Receipt were acknowledged by WILLIAM MECHIE party
thereto & ordered to be recorded

pp.   THIS INDENTURE made the fourteenth day of June in year of our Lord One thou-
190-   sand seven hundred & Seventy Between HUGH ALEXANDER of Albemarle County
191   & Colony of Virginia of one part & JOHN ALEXANDER of County & Colony afore-
           said of other part Witnesseth that HUGH ALEXANDER for sum of Sixty pounds

current money of Virginia to him in hand paid by sd JOHN ALEXANDER by these presents doth bargain sell & confirm unto JOHN ALEXANDER & to his heirs one certain tract or parcel of land containing Five hundred & fifty acres lying & being in County of Albemarle in the Fork of MECHAMS RIVER and bounded Beginning at pointers in DAVID STOCKTONs line & with it South forty five degrees West two hundred & sixty eight poles to a Chesnut in SARAH STOCKTONs line and with her line North sixty one degrees West two hundred poles to pointers, new lines North sixty six degrees East sixty poles to pointers, North one hundred & forty poles to a Pine & North sixty five degrees East at fifty eight poles to a Branch, eighty eight poles to pointers in his own line & with it North eighty five degrees East nine poles to his Corner Shrub Oak & new line North twenty three degrees East ninety two poles to pointers in ROBERT ANDERSONs line, & with it South eighty degrees East One hundred & forty eight poles to a white Oak, the same Course continued on a new line one hundred & twenty two poles in all, then hundred & twenty poles to a Pine in SAMUEL BLACKs line & with it forty five degrees West one hundred & sixty poles to the Beginning & all houses orchards gardens fences to the same belonging To have & to hold the said Five hundred & fifty acres of land with their appurteances to said JOHN ALEXANDER & his heirs and HUGH ALEXANDER & his heirs will forever warrant & defend the sold premises unto JOHN ALEXANDER In Witness whereof said HUGH ALEXANDER hath hereunto set his hand & Seal ye day & year first above written

Signed Sealed & Delivered in presence of

(no witnesses shown)

HUGH ALEXANDER

JANE her mark X ALEXANDER

Memorandum that on ye fourteenth day of June in year of our Lord One thousand seven hundred & Seventy Quiet & peaceable possession & Seizen was had & taken by HUGH ALEXANDER & by him was delivered to JOHN ALEXANDER and his heirs

HUGH ALEXANDER

JANE her mark X ALEXANDER

June ye fourteenth Then received of JOHN ALEXANDER the sum of Sixty pounds current money of Virginia being in full for the consideration money in this Deed mentioned, I say received by me

HUGH ALEXANDER

JANE her mark X ALEXANDER

At Albemarle June Court 1770

This Indenture memorandum & receipt were ackd. by HUGH ALEXANDER party thereto & ordered to be recorded

pp.
191-
192

THIS INDENTURE made the Thirty first day of March in year of our Lord One thousand seven hundred & Seventy Between JOHN LEWIS of HALIFAX County of one part and THOMAS GARTH of Albemarle County of other part Witnesseth that JOHN LEWIS for sum of Two hundred & Eighty pounds current money to him in hand paid by THOMAS GARTH doth bargain & sell THOMAS GARTH & his heirs one certain tract of land containing by Estimation nine hundred acres be the same more or less lying in County of Albemarle amongst the SOUTH WEST MOUNTAINS on the head of BLUE RUN, it being that tract of land said JOHN LEWIS purchased of STEPHEN HOMES deced except what hath been already sold to HENRY SHELTON and JOSIAH BUSH and bounded on the North East side by the SHELTONs & BUSHs lines, on the Southwest by THOMAS WALKERs and on the North West by RICHARD DURRETs together with the appurtenances thereto belonging To have & to hold the said tract of land with its appurteances unto THOMAS GARTH & his heirs and JOHN LEWIS will forever warrant & defend In Witness whereof said JOHN LEWIS hath hereunto subscribed his name & affixed his Seal the day & year first above written

Signed Sealed & delivered in presence of
     THOS. WALKER, DANL. SMITH,   JOHN LEWIS JUNR.
     THOS. WALKER JUNR., JOHN WALKER
  Memorandum that on the day & year within written peaceable & Quiet possession of
the within mentioned land was given by JOHN LEWIS to THOMAS GARTH according to the
true intent and meaning of these presents Witness my hand
Test THOMAS. WALKER, THOS. WALKER JUNR.,   JOHN LEWIS JUNR.
     JOHN WALKER, DANL. SMITH
  At Albemarle June Court 1770
This Indenture & memorandum were proved by the Oath of DANL. SMITH a Wits. thereto
& the same having been before proved by two other wits. were ordered to be recorded

pp.   THIS INDENTURE made on the thirty first day of March in year of our Lord One
192-   thousand seven hundred & Seventy between JOHN LEWIS of HALIFAX COUNTY
193   of one part and HENRY SHELTON of Albemarle County of other part Witnesseth
        that JOHN LEWIS for sum of Two hundred & five pounds current money to him in
hand paid doth bargain & sell HENRY SHELTON & his heirs a tract of land containing
Four hundred & sixteen acres lying in Albemarle County on both sides of BLUE RUN, it
being part of a tract the said JOHN LEWIS bought of STEPHEN HOMES deced, and bounded
beginning at pointers near a Spring called WILSONS SPRING, running thence South
thirty eight degrees East two hundred & sixty three poles crossing BLUE RUN at pointers
on the low grounds, South twenty eight degrees East ninety four poles to pointers round
some rocks and a Sassafras saplin mark'd E South twenty five degrees East twenty one
poles to some small Locust bushes, South Seventy nine degrees & an half at one hundred
& fifty poles to a Sassafras in HOMES's SPRING BRANCH thence down said Branch according to the meanders thereof to its confluence with BLUE RUN and down said Run
according to the meanders to the place where the line that divides ORANGE & Albemarle
crosses at, thence with the said County Line North seventy one degrees West two hundred & twenty poles to a Pine, Corner to RICHARD WILSONs Land and has the said WIL-
SONs name cut thereon, thence South forty seven degrees West one hundred & eight
poles to the Beginning together with the appurtenances thereto To have & to hold the
said tract of land with the appurtenances unto HENRY SHELTON & his heirs and JOHN
LEWIS from all persons will forever warrant & defend In Witness whereof said JOHN
LEWIS hath hereto subscribed his name & affixed his Seal the day & year above written
Signed Sealed & Delivered in presence of
     THOMAS WALKER, JOHN WALKER,   JOHN LEWIS JUNR.
     DANL. SMITH, THOS. WALKER JUNR.
  Memorandum on the day & year within written peaceable & Quiet possession of the
land and premises was given by JOHN LEWIS to HENRY SHELTON according to the true
intent and meaning of these presents Witness my hand
Witness THOMAS WALKER, JOHN WALKER,   JOHN LEWIS JUNR
     DANL. SMITH, THOS. WALKER JUNR.
  At Albemarle June Court 1770
This Indenture & memorandum were proved by Oath of JOHN WALKER, THOS. WALKER
JUNR. & DANL. SMITH, Wits. thereto, & ordered to be recorded

pp.   THIS INDENTURE made this fifth day of December One thousand seven hundred &
194-   Sixty nine Between THOMAS CAWTHORN of HANOVER COUNTY of one part and
195   JOHN WINN JUNR. of aforesaid Conty of other part Witnesseth that THOMAS CAW-
        THORN for the valuable consideration of Twenty five pounds Currt. money of

Virginia to him in hand paid doth by these presents bargain sell & confirm unto said
JOHN WINN JUNR. his heirs one parcel of land containing Three hundred & fifty acres
of land lying & being in County of Albemarle in the Fork of JAMES RIVER adjoining to
the East side BREMORE CREEK and bounded Beginning at pointers on the bank of the
said Creek and runing thence new lines East seventy poles crossing Long Branch to a
Pine on a Ridge, North fifty degrees East four hundred poles crossing three branches to
pointers & North forty one degrees West one hundred & Sixteen poles crossing the
aforesaid Branch to pointers in JOSEPH GOODEs Line and on the same South sixty degrees
West one hundred & forty five poles to pointers, thence on JOHN PAYNEs line South one
hundred & fifty poles to pointers, South twenty degrees West sixty four poles to a Pine,
South fifty five degrees West eighty six poles to a Pine, thence a new line South thirteen degrees West twenty two poles to pointers on the bank of said Creek and thence
down the same according to its meanders to the beginning To have & to hold the above
granted premises with all its rights members & appurtenances together with all houses
Orchards profts & commodities whatsoever thereupon belonging and THOMAS CAW-
THORN doth for himself his heirs warrant & defend the granted premises unto said JOHN
WINN JUNR. his heirs discharged of all manner of Incumbrances In Witness whereof I
have hereunto set my hand and fixed my Seal the day & year above written
Signed Sealed & Delivered in presence of
      ROBERT ELLIT, THOMAS BOWLES,   THOMAS CAWTHORN
      JOHN WINN, THOMAS BOWLES JUNR.
  Memorandum that quiet & peaceable possession was granted of the within mentioned
land to JOHN WINN JUNR by these presents
In presents of ROBERT ELLIT, THOMAS BOWLES   THOMAS CAWTHORN
      JOHN WINN, THOMAS BOWLES JUNR.
  At Albemarle July Court 1770
This Indenture & memorandum were ackd. by THOMAS CAWTHORN party thereto &
ordered to be recorded

pp.   THIS INDENTURE made the twelvth day of July in year of our Lord One thousand
195-   seven hundred & Seventy Between MICHAEL ISRAEL of County of Albemarle &
196   SARAH his Wife of one part & WILLIAM WILLIAMS of GOOCHLAND COUNTY of the
      other part Witnesseth that MICHAEL ISRAEL & SARAH his Wife for sum of Forty
pounds to them in hand paid by said WILLIAM WILLIAMS by these presents do bargain
& sell unto WILLIAM WILLIAMS his heirs a certain tract or parcel of land containing
by estimation Eighty acres be the same more or less lying & being in County of Albemarle and bounded Beginning at THOMAS DOLLINS Corner Chesnut on the side of a
Mountain, thence on new lines South forty degrees West sixty poles to pointers, North
Eighty six degrees West sixty two poles to a Hicory, South fifty eight degrees West twenty six poles to a red Oak, North six degrees West eighty poles to a Chesnut, North sixty
four degrees East one hundred & twelve poles to pointers on the side of DOLLINS line,
thence on his line South forty five degrees West eighteen poles to pointers, South twenty five degrees East twenty six poles to the first station with all woods profits commodities & appurtenances whatsoever to the parcel of land belonging and MICHAEL ISRAEL
his heirs will warrant & forever defend by these presents In Witness whereof said
MICHAEL ISRAEL & SARAH his Wife have hereunto interchangable set their hands &
affixed their Seals the day & year first above written
Sealed & Delivered in the presence of
      JOHN WOODSON,   MICHAEL ISRAEL
      WILLIAM WOODS, RICHD. WOODS   SARAH her mark X ISRAEL

Received the day & date of the within written Deed of WILLIAM WILLIAMS the sum of
Forty pounds current money of Virginia it being the full consideration of the within
mentioned lands & Tenements
Test RICHD. WOODS,   MICHAEL ISRAEL
      JOHN WOODSON, WILLIAM WOODS
  At Albemarle July Court 1770
This Indenture was ackd. by MICHAEL ISRAEL & SARAH his Wife parties thereto &
ordered to be recorded

pp.   THIS INDENTURE made the 27th day of November in year of our Lord One thou-
197-   sand seven hundred & Sixty nine Between BEN BROWN & SUSAN his Wife of
198   HANOVER COUNTY of one part and BARNARD BROWN of Albemarle County of
        other part Witnesseth that BEN BROWN for and in consideration of One hundred
& forty seven pounds thirteen Shillings current money of Virginia to him in hand paid
by these presents do bargain sell & confirm unto said BERNARD BROWN his heirs one
certain tract or parcel of land and Plantation containing by estimation Four hundred
acres be the same more or less lying & being in Albemarle County on both side of
DOYLES RIVER and bounded Begining at a Poplar on the North side of a branch called
the DEEP CREEK at BENAJAH BROWNs corner on the said Creek, runing thence North
fifteen degrees West one hundred & twelve poles to pointers, thence North twenty eight
degrees East seventy seven poles to pointers on a nole on the top of a Mountain, North
nine degrees & a half West sixty two poles to a Pine, thence North Eighty eight degrees
East One hundred & forty seven poles to five Chesnuts in a branch, thence South two degrees East One hundred & four poles to pointers, thence South eighty five degrees East
One hundred & thirty four poles to a Hickory, thence South Seven West seventy poles to
a Chesnut Oak, thence South forty nine West twenty two poles to a Chesnut Oak, thence
South nine degrees West seventy seven poles to a dead Gum, thence North 74 1/2 degrees West 80 poles to a Chesnut Oak, thence North 85 degrees West 168 poles to a red
Oak, thence North 3 degrees West 18 poles to a Maple, thence North 88 1/2 degrees East
twelve poles to the begining with all houses orchards improvements and appurtenances to said tract of land belonging unto BERNARD BROWN his heirs In Witness
whereof said BEN BROWN & SUSAN his Wife hath hereunto set their hands & Seals the
day & year first above written
Signed Sealed & Delivered in the presence of
      JOHN PRICE,   BEN BROWN
      BENAJAH BROWN, JOHN CAVE
  Memorandum that on the day & year first within written peaceable & Quiet possession
& Seizen of within granted land was had & taken by BEN BROWN & by him delivered
unto BERNARD BROWN to the purport intent & meaning of the within Indenture
Test   JOHN PRICE,   BEN BROWN
        BENAJAH BROWN, JOHN CAVE
  27th of November 1769 Then received of BERNARD BROWN the consideration money
within mentioned in full for the land within mentioned
Test   JOHN PRICE,   BEN BROWN
        BENAJAH BROWN, JOHN CAVE
  At Albemarle July Court 1770
This Indenture memorandum & Receipt was proved by the Oath of JOHN CAVE, a Wits.
thereto, & the same having been before proved by two other Wits. were ordered to be
recorded

pp.

pp.   THIS INDENTURE made this 27th day of November in year of our Lord One thou-
198-   sand seven hundred & Sixty nine Between BEN BROWN of HANOVER COUNTY of
199   the one part and BENAJAH BROWN of Albemarle County of other part Witnesseth
        that BEN BROWN for sum of Thirty pounds current money of Virginia to him in
hand paid by these presents do bargain sell & confirm unto BENAJAH BROWN his heirs
one certain tract of land containing by estimation seventy five acres be the same more
or less lying & being in Albemarle County on North side of DEEP CREEK joining the
lands of sd BENAJAH BROWN, BERNARD BROWN BERNICE BROWN & bounded begining at a
Chesnut & red Oak on the North side of said Branch & running thence North eighty
seven degrees East one hundred & four poles to a Poplar in a deep valley, thence South
fifteen degrees East one hundred ninety three poles to pointers on North side of said
Branch, thence up the said Branch by the sundry meanders thereof to the begining
with all woods ways & all Improvements & appurtenances to said tract of land
belonging In Witness whereof said BEN BROWN hath hereunto set his hand & Seal the
day & year first above written
Signed Sealed & Delivered in the presence of
        JOHN PRICE,   BEN BROWN
        BERNARD BROWN, JOHN CAVE
  Memorandum that on the day & year first within written peaceable & Quiet possession
& Seizin of within granted land was had & taken by BEN BROWN & by him delivered to
BENAJAH BROWN to the purport sence intent & meaning of the within Indenture
Test JOHN PRICE,   BEN BROWN
        BERNARD BROWN, JOHN CAVE
  27th of November 1769 Then received of BENAJAH BROWN the consideration within
mentioned in full for the land within mentioned
Test JOHN PRICE,   BEN BROWN
        BERNARD BROWN, JOHN CAVE
  At Albemarle July Court 1770
This Indenture memorandum & receipt were proved by the Oath of JOHN CAVE a Wits.
thereto & the same having been before proved by two other Wits. were ordered to be
recorded

p.   THIS INDENTURE made this ii day of February One thousand seven hundred &
200   Seventy Between JOHN DOLTON JUNR. of PITTSYLVANIA COUNTY of one part &
        THOMAS CARR of County of Albemarle of other part Witnesseth that said JOHN
DOLTON for sum of Three pounds Fifteen Shillings to him in hand paid by THOS. CARR
by these presents bargain sell & make over to said THOS. CARR his heirs one certain
tract of land lying & being in County of Albemarle containing by estimation One hundred acres be the same more or less (being one moiety of Two hundred acres that was
gave by JOHN KEY to MARY DALTON the Mother of said JOHN) lying & being in the Coty.
of Albemarle on the head branches of Keys Mill Run, on the North side of the SOUTH
WEST MOUNTAINS & is bounded by the lands of WM. GILLUM, MARTIN KEY & a new line
run for Boundary of THOMAS TERRYs purchase of the other moiety & the reversion title
& emolument of said One hundred acres of land more or less in fee simple to said THOS.
CARR & his heirs the said JOHN DALTON will forever warrant & defend by these presents
as Witness the hand & Seal of said JOHN DALTON the day & year above written
Signed Sealed & Delivered in presence of
        JNO. MOORE,   JOHN DALTON
        ROBERT ANDERSON, GILES ALLEGRE JUNR.
        JNO. MOORE JUNR., THOS. TERRY

Memorandum that on the day & year within written full possession & Seisen was had &
taken of within one hundred acres of land by JOHN DALTON & by him made over to THOS.
CARR to hold to him his heirs according to the contents & true meaning of the within
Indenture In presence of JNO. MOORE,
      ROBERT ANDERSON, GILES ALLEGRE JUNR.   JOHN DALTON
      JNO. MOORE JUNR., THOS. TERRY
  At Albemarle July Court 1770
This Indenture memorandum & receipt were proved by the Oath of ROBT. ANDERSON,
JOHN MOORE JUNR. & THOS. TERRY Wits. thereto & ordered to be recorded

pp.   THIS INDENTURE made the ninth day of August in year of our Lord Christ One
201-   thousand seven hundred & Seventy between MUNFORD ROBINSON of County of
202   Albemarle of one part & BENJAMIN COKE of other part Witnesseth that said
          MUNFORD ROBINSON for sum of Fifteen pounds current money of Virginia to
him in hand paid by these presents doth bargain sell & confirm unto said BENJAMIN
COKE his heirs all that dividend or parcel of land lying and being on the branches of
GREAT BYRD in the County aforesaid containing by estimation Two hundred acres be
the same more or less and bound Begining at pointers in ROBINSONs line, running
thence a new line North twenty five degrees West ninety poles to a Pine, South forty
seven degrees West One hundred & nine poles to a white Oak, South forty degrees West
two hundred & ten poles to three small saplins on ROBINSONs line, thence on his line
South fifty degrees East one hundred poles to pointers, North forty degrees East three
hundred & fifty poles to the beginning, Together with all woods commodities & appurtenances whatsoever to the same belonging To have & to hold the said tract of land and
every of their appurtenandces unto BENJAMIN COKE his heirs and MUNFORD ROBINSON
his heirs will warrant & forever defend by these presents In Witness whereof said
MUNFORD ROBINSON hath hereunto set his hand & Seal the date above written
Signed Sealed & Delivered in presents of
      WILLIAM PAYNE,   MUNFORT ROBINSON
      HENRY his mark R RANDOLPH,
      WM. PHILLIPS
Received the ninth day of August One thousand seven hundred & Seventy of BENJA-
MIN COKE the sum of Fifteen pounds it being in full for the land and appurtenances
within mentioned, I say received by me   MUNFORD ROBINSON
  At Albemarle August Court 1770
This Indenture & Receipt were ackd. by MUNFORD ROBINSON party thereto and ordered
to be recorded

pp.   THIS INDENTURE made the sixth day of August in year of our Lord One thousand
202-   seven hundred & Seventy & in the Tenth year of the Reign of our Sovereign
203   Lord George the Third Between RICHARD BENNETT of County of Albemarle of one
          part and MARBEL STONE of the same County of other part Witnesseth that for
sum of Sixty pounds current money of Virginia by said MARBEL STONE in hand paid
unto RICHARD BENNETT by these presents doth bargain sell & confirm unto MARBEL
STONE one certain tract of land lying & being in County of Albemarle on both sides of
CUNNINGHAM CREEK bounded Beginning at pointers near a branch of said Creek on the
East side thereof, thence North twenty five degrees East ninety two poles crossing a
branch to pointers North sixty five degrees West twenty four poles to pointers, thence
North fifty degrees West one hundred poles crossing CUNNIGHAMS CREEK to pointers,
thence Sixty degrees West two hundred poles to pointers, South ninety poles to a

Hickory, thence North eighty three degrees crossing CUNNINGHAMS CREEK to a Poplar on INDIAN CAMP BRANCH, thence up the said branch to a Maple on said Branch in WILLIAM AMOSS's line, thence on his line to pointers, thence new lines to the first station by estimation to contain three hundred acres of land be the same more or less with all woods gardens commodites & appurtenances thereon being or thereunto belonging and all Deeds evidences & wrightings touching the same To have & to hold the bargained & sold premises with every of their appurtenances to MARBEL STONE his heirs and RICHARD BENNETT will warrant & forever defend by these presents In Witness whereof said RICHARD BENNETT hath hereunto set his hand & affixed his Seal the day & year above written
Sealed & Delivered in presence of
    ELIJAH STONE,   RICHARD BENNETT
    HEZEKIAH STONE, WM. STONE   ANN her mark ✝ BENNETT
  At Albemarle August Court 1770
This Indenture was proved by the Oath of ELIJAH STONE, HEZEKIAH STONE & WM. STONE
Wits. thereto & ordered to be recorded

pp.   THIS INDENTURE made the ninth day of August in year of our Lord One thousand
203-   seven hundred & Seventy Between ADAM DEAN of Albemarle County of one part
204   and WILLIAM TWYMAN of CULPEPER COUNTY of other part Witnesseth that said
         ADAM DEAN for sum of Three hundred & fifty pounds current money to him in
hand paid by these presents doth bargain sell & confirm unto WILLIAM TWYMAN his
heirs one tract or parcel of land included in two Patents which said ADAM DEAN
purchased of WILLIAM WHITESIDES containing Four hundred and forty acres be the
same more or less lying and being in County of Albemarle on branches of MECHAMS
RIVER and bounded Beginning at a Hickory Corner to WILLIAM MOOR thence South
forty five degrees West fifty nine poles to a red Oak, thence North forty six West fifty
five poles to pointers, thence North fifty two East eighty fore poles to a whtie Oak,
thence North one and half East two hundred & fifty five poles to pointers, thence North
thirty two West seventy fore poles to pointers, thence South eighty three East one hundred thirty fore poles to pointers thence South forty nine East one hundred & thirty
poles to pointers, thence North seventy two East thirty fore poles to a Pine Corner to
GEORGE BERREY, thence South three East two hundred ninety fore poles to pointers,
thence South eighty three West two hundred thirty four poles to a Chesnut thence
North fifty fore poles to the first station Together with all houses orchards & all other
appurtenances whatsoever to the same belonging To have & to hold said premises
together with the appurtenances thereunto belonging to WILLIAM TWYMAN In Witness whereof said ADAM DEAN & ELENER DEAN hath hereunto set their hands & Seals
the day & year above written
Signed Sealed & Delivered in presence of us
    (no witnesses shown)   ADAM DEAN
                                                ELEANER DEAN
  Ninth day of August One thousand seven hundred & Seventy Then received three hundred & fifty pounds of WM. TWYMAN for the within mentioned land as witness our
hands   ADAM DEAN
                                                ELEANER DEAN
  At Albemarle August Court 1770
This Indenture & receipt were ackd. by ADAM DEAN & ELEONER his Wife parties thereto
& ordered to be recorded

p.   THIS INDENTURE made the ninth day of August One thousand seven hundred &
205 Seventy Between MARTIN TRAP of the Parish & County of AMHERST of the one
part & HENRY KEY of same County & Parish of other part Witnesseth that said
MARTIN TRAP for sum of Thirty pounds Currt. money of Virginia to him in hand paid
by said HENRY KEY by these presents doth bargain sell & confirm unto HENRY KEY his
heirs one certain tract of land containing One hundred & fifty acres be the same more
or less which said parcell of One hundred & fifty acres was granted unto said MARTIN
TRAP by Patent at WILLIAMSBURG bearing date the Tenth day of September MDCCLV
lying & being in County of Albemarle on the branches of STONES CREEK & bounded beginning at pointers in JOHN DAVIS & running on him North eighty degrees East two
hundred & twenty poles to pointers, North twenty two poles to a Spanish Oak, North
seventy eight degrees West one hundred & twenty poles to pointers, North thirty five
poles to a red Oak, West one hundred & ninety six poles to pointers, South one hundred
poles to a Hickory, East one hundred poles to pointers & South twenty two poles to the
Beginning Together with all houses orchards & appurtenances to the same belonging
To have & to hold the said Hundred & fifty acres of land with every of their appurtenances to said HENRY KEY his heirs and MARTIN TRAP his heirs will by these presents
warrant & defend In Witness whereof sd MARTIN TRAP hath hereunto set his hand &
Seals the day & year above written
Signed Sealed & Delivered in presence of
   (no witnesses shown)   MARTIN his mark + TRAP
 At Albemarle August Court 1770
This Indenture was acknowledged by MARTIN TRAP party thereto & ordered to be re-
corded. MARY his Wife came into Court & having first been privately examiend as the
Law directs voluntarily relinquished her right of Dower in the lands conveyed by this
Indenture

pp. THIS INDENTURE made this sixteenth day of July in year of our Lord One thou-
206- sand seven hundred & seventy Between HUGH DOUGHERTY of County of Albe-
207 marle of one part & JOHN HENDERSON JUNR. of sd County of other part Witnesseth that HUGH DOUGHERTY for sum of Eighty pounds currt. money of Virginia
to him in hand paid one certain tract or parcel of land lying & being in County of Albemarle on the waters of BISKIT RUN being the remainder of a tract Patented to HUGH
DOUGHERTY after Two hundred acres were laid off for MARSHALL DOUGHERTY's heirs,
Beginning at pointers running thence along the line of MARSHAL DOUGHERTY's heirs
South thirty & a half East One hundred & eighty nine poles to pointers, thence South
thirty & a half degrees West two hundred & forty five poles to a Hickory, North thirty &
a half degrees West one hundred & thirty seven poles to pointers, North thirty one East
two hundred & eighty nine poles to the beginning containing by Estimation two hun-
dred & fifty three acres be the same more or less To have & to hold said Plantation &
Tract of land with the appurtenances unto JOHN HENDERSON JUNR. his heirs free & discharged of all manner of Incumbrances In Witness whereof I have hereunto set my
hand & affixed my Seal the year & day above written
Signed Sealed & Delivered in presents of
   CHARLES LAMBERT,   HUGH his mark DOUGHERTY
   ALEXANDER BLANE, GEORGE BLANE,
   GEORGE his mark   DOUGLASS
Received on the day of the date of the within written Indenture of JOHN HENDERSON
JUNR. the sum of Eighty pounds currt. money of Virginia it being the consideration
money within mentioned I say reced p me

CHAS. LAMBERT,   HUGH his mark C DOUGHERTY
ALEXANDER BLANE, GEORGE BLANE
    Memorandum on the day of the date of the within written Indenture peaceable posses-
sion of the premises was had & taken by HUGH DOUGHERTY & by him delivered unto
JOHN HENDERSON JUNR. Witness my hand
Test   CHAS. LAMBERT   HUGH his mark C DOUGHERTY
        ALEXR. BLANE, GEORGE BLANE
    At Albemarle August Court 1770
This Indenture memorandum & receipt were proved by the Oath of CHARLES LAMBERT,
ALEXANDER BLANE & GEORGE BLANE, Wits. thereto, & ordered to be recorded

pp.   THIS INDENTURE made the Eighth day of August in year of our Lord One thou-
207-   sand seven hundred & Seventy Between JOHN HENSON & JUDITH his Wife of
208   County of Albemarle of one part & WILLIAM MARTIN of said County of other
        part Witnesseth that JOHN HENSON & JUDITH his Wife for sum of Twenty & five
pounds currt. money of Virginia to him in hand paid by these presents doth bargain
sell & confirm unto WILLIAM MARTIN his heirs a parcel or tract of land lying & being
in County of Albemarle on North side of RIVANNA RIVER being part of a tract of land
Patented to BENJAMIN DENNY bearing date the Tenth day of March One thousand seven
hundred & Fifty six begining at a Pine in THOMAS APPLEBURYs line, thence by a strait
line of mark't trees to PHILIP THURMANs line, thence along his line to SAML. MARTINs
line, down the River thence up the River to WM. MARTINs own line, thence along his
line to THOS. APPLEBURYs line where it began Together with all woods houses orchards
& appurtenances unto said land belonging and JOHN HENSON & JUDITH his Wife will
warrant & forever defend the sd land from all persons freely & clearly kept save harmless & Indemnified to sd WM. MARTIN his heirs saving the Quit rents that shall become
due to our Sovereign Lord the King his heirs & Successors In Witness whereof said JOHN
HENSON & JUDITH his Wife hath hereunto set their hands & seals the day & year first
above written
Signed Sealed & Delivered in the presence of
        (no witnesses shown)   JOHN HENSON
    At Albemarle August Court 1770
This Indenture was ackd. by JOHN HENSON party thereto & ordered to be recorded

pp.   THIS INDENTURE made the Ninth day of August in year of our Lord Christ One
209-   thousand seven hundred & Seventy between ANDREW RAY of the Parish of
210   Fredericksville in the County of Albemarle of one part and JOHN BOYD of the
        Parish of Fredericksville and County of Albemarle of other part Witnesseth that
ANDREW RAY for sum of Forty pounds current money of Virginia to him in hand paid
by JOHN BOYD by these presents doth bargain sell & confirm unto JOHN BOYD all that
parcell of land lying & being in County of Albemarle and Fredericksville Parish containing Eighty two accress be the same more or less and bounded Begining at WADDEYs
Corner Gum, from thence on WADDEYs line to CHARLES GOODMANs line to FRANCIS
GRAHAMs line, from thence on GRAHAMs line to ROBERT MECHIEs line, from thence in
MECHIEs line to the first Station together with all houses orchards improvements whatsoever & all profits commodites and advantages to the same belonging To have & to hold
the said Plantation, land & houses and every of their appurtenances unto JOHN BOYD his
heirs free and clear of all Incumbrances and ANDREW RAY his heirs unto said JOHN
BOYD will warrant & ever defend by these presents In Witness whereof the partie to
these presents his hand & Seal have set the day & year first above written

Signed Sealed & Delivered in presents of
        (no witnesses shown)   ANDREW RAY
  August 9th 1770 Received of JOHN BOYD forty pounds current money of Virginia it
being full satisfaction for the within land as witness my hand the day of the year first
above written   ANDREW RAY
  At Albemarle August Court
This Indenture memorandum & Receipt were acknowledged by ANDREW RAY party
thereto & ordered to be recorded. MARY, his Wife, came into Court and being first
privately Examined as the Law directs, voluntarily relinquished her right of Dower in
the Estate conveyed by the said Indenture

pp.   THIS INDENTURE made this 9th day of August in year of our Lord One thousand
210-   seven hundred & seventy Between JOHN RODES JUNR. & SARAH his Wife of Albe-
211   marle County & Fredericksville Parish of one part & JOHN MOORE of the same
           County & Parish of other part Witnesseth that JOHN RODES & SARAH his Wife for
& in consideration of Forty pounds current money of Virginia to them in hand paid by
JOHN MOORE by these presents doth bargain sell & confirm unto JOHN MOORE his heirs a
certain tract of land containing by estimation two hundred acres lying & being in
Albemarle County & Fredericksville Parish in the Fork of MOREMANS RIVER as bounded
begining at a Rock on the North side of MOREMANS RIVER known by the name of HER-
CULES PILLAR thence new lines North thirty degrees East thirty eight poles to a white
Oak, then North forty degrees West eighty poles to a white Oak, thence North sixty five
degrees West eighty poles to pointers, thence South fifty three degrees West at fifty
eight poles the N. Fork of MOREMANS RIVER at One hundred and fifty poles to a Chesnut
on the Middle Fork, thence South twenty five degrees West thirty four poles to a red Oak
thence South five degrees West eighty two poles to a Chesnut, thence East seventy poles
to a Spruce Pine on the South fork, then down the same to the first Station To have & to
hold said Two hundred acres of land contained within the said bounds be the same more
or less with all priviledges advantages and Improvements to the same belonging unto
JOHN MOORE & his heirs and JOHN RODES doth hereby for himself his heirs warrant said
land unto JOHN MOORE his heirs In Witness whereof said JOHN RODES & SARAH his Wife
doth hereunto set their hands & Seals the day & year above written
Signed Sealed & Delivered in presence of
        (no witnesses shown)   JOHN RODES
                                                     SARAH RODES
  Memorandum that Quiet & peaceable possession was taken and had of the land by said
JOHN RODES & SARAH his Wife by them was given to JOHN MOORE according to the true
intent & meaning of the within Indenture   JOHN RODES
                                                     SARAH RODES

  At Albemarle August Court 1770
This Indenture & memorandum were ackd. by JOHN RODES & SARAH his Wife parties
thereto & ordered to be recorded

pp.   THIS INDENTURE made on the fourth day of August in year of our Lord One thou-
211-   sand seven hundred & Seventy Between JOSEPH GRAVES of ROWAN COUNTY in
212   the Province of NORTH CAROLINA of one part & PATRICK FISHER of Albemarle
           County in the Colony of Virginia of other part Witnesseth that said JOSEPH
GRAVES for sum of Forty pounds current money to him in hand paid by PATRICK
FISHER doth bargain & sell unto PATRICK FISHER & to his heirs a tract of land contai-

ning by estimation one hundred acres be the same more or less lying in Albemarle County on the North West side of the SOUTHWEST MOUNTAINS on the waters of the North Fork of JAMES RIVER and bounded on the North side by EDWARD BABERs & WM. BRICK-MANs land on the East side by JAMES WATSONs land & on the South & West sides by the land belonging to the heirs of JOHN HAMMOCK deced To have & to hold said tract of land with its appurtenances unto said PATRICK FISHER & his heirs and JOSEPH GRAVES & his heirs will warrant & defend In Witness whereof said JOSEPH GRAVES hath hereunto subscribed his name & affixed his Seal the day & year first above written
Signed Sealed & Delivered in presence of
      DAVID WATTS, WILLIAM WATSON,   JOSEPH his mark GRAVES
      DANL. SMITH, CLABON ROATHWELL
      ROBERT POWELL

    Memorandum on the day & year within written peaceable & Quiet possession of the within land was given by JOSEPH GRAVES to PATRICK FISHER according to the true intent and meaning of these presents
Test   DAVID WATTS, WILLIAM WATSON,   JOSEPH his mark GRAVES
      DANL. SMITH, CLABON ROATHWELL
      ROBERT POWELL
  At Albemarle August Court 1770
This Indenture & memorandum were proved by the Oath of DAVID WATTS, WM. WATSON & CLABOURN ROUTHWELL Wits. thereto & ordered to be recorded

pp.   TO ALL TO WHOM these presents shall come Greeting. Know ye that we WM. &
212-   JAMES HOPKINS of the Parish of St. Anns in the County of Albemarle for the
213   sum of Forty pounds Nine Shillings current money of Virginia to us in hand
        paid by these presents do bargain sell & make over unto JAMES MARTIN & his
heirs one certain tract of land lying & being in County aforesaid containing Two hundred & three acres which said land was part of a great tract containing originally two thousand acres known by the name DRY BRANCH belonging to the Estate of Collo. ARTHUR HOPKINS deced & left by his Will to be sold by us his heirs and we WM. & JAMES HOPKINS the said two hundred & three acres hath sold to the said JAMES MARTIN which said land is bounded Beginning at pointers of Pines in the old line, running thence N. 35 W. 23 poles to a corner Pine in the old line, thence a new line S. 60 W. 120 poles to a corner Pine, thence another new line S. 14 E. 100 poles to pointers Oak & Pine, thence another new line S. 47 E. 162 poles to a corner Pine in another old line thence along the old line to the beginning with all houses orchards fences and all Estate right of us WILLIAM & JAMES HOPKINS our heirs unto the premises To have & to hold the tract of land according to the bounds aforesaid and WILLIAM & JAMES HOPKINS & heirs will warrant & forever defend by these presents In Witness whreof we have hereunto set our hands & Seals this (blank) day of August in year of our Lord One thousand seven hundred & Seventy in the Tenth year of our Reign
Signed Sealed & delivered in presence of
      JOHN MARTIN,   WILLIAM HOPKINS
      HUDSON MARTIN, WILLIAM PAYNE   JAMES HOPKINS
  At Albemarle August Court 1770
This Indenture memorandum & Receipt were ackd. by WM. & JAMES HOPKINS parties thereto & ordered to be recorded

pp.   THIS INDENTURE made the Ninth day of August in year of our Lord One thousand
214-   seven hundred & Seventy Between JOHN GOODALL of ORANGE COUNTY and
215   ELINOR his Wife of one part and SAMUEL OVERTON of the other part Witnesseth

that for the sum of (blank) pounds Virginia Currencey to them the said CHARLES
GOODALL & ELLENOR his Wife in hand paid by SAMUEL OVERTON and for divers other
good causes and considerations them thereunto moving by these presents bargain sell
& confirm unto SAMUEL OVERTON his heirs one certain tract of land containing Six
hundred & ninety acres lying and being in County of Albemarle on ROCKEY CREEK,
Four hundred acres a part thereof was granted by Patent bearing date the fifteenth day
of October 1741 to JAMES MEREDITH & Two hundred & ninety acres on this part thereof
was granted by Patent bearing date the twelfth day of January 1746 to JOHN EUBANKS &
the property since became vested in said JOHN GOODALL the particular bounds of the six
hundred & ninety acres of land being set forth in the said Patents reference being
thereunto had Together with all houses Orchards profits commodities & appurtenances
whatsoever to said Six hundred & ninety acres of land belonging To have & to hold the
said land with their appurtenances unto SAMUEL OVERTON his heirs In Witness whereof JOHN GOODALL & ELLINOR his Wife hath hereunto set their hands & Seals the day &
year first above written
Signed Sealed & Delivered in presence of
          (no witnesses shown)   JOHN GOODALL
                                                         ELIONER GOODALL
   Received the 9th day of August 1770 from SAMUEL OVERTON Two hundred pounds Virginia Corrency being the consideration within mentioned
                                                         JOHN GOODALL

   At Albemarle August Court 1770
This Indenture memorandum & receipt were ackd. by JOHN GOODALL & ELINOR his Wife
parties thereto & ordered to be recorded

pp.   THIS INDENTURE made this ninth day of August in year of our Lord One thousand
215-   seven hundred & Seventy Between EDMUND PRICE of County of CUMBERLAND of
216   the one part and ISHAM DAVIS of Albemarle County of other part Witnesseth
         that EDMUND PRICE for consideration of Thirty pounds current money to said
EDMUND PRICE in hand paid by said ISHAM DAVIS by these presents doth bargain sell &
confirm unto ISHAM DAVIS his heirs one certain tract or parcel of land containing
ninety nine acres be the same more or less bounded Beginning at JOHN SCOTTs corner
white Oak runing thence on said SCOTTs line North two degrees West seventy eight poles
to a Pine, then the same Course continued ninety six poles to a new line to pointers,
then due East ninety poles to an Oak, then South two degrees two hundred poles to pointers in the River at the mouth of a small branch, thence up the River and meanders to
the first Station Together with all houses orchards fences profits & all other appurtenances belonging To have & to hold said tract of land together with every of their
appurtenances unto ISHAM DAVIS his heirs and EDMUND PRICE his heirs will warrant
& forever defend In Witness whereof said EDMUND PRICE hath hereunto set his hand
this ninth day of August One thousand seven hundred & Seventy
Signed Sealed & Delivered in presence of
     MARK LEAK,   EDMUND PRICE
     WILLIAM HOPKINS, JOHN NASH
   Received of ISHAM DAVIS the day & year aforesaid the sum of Thirty pounds current
money it being the consideration within mentioned
                                                         EDMUND PRICE

   At Albemarle August Court 1770
This Indenture memorandum & receipt were ackd. by EDMUND PRICE party thereto &
ordered to be recorded

pp.   THIS INDENTURE made the ninth day of August in year of our Lord One thousand
217-   seven hundred & Seventy Between WILLIAM WOOD of County of Albemarle of
218   one part and JOHN MORRISS of same County of other part Witnesseth that said
        WILLIAM WOOD for sum of Seventy five pounds of lawfull money of Virginia by
him the said JOHN MORRISS to him the said WILLIAM WOOD in hand paid by these presents doth bargain sell & confirm unto JOHN MORRISS his heirs a certain parcell of land
where of the said WILLIAM WOOD formerly lived lying & being in the RAGED MOUN-
TAIN on the waters of MEACHUMS RIVER in the aforesaid County & containing by Estimation One hundred acres be the same more or less and bounded Begining at a Corner
Elm of JOHN WOOD on RUBIN TERRELLs line on a branch, thence up the branch to a
Locus Stake, thence up the Ridge on a new line of JOHN WOOD to WILLIAM SMITH,
thence on his line to RICHARD DOLLINS line thence on RICHARD DOLLINS line to RUBIN
TERRELLs line, thence down RUBIN TERRELLs line to the place begun at and all rents
issues & profits thereof with the appurtenances To have & to hold said Plantation &
tract of land with the appurtenances unto JOHN MORRISS his heirs and WILLIAM WOOD
his heirs will warrant & forever defend by these presents against the claims of every
person free and discharged of all Incumbrances In Witness whereof the party aforesaid to these presents hath Interchangably set his hand & affixed his Seal the day &
year above written
Signed Sealed & Delivered in presence of
        DANL. SMITH,
        JOHN WHITE   WILLIAM WOOD
  Received on the day of the date of the within Indenture of the within named JOHN
MORRIS the sum of Seventy five pounds current money being the consideration money
within mentioned   Reced by me
Test DANL. SMITH,   WILLIAM WOOD
        JOHN WHITE
  At Albemarle August Court 1770
This Indenture memorandum & receipt were ackd. by WILLIAM WOOD party thereto &
ordered to be recorded

pp.   THIS INDENTURE made on the Seventeenth day of April in year of our Lord One
218-   thousand seven hundred & Seventy Between WILLIAM WOODS of the County of
219   Albemarle of one part and RICHARD WOODS of same County of other part Witnes-
        seth that WILLIAM WOODS for sum of Two hundred & forty pounds current
money to him in hand paid by RICHARD WOODS doth bargain & sell to said RICHARD
WOODS & his heirs one tract of land containing four hundred acres lying in the aforesaid County on both sides of IVY CREEK a branch of the RIVANNA RIVER bounded Beginning at a white Oak a corner to Capt. CHARLES HUDSON and running thence new
lines South seventy three degrees West One hundred & sixty eight poles to a red Oak,
North thirty seven degrees West four hundred & twelve poles crossing IVY CREEK to a
Hickory, North seventy three degrees East one hundred & sixty eight poles to pointers
in Capt. CHARLES HUDSONs line, thence on his line South thirty seven degrees East four
hundred & twelve poles crossing IVY CREEK to the beginning Together with all appurtenances thereto belonging To have & to hold said tract of land with its appurtenances
to said RICHARD WOODS & his heirs and WILLIAM WOODS will forever warrant & defend
In Witness whereof said WM. WOODS hath hereto subscribed his name & affixed his Seal
the day & year above written
Signed Sealed & Delivered in presence of
        JOHN WOODS,   WILLIAM WOODS
        MICAJAH CHILES, ARCHIBALD WOODS

Memorandum on the day & year within written peaceable & Quiet possession of the
land was given by WILLIAM WOODS to RICHARD WOODS according to the true intent &
meaning of these presents Witness my hand
     JOHN WOODS,   WILLIAM WOODS
     MICAJAH CHILES, ARCHIBALD WOODS
  At Albemarle Augsut Court 1770
This Indenture & memorandum were ackd. by WM. WOODS party thereto & ordered to be
recorded. SUSANNAH, his Wife, came into Court & being first privately Examined as the
Law directs voluntarily relinquished her right of Dower in the Estate conveyed by this
Indenture

pp.   Albemarle County Sc
219- GEORGE ye 3d by the Grace of God of Great Britain France & Ireland King defen-
220   der of the faith &c. To JOHN DIX & ROBERT PAYNE three of his Majesties Justices
      of the Peace for the County of PITTSYLVANIA or any two of them in pursuance
of an Act of Assembly of the Colony of Virginia intitled An act for settling the title &
bound of land &c. We commission you or any two of you to come before you JANE
HARRISON, the Wife of ANDREW HARRISON, but if she is unable to attend you that then
do you go to her & privately examine her & apart from her said Husband touching her
consent to her relinquishment of her right of Dower to a certain piece of land in Ablemarle County sold by her said Husband to SAMUEL MARTIN containing One hundred &
Eighty acres lying on the North Fork of JAMES RIVER and whether she be willing the
Deed made by ANDREW HARRISON to the said SAMUEL MARTIN Esqr. shall be recorded in
our Court of Albemarle for the said land shall be recorded bearing date the (blank) day
of (blank) 1769 and after her examination you are on the back hereof to the Indenture
aforesaid such her privy Examination or her refusal fail not & return the Commission
to our said Court at Ablemarle Witness   T. WOODSON Dy. Clk.
  PITSILVANIA to wit
In pursuance of the within Commission to us directed, we the Subscribers have
privately examained JANE HARRISON, the Wife of ANDREW HARRISON, touching her relinquishment of her right of Dower to a certain tract of land & she freely & willingly
relinquishes her right of Dower in the said lands and that the Deed made by her Husband ANDREW HARRISON to SAMUEL MARTIN Esqr. be recorded. Certified under our
hands this 1st day of Octr. 1770   JOHN DIX
                     ROBT. PAYNE

  At Albemarle October Court 1770
This Commission was returned to Corut & ordered to be recorded

pp.   THIS INDENTURE made this fifteenth day of September in year of our Lord Christ
220- one thousand seven hundred & Seventy Between JAMES DAVENPORT of County of
221   HANOVER & his Wife, FRANCES, of one part and RICHARD GILLIAM of Parish of
      St. Anns & County of Albemarle of other part Witnesseth that JAMES DAVENPORT
& FRANCES his Wife for sum of Fifty five pounds to them in hand paid by these presents
doth bargain sell & confirm unto RICHARD GILLIAM his heirs one certain tract or parcel of land containing Three hundred & twelve acres more or less lying & being in
County of Albemarle on the East side of the RAGGED MOUNTAIN adjoining the lands of
JAMES JONES formerly the land of JOSEPH ANTHONY & STEPHEN HUGHES formerly the
land of JOHN GRILLS and lies on the branches of BISKET RUN a branch of MOORES CREEK
it being the same land that was granted by Letters Patent to JAMES DAVIS bearing date
the first day of October One thousand seven hundred & Forty seven & by said DAVIS

conveyed to PATRICK BISHOP & by said BISHOP convey'd to JAMES DAVENPORT by Deed
bearing date the nineteenth day of August in year of our Lord Christ One thousand
seven hundred & Fifty four and JAMES DAVENPORT & FRANCES his Wife hath forever
remised & quit claim unto RICHARD GILLIAM his heirs all the Estate right tile or
demand whatsoever of him said JAMES DAVENPORT & FRANCES his Wife to the above
mentioned tract of land containing by estimation Three hundred & twelve acres with
the appurtenances To have & to hold the said Three hundred & twelve acres of land
with the appurtenances unto RICHARD GILLIAM his heirs In Witness whereof said
JAMES DAVENPORT & FRANCES his Wife hath set their hands & affixed their Seals the
day & year above written
Signed Sealed & Delivered in presence of
     NICHS. HAMNER,   JAMES DAVENPORT
     CHARLES DAVENPORT, RICHARD DAVENPORT   FRANCES DAVENPORT
  Received of RICHARD GILLIAM Fifty five pounds Currt. money being the consideration
for the land within sold Witness my hand & Seal
     NICHS. HAMNER,   JAMES DAVENPORT
     CHARLES DAVENPORT
  At Albemarle October Court 1770
This Indenture & receipt were acknowledged by JAMES DAVENPORT & FRANCES his Wife
parties thereto & ordered to be recorded

pp.   THIS INDENTURE made this Eight day of Sept. One thousand seven hundred &
222-   Seventy Between NATHAN BOND of AMHERST COUNTY of one part & GEORGE
223   PERRY JUNR. of Albemarle County of other part Witnesseth that NATHAN BOND
       for sum of Seventy five pounds current money to him in hand paid by these
presents doth bargain sell & confirm unto GEORGE PERRY JUNR. & his heirs one track
or parcell of land in ye County of Albemarle on the north side of HARDWARE RIVER in
the Branches of SHEPHERD CREEK containing One hundred & Eighty six acres & bounded
begining at a Pine in JOHN DAMERONs & runing with same South eighty nine degrees
West one hundred & Seventy two poles to pointers, then on RICHARD DAMERONs line
South ten degrees West One hundred & fifty poles to a red Oak, then on CHARLES BONDs
line South eighty four & a half degrees East one hundred & ninety six poles crossing
two branches to SHEPHERDS CREEK to a pine & North one hundred & seventy poles to ye
first station the said One hundred & eighty six acres of land granted to GEORGE PERRY
JUNR. to have & to hold together with all houses orchards & all other appurtenances
thereunto belonging and NATHAN BOND & his heirs will warrant & forever defend by
these presents In Witness whereof ye said NATHAN BOND hath hereunto set his hand &
Seal the day & year above written
Sign'd Seal'd & Deliver'd in presence of
     FRANCIS SATTERWHITE,   NATHAN BOND
     FRANKLYN BOWLING, THOS. RIGHLEY
  Received of the within named GEORGE PERRY JUNR. the full & just sum of Seventy five
pounds currt. money being the consideration money within mentioned
Test FRANCIS SATTERWHITE,   NATHAN BOND
     FRANKLYN BOWLING, THOS. RIGHLEY
  At Albemarle October Court 1770
This Indenture memorandum & receipt were ackd. by NATHAN BOND party thereto &
ordered to be recorded. ELIZABETH, the Wife of said NATHAN, personally appeared in
Court & being first privately Examined as the Law directs, voluntarily relinquished her
right of Dower in the Lands conveyed by the said Indenture

pp.   THIS INDENTURE made this Eleventh day of September in year of our Lord God
223-   One thousand seven hundred & Seventy Between THOMAS McCULLOCK of ye
225   Parish of St. Ann, County of Albemarle, Colony & Dominion of Virginia & ISABLE
         his Wife of one part & MOSES EDGAR of AUGUSTA COUNTY & Colony & Dominion
aforesaid, Weaver, of other part Witnesseth that said THOS. McCULLOCK & ISABLE his
Wife for consideration of the Quantity of Fourty one acres lying given in exchange and
alreddy acknowledged to them by MOSES EDGAR by these presents doth bargain & sell
exchange & confirm unto said MOSES EDGAR his heirs a certain tract or parcel of land
lying & being in Albemarle County on both sides of the main Branch or head Branch of
MECHUMS RIVER Forty five acres & is bounded Begining at a red Oak in BARTHOLOMEW
RAMSAY's line and runing with it North forty nine degrees East ninety eight poles to a
Hickory pointers in ADAM DEANs line, thence with ADAM DEANs line runing South
forty eight degrees East to cross the main branch aforesaid fifty five poles to a black
Oak in WILLIAM WINSTONEs line thence with WINSTONEs South forty five degrees West
one hundred & sixty two poles to Gum pointers in ROBERT TERRELLs line, thence with
ROBERT TERRELLs down the branch with its several courses to where it empties into a
larger branch of MECHAMS RIVER at a large Pine, thence North seventy three degrees
West fifty one poles to a Pine in JOHN RODES line, thence North eighteen degrees West
forty three poles to a Pine in BARTHOLOMEW RAMSAYs line, thence with RAMSAYs line
South sixty nine degrees East fifty poles to the first station being part of sixty nine
acres Pattented to THOMAS McCULLOCK bearing date at WILLIAMSBURG the twenty
seventh day of August One thousand seven hundred & Seventy may more fully appear
the said tract of land exchanged by said THOMAS McCULLOCK containing forty five
acres be the same more or less Together with all houses barns stables orchards profits &
appurtenances whatsoever belonging In Witness whereof said THOS. McCULLOCK &
ISABLE his Wife hath to these presents set their hands & Seals the day & year above
written
Signed Sealed & Delivered in the presents of
         (no witnesses shown)   THOS. McCULLOCK
                                                     ISABLE McCULLOCK
   Received September ye Eleventh day One thousand seven hundred & Seventy full
satisfaction of EDGAR for the within mentioned land   THOS. McCULLOCK
   At Albemarle October Court 1770
This Indenture memorandum & receipt were acknd. by THOS. McCULLOCK & ISABLE his
Wife parties thereto & ordered to be recorded

pp.   THIS INDENTURE made the Eleventh day of October in year of our Lord One thou-
225-   sand seven hundred & Seventy Between THOMAS McCULLOCK & ISABLE his Wife
226   of ye Parish of St. Anns in the County of Albemarle of one part & ROBERT TER-
         RELL of ye Parish of St. Thomas's in County of ORANGE of ye other part Witnes-
seth that said THOMAS McCULLOCK & ISABLE his Wife for ye sum of Seven pounds currt.
money of Virginia to them in hand paid by ye sd ROBT. TERRELL by these presents doth
bargain sell & confirm to ye sd ROBERT TERRELL his heirs one certain tract or parcel of
land lying in Albemarle County & bounded Begining at a Pine, Corner to JNO. ROADES,
thence South eighteen degrees East One hundred & fourty poles, thence to a corner of
ye sd TERRELLs in ye MORE BRANCH then down ye MORE BRANCH ye several courses to
where it empties into a larger branch of MEACHUMS RIVER at a large Pine, thence
North seventy three degrees West fifty one poles to the begining, the sd Tract of land
doth contain twenty acres more or less together with all houses gardens profits & appurtenances to the tract of land To have & to hold ye tract of land with appurtenances

unto ye sd ROBERT TERRELL his heirs and THOMAS McCULLOCK his heirs will warrant & forever defend by these presents In Witness whereof ye sd THOMAS McCULLOCK & ISABLE his Wife have hereunto set their hands & affixed their Seals the day & year above written

Signed Sealed & Delivered in presence of

REUBEN TERRELL,   THOS. McCULLOCK
GEORGE BOURN, MARK CARRELL   ISABLE McCULLOCK

Received of ROBERT TERRELL the consideration money within mentioned this Eleventh day of October 1770   THOS. McCULLOCK

At Albemarle October Court 1770

This Indenture & receipt were ackd. by THOS. McCULLOCK & ISABLE his Wife parties thereto & ordered to be recorded

pp. 227-228   THIS INDENTURE made this twelvth day of Septem. in year of our Lord One thousand seven hundred & Seventy Between RICHARD ESTES of Albemarle County &c. of one part and BARTLETT BENNETT &c. of other part Witnesseth that RICHARD ESTES for sum of Fifty five pounds current money to him in hand paid by BARTLETT BENNETT by these presents doth confirm unto said BARTLETT & his heirs one certain tract or parcel of land containing Two hundred acres lying & being in Albemarle and bounded beginning at JOHN WOODS corner pointers Cedar and Rock & STOCKTONS BRANCH, runing thence on his line North fifty five degrees East thirty two poles to a white Oak saplin, thence on new lines North thirty three degrees West sixty six poles to a white Oak, North seventy degrees West eighty three poles to a red Oak & South forty degrees West one hundred & seventy three poles to WILLIAM WHITESIDES Corner poynters thence on his line South fourteen degrees East one hundred & twelve poles crossing STOCKTONS BRANCH to his corner two white Oaks, thence on new lines South fourteen degrees East sixty poles to a Pine saplin and North eighty degrees East ninety nine poles to a white Oak in WOODS line, then on the same fourteen degrees East one hundred & forty eight poles to the first station, Together with all houses orchards & water courses thereunto belonging unto sd BARTLETT BENNETT his heirs In Witness whereof the sd RICHARD ESTES hath hereunto set his hand & Seal the day & year first above written

Signed Sealed & Delivered in presence of
(no witnesses shown)   RICHARD ESTES

At Albemarle November Court 1770

This Indenture was ackd. by RICHARD ESTES party thereto & ordered to be recorded

p. 228   THIS INDENTURE made on the Eighth day of November in year of our Lord One thousand seven hundred & Seventy between CHRISTOPHER JOHNSON & BETTY his Wife of BEDFORD COUNTY of one part & THOMAS WALKER of Albemarle of other part Witnesseth that CHRISTOPHER JOHNSON for sum of One hundred pounds Currt. money to him in hand paid by said THOS. WALKER doth bargain & sell unto THOMAS WALKER & his heirs a tract of land containing by estimation Five hundred acres be the same more or less lying in Albemarle County on both side of TURKEY RUN & joining the lands of said THOMAS WALKER, the lands of THOMAS WALKER Esqr. & also the lands belonging to the Estate of ROBT. COBBS deceased Toegther with the appurtenances thereto belonging To have & to hold the said tract of land with its appurtenances unto said THOMAS WALKER & his heirs and CHRISTOPHER JOHNSON & BETTY his Wife will forever warrant & defend In Witness whereof said CHRISTOPHER JOHNSON & BETTY his Wife have hereto subscribed their names & affixed their Seals the day & year first above written

Signed Sealed & Delivered in the presence of
    DAVID RODES,   CHRISTR. JOHNSON
    NICHOLAS LEWIS, EDMUND COBBS
  At Albemarle November Court 1770
This Indenture was ackd. by CHRISTOPHER JOHNSON party thereto & ordered to be
recorded

p.   THIS INDENTURE made the Eight day of November in year of our Lord One thou-
229   sand seven hundred & Seventy in the Tenth year of the Reign of our Sovereign
          Lord George the third Between JAMES MARTIN of County of Albemarle of one
part & FISHER RICE BENNETT of same County of other part Witnesseth that for sum of
Forty pounds current money of Virginia by said FISHER RICE BENNETT in hand paid
unto JAMES MARTIN said JAMES MARTIN by these presents doth bargain sell & confirm
unto FISHER RICE BENNETT one certain tract or parcel of land lying & being in County
of Albemarle containing Two hundred & three acres, part of a larger tract known by
the name of DRY BRANCH TRACT belonging to the Estate of ARTHUR HOPKINS deced &
left by his Will to be sold by his Trustees, WM. & JAMES HOPKINS, which said parcell of
land was by sd Trustees convey'd to sd JAMES MARTIN begining at pointers of Pine and
thence runing N. 35 West 232 poles to a Corner Pine in the Old Line, thence into the
Woods & new line South 60 W. 120 poles to a Corner Pine, thence another new line S 14
E. 100 poles to pointers of Oak, thence another new line S. 47 E. 162 poles to pointers in
the Old Line, thence along the Old Line No. (this line is scratched out) E.   to the begining
with all houses gardens & appurtenances thereon belonging To have & to hold the
hereby bargained & sold premises with every of their appurtenances unto FISHER RICE
BENNETT his heirs and JAMES MARTIN his heirs will warrant & forever defend by these
presents In Witness whereof said JAMES MARTIN hath hereunto set his hand & affixed
his Seal the day & year above written
Seald & Deliverd. in presence of
    WHILFD. WILSON,   JAMES MARTIN
    JOSEPH LEA
  At Albemarle November Court 1770
This Indenture was ackd. by JAMES MARTIN party thereto & ordered to be recorded

p.   KNOW ALL MEN by these presents that I JOHN FORD of County of Albemarle for
230   sum of Twenty pounds current money of Virginia to me in hand paid by JOHN
          FORD JUNR. hath bargained & sold for the consideration aforesaid unto JOHN
FORD JUNR. for himself & his heirs one Negro boy named Jack about six years forever to
him said JOHN FORD JUNR and I do hereby acknowledge the right and title to the said
Negro boy Jack to be free from all claims of me my Executors or any other persons
whatsoever In Witness whereof I have hereunto set my hand and Seal this Seventh day
of November 1770
Test ANDREW WALLACE,   JOHN FORD
    JAMES SHAW
  Received November 7th 1770 of JOHN FORD JUNR. twenty pounds current money of
Virginia it being the consideration within mentioned I say reced p me
Test ANDREW WALLACE,   JOHN FORD
    JAMES SHAW
  At Albemarle November Court 1770
This Indenture & Receipt were ackd. by JOHN FORD party thereto & ordered to be re-
corded

pp.   THIS INDENTURE made this fifth day of September in year of our Lord One thou-
230- sand seven hundred & Seventy Between JOHN GOODALL & ELIONER his Wife,
232   TRISTAN SNOW & ELIZABETH his Wife, FRANCES JOHNSON & MARY JOHNSON co-
heirs of JOHN JOHNSON deced of County of ORANGE & Parish of St. Thomas of one
part & EPHRAIM SIMONDS of the County & Parish aforesaid of other part Witnesseth
that JOHN GOODALL & ELIONER his Wife, TRISTAN SNOW & ELIZABETH his Wife, FRANCES
JOHNSON & MARY JOHNSON for sum of Forty pounds Currt. money of Virginia to them in
hand paid by EPHRAIM SIMONDS by these presents do bargain sell and confirm unto
said EPHRAIM SIMONDS his heirs one certain tract or parcel of land containing by estimation Four hundred acres lying & being in Albemarle County on the Branches of
BEVERDAM SWAMP and bounded beginning at MILLS's Corner Poplar runing thence on
new lines West one hundred & twenty poles to two Hiccory saplins, North twenty five
degrees East two hundred & thirty poles crossing two branches to a Pine & Gum saplin
on the side of a Mountain, thence East two hundred & three poles to a red Oak in Mr. .
WEBBs line, thence on the same South two hundred poles to WEBBS & MILLS corner two
red Oaks, thence on MILLS line South sixty four degrees West one hundred & thirty
nine poles to the first station, Together with all houses gardens watercourses thereunto
belonging To have & to hold the said land with their appurtenances unto said EPHRAIM
SIMONDS his heirs and (the Grantors above named) will warrant & forever defend by these
presents In Witness whereof they the said JOHN GOODALL & ELIONER his Wife, TRISTAN
SNOW & ELIZABETH his Wife, FRANCES JOHNSON & MARY JOHNSON hath hereunto set
their hands & Seals the day & year above written
Signed Sealed & Delivered in presence of

W. BELL,	JOHN GOODALL	ELIONER GOODALL
ELIZABETH BELL	TRISTAN SNOW	ELIZABETH SNOW
ANN RHODES	FRANCES JOHNSON	MARY JOHNSON

    Received of Mr. EPHRAIM SIMANDS Forty pounds currant money of Virginia in full
satisfaction for the consideration money in the within written Deed on the day & year
within written
In presence of

	JOHN GOODALL	TRISTAN SNOW
(no witnesses shown)	FRANCES JOHNSON	MARY JOHNSON

  At Albemarle November Court 1770
This Indenture & receipt were ackd. by JOHN GOODALL & ELIONER his Wife, TRISTAN
SNOW & ELIZABETH his Wife, FRANCES JOHNSON & MARY JOHNSON parties thereto &
ordered to be recorded

p.   THIS INDENTURE made this Eighth day of November in year of our Lord One
233   thousand seven hundred & Seventy Between JOHN LEWIS of Parish of St. Anns &
      County of Albemarle of one part & JOHN LEWIS JUNR. of the same County &
Parish of other part Witnesseth that JOHN LEWIS SENR. for and in consideration of the
love & respect as well as the sum of Five Shillings Sterl. to him in hand paid by JOHN
LEWIS JUNR. by these presents doth give sell & confirm unto said JOHN LEWIS JUNR. his
heirs one certain tract or parcel of land containing Four hundred & Thirty seven acres
lying & being in County of Albemarle and bounded Beginning at THOMAS GOLSBY corner pointers & running thence on new lines North forty degrees East ninety six poles
to a Pine & North ten degrees West one hundred & twelve poles to pointers on the
REVEREND WILLIAM STITHs line, thence on his line Eighty five degrees West one hundred & forty five poles to a Pine, North twenty five degrees West sixty four poles to
pointers, North ten degrees West twenty four poles to a Pine, North forty degrees West
forty two poles to a Pine, South eighty six degrees West two hundred poles to pointers on
the side of a knole, South thirty three degrees East three hundred & twenty two poles to

pointers in THOMAS GOLSBYs line, thence on the same North eighty eight degrees East One hundred & eighty four poles to the Begining & now in possession of said JOHN LEWIS JUNR. with all houses & advantages whatsoever to the same land & premises belonging To have & to hold sd land & premises with the appurtenances unto JOHN LEWIS JUNR. his heirs and JOHN LEWIS SENR. & his heirs & all other persons will warrant & forever defend by these presents In Witness whereof the said JOHN LEWIS SENR. hath set his hand & Seal

                                                   JOHN LEWIS

  At Albemarle November Court 1770
This Indenture was ackd. by JOHN LEWIS party thereto & ordered to be recorded

pp.   THIS INDENTURE made this (blank) day of (blank) in year of our Lord One thou-
234-   sand seven hundred & Seventy Between JOHN DICKASON & MARY his Wife of
235   Albemarle County of one part and JOHN RIPPITO of County aforesaid of other
         part Witnesseth that JOHN DICKASON & MARY his Wife for sum of Seventeen
pounds current money of Virginia to him in hand paid by said JOHN RIPPITO by these
presents do bargain sell & confirm unto JOHN RIPPITO his heirs one certain tract or
parcel of land containing by supposition Five hundred acres lying & being in Albemarle County on the South side of the PAYNE MOUNTAIN and bounded Begining at a
Pine Corner in JACOB WATTS cleared ground & runing thence South sixty nine degrees
East one hundred & fifty eight poles to a Pine & some Oak saplins, thence South thirty
one degrees West two hundred & twenty & a half poles to several Pine pointers, thence
North fifty degrees West one hundred & eighty poles to a Pine, thence North fifty four
degrees East sixty four poles to a Pine, thence North thirty degrees East one hundred &
fourteen poles to several saplins which now is cut down and a Pine marked for the Beginning which is the first station in this Deed, together with all houses orchards and
appurtenances whatsoever to the same belonging and JOHN DICKASON & MARY his Wife
for themselves & their heirs the said lands & premises with the appurtenances to said
JOHN RIPPITO his heirs will warrant & forever defend by these presents In Witness
whereof JOHN DICKASON & MARY his Wife hath hereunto set their hands & Seals the
day & year above written
Signed Sealed & Delivered in the presence of
     JAMES MARKS,   JOHN DICKASON
     ROBERT MECHIE, JEREMIAH YANCEY   MARY her mark ⅄ DICKASON
 Received of Mr. JOHN RIPPITO Seventeen pounds Currt. money being in full satisfaction of the consideration mentioned in the within written Deed on the day & year
within written   p me   JOHN DICKASON
                                          MARY her mark ⅄ DICKASON

  At Albemarle November Court 1770
This Indenture & receipt were ackd. by JOHN DICKASON & MARY his Wife parties thereto
& ordered to be recorded

pp.   THIS INDENTURE made this Eighth day of Octr. in year of our Lord One thousand
236-   seven hundred & Seventy & in the ninth year of our Sovereign Lord George the
237   third by the Grace of God of Great Britain King defender of the faith &c. Between
         BOND BURNETT & ISBELL his Wife of Fredericksville Parish & County of Albe-
marle of one part & NATHANIEL HARLOW of the Parish & County aforesaid of other part
Witnesseth that said BOND BURNETT & ISBELL his Wife for sum of Twelve pounds Ten
Shillings current money of Virginia to them in hand paid by these presents do bargain
sell & confirm unto NATHANIEL HARLOW his heirs one certain tract or parcell of land
lying & being in the Parish & County aforesaid on the South side of the South Branch of

the North Fork of JAMES RIVER containing Fifty acres be the same more or less bounded Beginning at a white Oak on the River bank joining of WM. VICE from thence runing a West Course along VICEs line to a Corner white Oak, from thence runing a North Course to the above NATHANIEL HARLOWs corner red Oak & Pine saplins from thence down sd HARLOWs line to a white Oak sapling in the Fork of a branch, thence down the sd Branch to the River from thence down the River to the begining with all houses orchards & appurtenances to the sd land belonging and BOND BURNETT & ISBEL his Wife their heirs will warrant & forever defend by these presents In Witness whereof said BOND BURNETT & ISBEL his Wife have hereunto set their hands & Seals this day & year first above written

Signed Sealed & Delivered in presence of   BOND his mark   BURNETT
          (no witnesses shown)   ISABEL her mark   BURNETT

     At Albemarle November Court 1770
This Indenture was ackd. by BOND BURNETT & ISABEL his Wife parties thereto & ordered to be recorded

pp.   THIS INDENTURE made this Eighth day of Nov. in year of our Lord One thousand
237-   seven hundred & Seventy & in the Tenth year of the Reign of our Sovereign
239   Lord George the Third by the Grace of God of Great Britain King Defender of the
        faith &c., Between ROWLAND HORSLEY of Parish of Fredericksville & County of
Albemarle of one part & NATHANIEL HARLOW of County aforesaid of other part Witnesseth that RICHARD HORSLEY in consideration of the sum of Eight pounds current money of Virginia to him paid by these presents do bargain sell & confirm unto NATHANIEL HARLOW his heirs one certain tract or parcel of land lying & being in the Parish aforesaid containing forty acres be the same more or less bounded Begining at a Dogwood & white Oak saplings on the River bank at the mouth of a Gut below the mouth of IVY CREEK thence runing a West course to a Poplar on a branch cornering on the said Poplar thence down the said Branch to IVY CREEK crossing said Creek thence up said Creek to a white Oak joining NATHANIEL HARLOW entry thence runing an East course down the said HARLOWs line to WILLIAM VICE corner Pine thence along VICE line crossing the Creek to the River thence down the River to the first station with all improvements & appurtenances to the same belonging free & clear from all Incumbrances the Quitrents henceforth coming due to our Sovereign Lord the King his heirs & Successors only excepted and ROWLAND HORSLEY for himself his heirs will warrant & forever defend by these presents In Witness whereof sd ROWLAND HORSLEY have hereunto set his hand & Seal the day & year first above written

Signed Sealed & Delivered in presents of
          (no witnesses shown)   ROWLAND HORSLEY

 Received the (blank) day of October One thousand seven hundred & Seventy of NATHANIEL HARLOW Eight pounds current money of Virginia being the consideration money for the within granted land Witness my hand this day & year above written
                                                       ROWLAND HORSLEY

     At Albemarle November Court 1770
This Indenture memorandum & receipt were ackd. by ROWLAND HORSLEY party thereto & ordered to be recorded

pp.   THIS INDENTURE made this seventh day of April One thousand seven hundred &
239-   Seventy Between JOHN SINTER of County of Albemarle & Parish of Fredericks-
240   ville of one part & PETER CLARKSON of aforesaid County & Parish of other part
        Witnessesth that for sum of Fifty pounds current money of Virginia by said

PETER CLARKSON paid to said JOHN SINTER do release & confirm unto PETER CLARKSON his heirs one tract or parcel of land containing two hundred & fifty acres more or less lying and being in aforesaid County & bounded Begining at a corner white Oak on the North side of a Branch crossing the same about one pole from the corner and running thence up the Branch on new lines South thirty nine degrees West fifty eight poles to pointers, South thirty degrees West forty eight pooles to a white Oak, South eighteen degrees West eighty eight poles to a red Oak South forty four degrees West forty six poles to a Pine, North seventy one degrees West one hundred & two poles to a Pine, North thirty four poles to pointers in JOHN WILLIAMSONs line & with his line North thirty seven Degrees East sixty tw poles to pointers and North fifteen degrees West one hundred & thirty one poles to pointers, new lines North seventy six degrees East forty eight poles to pointers, South twenty degrees twenty poles to the beginning To have & to hold the said parcel of land together with all houses orchards & all appurtenances whatsoever to said premises belonging In Witness my hand the day & year above written

Test THOMAS CARR,   JOHN his mark SINTER
    WILLIAM CHISHOLM,
    JOHN his mark RANDOLPH
  At Albemarle November Court 1770
This Indenture was proved by the Oath of THOMAS CARR, WM. CHISHOLM & JOHN RAN-DOLPH wits. thereto & ordered to be recorded

pp.
240
242

THIS INDENTURE made this Eight day of October in year of our Lord One thousand seven hundred & Seventy Between WILLIAM SEWELL of Albemarle County of part and DAVID NOWLIN of same County of other part Witnesseth that WILLIAM SEWELL for consideration of Thirty pounds Currt. money by him the said DAVID NOWLIN to him said WILLIAM SEWELL in hand paid by these presents doth bargain sell & confirm unto DAVID NOWLIN his heirs one certain tract of land lying & being in County of Albemarle on the Brances of HARDWARE RIVER and bounded Beginning at JOSEPH ANTHONY corner white Oak and run.g thence South forty degrees West two hundred poles to a red Oak saplin, North seventy degrees West one hundred & Sixty poles to pointers by a Branch, North forty degrees East wo hundred poles to pointers, South seventy degrees East fourteen poles to a Pine, thence on JOSEPH ANTHONYs line South seventy degrees East one hundred & fifty two poles to the Beginning containing by estimation One hundred & ninety two acres be the same more or less and the rents issues profits thereof with the appurtenances To have & to hold said Plantation & tract of land with the appurtenances unto DAVID NOWLIN his heirs discharged from all Incumbrances In Witness whereof I have hereunto set my hand & Seal ye day & year above written
Signed Sealed & Delivered in presents of
    WILLIAM his mark MORRAN,   WILLIAM SEWELL
    SOLOMON his mark NELSON, JOHN SEWELL
  At Albemarle November Court 1770
This Indenture memorandum & Receipt were ackd. by WM. SEWELL party thereto & ordered to be recorded

pp.
243-
244

THIS INDENTURE made this Sixteenth day of March Anno Dom. One thousand seven hundred & Sixty four Between NICHOLAS RICE of LOUISA COUNTY of one part & ALEXANDER BAINE, Merchant in HENERICO, of other part Witnesseth that NICHOLAS RICE for divers good causes & consideration him thereunto moving but more especially for the better securing paiment of the sum of Twenty seven pounds

Thirteen Shillings & Eleven pence Currency due by Bond bearing Interest from the 31. day of Jany. 1763 to said ALEXANDER BAINE & further for sum of Five Shillings like money to me in hand paid by ALEXANDER BAINE by these presents do bargain sell & confirm unto ALEXANDER BAINE his heirs one certain tract or parcel of land lying & being in County of Albemarle being my full share proportion & dividend of the land left to me by the Last Will & Testament of NICHOLAS MILLS SENR. deceased as may more fully appear reference thereto being had on the records of HANOVER COUNTY Court with all proffits hereditaments & emoluments whatsoever thereto belonging To have & to hold said Tract of land with the appurtenances unto ALEXANDER BAINE his Exrs. & assigns upon condition that if NICHOLAS RICE his heirs shall pay or cause to be paid unto ALEXANDER BAINE his heirs the said sum of Twenty seven pounds thirteen Shillings & Eleven pence & Interest to be computed from the 31st day of January 1763 upon or before the first day of May next ensuing the date hereof that then these presents & everything therein contained shall cease determine & be void In Witness whereof I have hereunto set my hand & afixed my Seal the day & year above written
Signed Sealed & Delivered in presence of
THOMAS PERKINS, NICHOLAS RICE
JOHN BULLOK, DAVID ROSS
Acknowledged the Eleventh day of Sept. 1770 before
MERTH. PRICE, JOHN WALKER
WM. GARROTT DABNEY CARR
WM. PETTITT
At Albemarle November Court 1770
This Indenture was proved by the Oaths of MEREDITH PRICE, JOHN WALKER & DABNEY CARR Wits. thereto & ordered to be recorded

p. 244 THIS INDENTURE made this tenth day of Decr. One thousand seven hundred & Seventy Between JACOB SNEED & MARY his Wife of one part & ARTHUR GRAHAM of other part Witnesseth that said JACOB SNEED & MARY his wife for sum of Ten pounds Currt. money by these presents doth bargain sell & confirm unto ARTHUR GRAHAM & his heirs a parcel of land containing Fifty acres lying & being in Albemarle County on the Branches of IVY CREEK and bounded Beginning at Mr. KEYs pointers on LEWIS's line & running thence South twenty eight degrees East ninety four poles on a branch to pointers, thence North sixty nine degrees West twenty four poles to HOLLANDs corner Pine, thence South twenty two degrees West eighty two poles to pointers thence North twenty eight degrees West one hundred & thirty poles to pointers in LEWIS's line, thence on his line to the first station, To have & to hold unto said GRAHAM & his heirs In Witness whereof the parties to these presents do set their hands & Seals the day above written

JACOB his mark F SNEED
MARY her mark X SNEED

At Albemarle Decr. Court 1770
This Indenture was ackd. by JACOB SNEED & MARY his Wife parties thereto & ordered to be recorded

pp. 245-246 THIS INDENTURE maid this Ninth day of July in year of our Lord MDCCLXX Between JOHN PARTREE BURK of County of BEDFORD, JOHN BURK, Son & heir of CHARLES BURK deced, & SAMUEL BURK of County of BUCKINGHAM of one part and OBEDIAH SMITH of County of CHESTERFIELD of other part Witnesseth that JOHN PARTREE BURK, JOHN BURK & SAMUEL BURK for sum of One hundred pounds Currt money of Virginia to them paid by OBEDIAH SMITH by these presents doth bargain &

sell unto OBEDIAH SMITH & his heirs one certain track or parcel of land containing Six hundred acres lying & being in County of Albemarle (formerly GOOCHLAND) on the North side & joining the RIVANNA RIVER Two hundred acres part of which was granted to SAML.BURK by Patent bearing date the twenty Eight day of September MDCCXXXII & four hundred acres, the other part thereof, was also granted to said SAMUEL BURK by Patent bearing date the fifth day of June MDCCXLIV & which was by the Last Will & Testament of said SAMUEL BURK which was proved & recorded in County Court of Albemarle devised to his Wife MARY BURK during her life & after her decease to be sold & the money arising therefrom to be applyed in the following manner, that is to say, one Shilling Sterling to his Daughter, ELIZABETH CABELL, One Shilling Sterling to his Son, SAMUEL BURK & one Shilling Sterling to his Son, RICHARD BURK, & the residue to be equally devided between his Sons, JOHN PARTREE BURK, CHARLES BURK and his Daughter MARY SMITH, Wife to the said OBEDIAH SMITH & his Grandson, SAMUEL BURK reference unto the Will being had will more fully appear and now in possession of said OBEDIAH SMITH with all houses & advantages to said land belonging To have & to hold the premises with the appurtenances unto OBEDIAH SMITH his heirs and JOHN PARTREE BURK, JOHN BURK & SAMUEL BURK & their heirs the land & premises above mentioned with the appurtenances to said OBEDIAH SMITH his heirs will warrant & forever defend by these presents In Witness whereof said JOHN PARTREE BURK, JOHN BURK & SAMUEL BURK hath hereunto set their hands & affixed their Seals the day and year before mentioned
Sealed & Delivered in presence of

WILLIAM HORSLEY, THOMAS HIGGINSON,	JOHN BURKS
NICHOLAS CABELL, JOHN HORSLEY,	SAML. BURKS
JOS. CABELL	

Then received of OBEDIAH SMITH the sum of One hundred pounds being the consideration within mentioned

Test WILLIAM HORSLEY, THOMAS HIGGINSON,	JOHN BURKS
NICHOLAS CABELL, JOHN HORSLEY,	SAML. BURKS
JOS. CABELL	

At Albemarle December Court 1770
This Indenture & Receipt were proved by the Oath of NICHOLAS CABELL, JOHN HORSLEY & JOSEPH CABELL wits. thereto & ordered to be recorded

pp.   TO ALL TO WHOM these presents shall come Greeting. Know ye that I JOHN MAR-
246-   TIN of County of HENERICO for sum of One hundred & fifty pounds current
248   money of Virginia by these presents do bargain sell & make over unto BARBARA
         RAMSAY of County of Albemarle Two hundred acres of land lying and being in
County of Albemarle near SCRATCH FACE MOUNTAIN & is the land whereon said MARTIN did dwell & said RAMSAY is now in possession of & which land was taken up by Mr. CHARLES LYNCH & sold by him to JONATHAN WOODSON and Patented in the said WOODSONs name being dated March the first One thousand seven hundred & forty three and the said WOODSON sold the same to WILLIAM HOOPER & the said HOOPER to HARDING BURNLEY & the said BURNLEY sold the same to said MARTIN, which land is bounded Beginning at EDWARD CARTER Esqr. corner white Oak thence new lines South sixty degrees West twenty two poles to an Ash in a Spring, thence down the said branch by its meanders making in a straight line One hundred & fifty two poles to a white Oak on the Branch, thence with the woods South eighty two poles to pointers, thence North Eighty four degrees East two hundred & thirty poles to pointers, thence North five degrees East thirty six poles to pointers of Pine in the said CARTERs line that formerly was JOHN BURWELLs line & thence along the said CARTERs line that was BURWELLs to the first

station as also another tract of land containing two hundred & forty acres adjoining the above mentioned tract which was granted to said MARTIN by Letters Patent bearing date the twenty third day of May One thousand seven hundred & Sixty three in the Third year of our Reign & is bounded Beginning at pointers on the bank of the North side of HARDWARE RIVER in JAMES TAYLORs line & runing with TAYLORs line North sixty one degrees East sixty two poles to pointers, South forty six degrees East twenty four poles to a white Oak, thence a new line North seven degrees East one hundred & seventy eight poles to pointers by a Branch, thence up the Branch according to its meanders in a sight line forty three poles to pointers on JOHN MARTINs Old Line & with it South eighty four degrees West one hundred & thirty eight poles to pointers, North one hundred & eight poles crossing a Branch to a white Oak on the late Secretarys line by a Branch and down the Branch with the Secretarys line one hundred & twenty poles to another Oak on the River, then cross the river to a white Oak in JOSHUA FRYs line & with FRYs line South twenty eight degrees West Fifty poles to a white Oak in BENJAMIN WHITE's line and with WHITE's South seventy one degrees East fifty one poles to Maples on the South side the River on the bank of said River then down the River according to its meanders to the first station with all houses orchards fences & estate right of JOHN MARTIN To have & to hold the said tract of land be the same more or less according to the bounds aforesaid and every of their appurtenances and JOHN MARTIN his heirs will warrant & forever defend by these presents
Signed Sealed & Delivered in presence of
          JNO. HARVIE,   JOHN MARTIN
      JOHN MARKS, THOS. WALKER JUNR.
  At Albemarle January Court 1771
This Indenture & memorandum were acknowledged by JOHN MARTIN party thereto & ordered to be recorded. MARY, Wife of said JOHN, personally appeared in Court & being first privately Examined as the Law directs voluntarily relinquished her right of Dower in the lands conveyed by this Indenture

pp.   KNOW ALL MEN by these presents that I JOSEPH FITZPATRICK of Albemarle
248-   County for sum of Seventy seven pounds nine Shillings & one Penny current
249   of Virginia to me in hand paid by JAMES & ROBERT DONALDS & CO., Merchants in
         GLASGOW, by these presents do bargain sell & deliver unto said DONALDS & CO.
one certain parcell of land containing Four hundred & twenty seven acres being the same land purchased by me of Mr. HARDON BURNLEY the Eleventh day of June in year of our Lord One thousand seven hundred & sixty three, and the same is recorded in Albemarle Court the Eleventh day of August in the aforesaid year lying on both sides of the Middle fork of CUNINGHAM CREEK and being the Plantation I now live on with all houses orchards & all other appurtenances thereunto belonging, & likewise hereby bargain sell & deliver unto said DONALDS & CO. one Negro wench named Phebe, one boy named Tobby, one Negro boy named Nick, one Negro girl named Jeanie, one Negro girl named Tiller, the two boys & two girls all the Children of the said Phebe & one Quart Mugg To have & to hold unto said DONALDS & CO. their heirs and JOSEPH FITZPATRICK shall warrant & forever defend from the claim of any person Provided that if said JOSEPH FITZPATRICK or assigns shall well & truly pay or cause to be paid unto said JAMES & ROBERT DONALDS & CO. their heirs the above mentioned sum of Seventy seven pounds Nine Shillings & one Penny current money with lawfull Interest on the same from this date on or before the Twentieth day of August in the year One thousand seven hundred & Seventy three for the Redemption of the within bargained land & slaves &c. This Indenture to be Void & of no effect In Witness whereof I have hereunto set my hand & Seal this Twentieth day of August in year of our Lord One thousand seven hun-

dred & Seventy
Signed Sealed & Delivered in presence of us
    THOMAS NAPIER, PETER DAVIE,   JOS. FITZPATRICK
    THOS. FITZPATRICK, ABRA. WOODSON,
 At Albemarle December Court 1770
This Indenture eas proved by the Oath of THOMAS NAPIER, THOS. FITZPATRICK & PETER
DAVIE wits. thereto & ordered to be recorded

pp.   THIS INDENTURE made this 13th day of December One thousand seven hundred &
250-   Seventy Between THOMAS PEMBERTON of Albemarle County & REBECCA his Wife
251   of one part & HUGH RICE MORRISS of said County of other part Witnesseth that
      for sum of Thirty pounds current money to them in hand paid doth bargain &
sell unto said MORRISS his heirs one parcel of land in Albemarle County in the NORTH
GARDEN in the Cove of the RAGGED MOUNTAINS Beginning at a white Oak thence South
sixty six degrees West one hundred & sixty six poles to a white Oak, North fifty degrees
West thirty four poles to a Chesnut Oak, North eighteen degrees West fifty two poles to
pointers, North eighteen degrees East one hundred Eighty five poles to a Stump, North
thirty three & a half degrees East forty two poles to a Hickory, South fifteen degrees
East thirty six poles to pointers, South thirty one degrees West forty six poles to the first
station containing Seventy eight acres To have & to hold the said land with appurte-
nances to said HUGH RICE MORRISS his heirs and THOMAS PEMBERTON & REBECCA his
Wife for themselves & their heirs will forever warrant & defend and will keep said
MORRISS his heirs harmless & Indemnified against all Incumbrances whatsoever In
Witness whereof THOMAS PEMBERTON & REBECCA his Wife hath hereunto subscribed
their names & affixed their Seals on the day & year above written
Signed Sealed & delivered in the presence of
    (no witnesses shown)   THOMAS PEMBERTON
                              REBECCA PEMBERTON
 Received December the 13th One thousand seven hundred & Seventy Thirty pounds
current money being the consideration of the within parcel of land p me
                            THOMAS PEMBERTON
 At Albemarle December Court 1770
This Indenture memorandum & Receipt were acknowledged by THOMAS PEMBERTON &
REBECA his Wife parties thereto & ordered to be recorded

pp.   THIS INDENTURE made this Sixth day of December in year of our Lord One thou-
251-   sand seven hundred & Seventy Between FOSTER WEBB Gent. of NEW KENT COUN-
253   TY & JOHN WEBB Gent. & JUDITH his Wife of County of HANOVER of one part &
      JACOB WATTS of County of Albemarle of other part Witnesseth that for sum of
Two hundred & two pounds Ten Shillings current money of Virginia to them in hand
paid by said JACOB WATTS by these presents do bargain sell & confirm unto JACOB
WATTS his heirs one certain tract or parcel of land containing Six hundred & twenty
five acres lying & being in Albemarle County on both side of the North Branch of the
NORTH RIVER joining the lands of Capt. DAVID MILLS deced and bounded Begining at a
white Oak & two red Oak saplins pointers, thence North sixty degrees East four hundred
poles crossing the River along the old line joining Capt. MILLS to two Oaks & Hickory
bush near a Pine Stump, the Old Corner, thence along the Old Line North twenty
degrees West two hundred & twenty poles to a large Pine on the Old Line, thence South
sixty degrees West four hundred & six poles crossing the River just below the Fork
Quarter to a white Oak by a branch thence South twenty three degrees East two hundred
& twenty poles to the begining Except one acre part thereof which has by Order of

Court been laid off for a MILL together with all houses Orchards fences and water
courses thereunto belonging To have & to hold the said land with the appurtenances
whatsoever to the same belonging to him the said JACOB WATTS his heirs said FOSTER
WEBB & JOHN WEBB and JUDITH his Wife for themselves and their heirs will warrant &
forever defend by these presents against all persons freely & clearly discharged of all
Incumbrances In Witness whereof FOSTER WEBB & JOHN WEBB & JUDITH his Wife hath
hereunto set their hands & Seals the day & year above written
Signed Sealed & Delivered in the presence of
          JOHN HAWKINS,   FOSTER WEBB
          ROBERT BAINE, GABRIEL MAUPIN   JOHN WEBB
   Received of Mr. JACOB WATTS the full & just sum of two hundred & two pounds Ten
Shillings lawfull money of Virginia it being the consideration mentioned in the within
written Deed on the day & year within written
In presence of JOHN HAWKINS,   Received by us) FOSTER WEBB
          ROBERT BAINE, GABRIEL MAUPIN   ) JOHN WEBB
   At Albemarle December Court 1770
This Indenture memorandum & receipt were proved by the Oath of JOHN HAWKINS,
ROBERT BAINE & GABRIEL MAUPIN Wits. thereto & ordered to be recorded

pp.   THIS INDENTURE made the 31st day of July in the Ninth year of our Sovereign
253-   Lord George the third by the Grace of God of Great Britain France & Ireland,
255   King Defender of the Faith &c. & in the year of our Lord Christ 1770 Between
          JACOB OGLESBY of the County of AMHERST of one part & SHADRICK OGLESBY of
the County of BUCKINGHAM of other part Witnesseth that JACOB OGLESBY for sum of
Twenty pounds current money of Virginia payd to him by SHADRICK OGLESBY by these
presents doth grant & confirm unto said SHADRICK OGLESBY his heirs all that tract or
parcel of land lying & being in County of Albemarle on the South side of HARDWARE
RIVER on both sides of DARBYS CREEK containing Three hundred & seventy acres &
bounded Beginning at pointers in STEPHENS line on the River bank and runing with
HUGH MORRISS's line North seventy degrees West One hundred & eighty three poles to a
red Oak thence new line North forty six degrees West nine poles to pointers in JOHN
HALLs line, & with HALLs line South eighty three degrees West forty seven poles to two
Pines crossing DARBYS CREEK then North thirty eight degrees West One hundred &
seventy two poles crossing two branches to a red Oak, North fifteen degrees East One
hundred & four poles crossing a branch to a white Oak & pointers, North seventy seven
degrees East One hundred & fifty poles crossing DARBYS CREEK to a Pine, South seventy
four degrees East forty four poles to a Pine in WILLIAM KEPPERS's line & with his line
South forty degrees West sixty six poles to pointers, South fifty degrees East one hundred & fifty two poles crossing a branch to a white Oak in STEPHENS Line & with his line
fifteen degrees East one hundred & eighty poles to the beginning which said tract of
land was granted to JACOB OGLESBY by Patent bearing date the fourteenth day of February One thousand seven hundred & Sixty one Together with all houses orchards & all
other appurtenances whatsoever to the same belonging To have & to hold the said
Three hundred & seventy acres of land with the appurtenances unto said SHADRICK
OGLESBY his heirs discharged from all Incumbrances whatsoever In Witness whereof
said JACOB OGLESBY hath hereunto set his hand & Seal the day & year above written
Signed Sealed & Delivered in the presence of
          WILLIAM OGLESBY,   JACOB OGLESBY
          DAVID OGLESBY, HEZEKIAH ATKINSON

Memorandum That on the 31st day of July One thousand seven hundred & seventy
livery & seizin was had & taken by JACOB OGLESBY & by him delivered to SHADRICK
OGLESBY according to the intent & meaning of the within written Deed
Signed Sealed & Delivered in presence of
    WILLIAM OGLESBY,   JACOB OBLESBY
    DAVIS OGLESBY, HEZEKIAH ATKINSON
At Albemarle December Court 1770
This Indenture & Memorandum were ackd. by JACOB OGLESBY party thereto & ordered to
be recorded

(Albemarle County Deed Book 5 contains 521 pages. Our book divides Deed Book 5 into two books,
one for pages 1 to 255 covering August Court 1768 through December Court 1770; and one for pages
255 to 521 covering January Court 1771 through August Court 1772).

ADAMS. Elizabeth (of Henerico Co. -28);
James 29, 35; Richard (of Henerico Co.-
28), 29; Robert 13, 27, 34, 56.
AGER (EGER). Moses 3, 87.
AHART. Michael (of Culpeper Co.-86).
ALEXANDER. Hugh 63, 95, 96; Jane 96;
John 95, 96.
ALLEGRE. Giles 49; Giles Junr. 84, 100, 101
ALLEN. Abraham 30, (of Augusta Co. -64), 91;
David 32; John 49, 50, 58, 69, 70;
Mary 30, 69, 70; Micajah 30; Richard 64.
AMOSS. William 14, 15, 102.
ANDERSON. Garland (of Hanover Co.-54), 55;
George 62; Joseph 30, 31; Matthew 65;
Robert 84, 96, 100, 101; Thomas 5, 49, 84.
ANTHONY. Joseph 109, 117.
APPLEBURY. Thomas 62, 104; William 62.
ARNOLD. Samuel 42.
ASHLEY. William 23, 24.
ATKINSON. Hezekiah 122, 123.
AUSTIN. William 93.

BABER. Edward 106.
BAILEY. Thomas 19, 20.
BAINE. Alexander (Mercht. of Henrico Co.-117),
118; Robert 122.
BAKER. John (of St. James Northam, Goochland
Co.-12), 13, 14; Susannah 13, 14.
BALLARD. Line 76; Thomas 9.
BALLOW. Jane or Johanna (Goolsbee -7);
Leoanrd 4; Leoanrd Senr. 7; Thomas 4.
BANKS. Line 19, 20; Thomas 19.
BARKSDALE. William 39.
BARTON. William 79.
BELL. Elizabeth 114; John 91; Thomas 50,
69; W. 38. 91, 114; William (of Orange
Co.-38).
BENBY. Edward 94.
BENGE. Samuel 79, 80.
BENGER. Benjamin 79.
BENNETT. Ann 102; Bartlett 28, 112;
Fisher Rice 113; Richard 14, 15, 101, 102.
BERNARD. Abner 67; Peter 67.
BERREY. Bradley 70; George 102.
BIRKS. Samuel 48.
BISHOP. Patrick 110.
BLACK. Samuel 50, 96.
BLACKBURN. Edward 74.
BLANE. Alexander 103, 104;
George 53, 65, 103, 104.

BOLEN. Property of 6.
BOND. Charles 110; Nathan (of Amberst
Co.-110).
BOSWELL. Matthew 34.
BOTETOURT -85.
BOURN. George 112.
BOWER(S). James 5, 17, 74.
BOWLES. Thomas 98; Thomas Junr. 98.
BOWLING. Franklyn 110.
BOYD. James 67; John 104, 105;
Samuel 3, 5, 24.
BRANCH: Bakers 93; Elm 80; Great 92, 93;
Homes Spring 97; Indian Camp 14, 102;
Jumping 64; Kids 75; Maple 92; Mirey 3, 93;
More 111; Owens 46; Piney 42; Plumbtree
79; Stocktons 8, 9, 36, 112; Virgin Spring 30.
BRADSHAW. William 15.
BRICKMAN. William 106.
BROCKMAN. Rebecca 62, 63; Samuel (of Orange
Co.- 62), 63; Samuel (the Older of Orange Co.-
62, 63; William 62, 63.
BROWN. Ben (of Hanover Co.-25), 54, 55, 86, 87,
89, 99, 100; Benajah 25, 86, 87, 89, 99, 100;
Bernard 86, 87, 89, 99, 100; Bernice 86, 87,
89, 100; Bezelia 25; Susan 54, 55, 99.
BRUCE. Caty 75; Richard 75.
BRYANT. Solomon 24, 82.
BULLOK. John 118.
BUNCH. Henry 5, 88.
BURGER. Benjamin 27, 28.
BURK. Charles (deced-118); John (of Augusta
Co.-87), 88, 94, 118; John Parteee (of Bedford
Co.-118), 119; Mary 119; Richard 119;
Samuel (of Buckingham Co.-118), 119.
BURNETT. Bond 115, 116; Isbell 115, 116.
BURNLEY. Harding 119; (Hardon -120).
BURROWS. John 78, 79.
BURRUS (BURRASS). William 22, 23, 61, 94.
BURWELL. John 119.
BUSH. Joseph 31, 32; Josiah 96.
BUSTER. Claudius 23, 70.

CABELL. Elizabeth 119; Joseph 119;
Nicholas 42, 119; William 72.
CAINE. Nicholas 1.
CAMPBELL. John 87; Neill 4, 7, 8.
CANNON. John 74.
CARDIN. Reubin 21.
CARR (KERR). Dabney 118; Henry 57;
James 9, 46, 47; Margaret 94, 95; (contd)

CARR (KERR) (contd). Samuel 5, 58, 87, 88, 94, 95; Sarah 47; Thomas 39, 83, 84, 100, 117.
CARRELL. Mark 112.
CARTER. Edward 56, 57, 64, 81, 119.
CARVER. Archibald 1; Joseph 1; William 1.
CARY (CAREY). Roger 93; Wilson Miles (of Elizabeth City Co.-90).
CAVE. John 26, 99.
CAWTHORN. Thomas (of Hanover Co.-97), 98.
CHAMBERLAIN. Edward Pie 16.
CHARLOTTESVILLE. Town of or called 24, 43,. 49.
CHILES. Micajah 42, 50, 70, 94.
CHISHOLM. William 117.
CHISWELL. Corner 30, 89; John (Parish of St. Martins Hanover Co.-47), 50, 69, 70.
CHURCH. Bellvoir 39; Vestrymen of Fredericksville Parish named -39.
CLARK. Ann 11, 12; Benjamin 11; Bolling 83; John 11, 12, 49; Jonathan 11; Mary 49; Robert 49.
CLARKSON. Peter 116, 117.
CLEVELAND. Alexander 35.
COBB(S). Edmund 113; John 16; Robert 112.
COCK. Benjamin 16; Richard 16.
COCKRAN. Line 75, 76.
COFFEY. Benjamin 33; Cleavland 78, 91; Edward 30, 64; Thomas 35.
COKE. Benjamin 101.
COLE(S). Isaac 4; John 3, 10, 44.
COLEMAN. James (of Louisa Co.-63); John 12.
COLLINS. Thomas 65.
COOKE. David 37.
COOPER. James 59, 60; John 59, 60.
COPELAND. Henry 82, 83.
COUNTY: Amherst 22, 24, 57, 66, 83, 87, 93, 110, 122; Augusta 5, 8, 30, 91; Bedford 34, 112, 118; Buckingham 6, 10, 122; Chesterfield 118; Culpeper 86; Elizabeth City 90; Goochland 7, 12, 18, 26, 41, 82, 119; Halifax 96, 97; Hanover 25, 37, 38, 49, 54, 55, 73, 86, 89, 99, 100, 109, 118, 121; Henrico 28, 117, 119; Louisa 6, 63, 68, 75, 92, 117; New Kent 37, 38, 121; Orange 38, 62, 97, 106, 114; Pittsylvania 83, 100, 109.
COWEN. John 57.
COX. Elisha 4; William 7, 47, 48, 91, 92.
CRAWFORD. David 50; William 88.

CREASEY. Charles 40; George 40; William 40. William Junr. (of Buckingham Co. -40), 48; William Senr. 40.
CREEK. Baileys 20; Ballengers 88; Beaver 22, 31; Bremore 98; Byrd 13, 29; Buck Island 81; Buck Mountain 17; Camping 15; Careys 62; Cunninghams 14, 48, 59, 60, 101, 102, 120; Darbys 122; Deep 99, 100; Edges 26; Great Byrd 13, 18, 19; Green 65; Hendersons 81; Hensleys 77; Ivy 17, 42, 47, 51, 73, 75, 76, 108, 116, 118; Lickinghole 35, 57; Lynches 1, 22; Meachums 27, 28; Mechunk 56, 67; Moores 6, 12, 25, 26, 53, 78, 109; Prettys 32; Raccoon 59, 60; Rich 42; Rockey 5, 86, 88, 107; Shepherds 110; Smiths 20; Stocktons Mill 87; Stowes 103; Taylors 22, 93, 94; Totier 83, 88; Whitesides 72.
CULL. James 30, 31.

DABNEY. Jane 21; William 12, 21, 22.
DAMERON. John 110; Richard 110.
DAVENPORT. Charles 110; Frances 109, 110; James 85 (of Hanover Co.-109), 110; Richard 110.
DAVID. Peter 4.
DAVIDSON. Samuel 27.
DAVIE. Peter 12, 56, 66, 81, 121.
DAVIS. Bartlet 75; Isaac 37, 38, 39, 94; Isham 107; James 109; John 87, 103; Patrick 51; Samuel 13; William 78.
DAY. Robert 42.
DEAN. Adam 87, 102, 111; Eleaner 102.
DEDMAN. Samuel (of Louisa Co.-6).
DENNY. Benjamin 104.
DICKASON. John 115; Mary 115; Thomas 30.
DICKSON. Mr. 60.
DIVERS. John 80.
DIX. John (of Pittsylvania Co.-109).
DOBBINS. John 1.
DOLLINS. Jno. 90; Presley 32, 33, 90; Richard 90, 108; Thomas 98; William 90.
DOLTON (DALTON). David 60; John Junr. (of Pittsylvania Co.-83), 84, 100, 101; Mary 83, 100; William 64.
DONALDS & CO. James & Robert (Merchts. of Glasgow) 3, 4, 12, 25, 56, 81, 120.
DOUGHERTY. Hugh 53, 54, 103, 104; Marshall 103.
DOUGLASS. George 103, 104; Thomas 32.

DOWELL. Ambrose (Planter-60), 61;
  John 64; Thomas 60, 61.
DUDLEY. George 24.
DURRETT. Richard 96.
DUVALL. Samuel (of Henrico Co.-28).

EADES. Abraham Junr. (of Amherst Co.-83),
  88; Jacob 83.
EAGLE. Archibald 25.
EARLEY. John 37.
EASTON. Thomas 1.
EDGAR. Moses (of Augusta Co.-111).
EDGE. Robert 25.
ELLIS. Bartlett 26.
ELLIT. Robert 98.
EPPERSON. James 75; John 26.
ESTES. Richard 112.
EUBANKS. John 107.

FARISH. Robert 18, 19, 20, 21.
FARRAR. Richard 7, 8.
FAUQUIER. Francis 85.
FENCHER. Francis 72, 73; Samuel 72, 73.
FERGUSON. Charles 43, 44; Daniel 63;
  William 66.
FIELDS. Peter 82; Robert 39, 40.
FISHER. Patrick 105, 106.
FITZPATRICK. Joseph 64, 120, 121;
  Thomas 45, 65, 68, 121.
FORD. John 67, 113; John Junr. 113.
FORD. Lynches 11.
FORSIE. Benjamin 67; John 67; John Junr. 67.
FRY. Henry (Court Clerk -1), 10, 11, 41, 54,
  55; John 3, 4, 10, 11, 44, 45; Joshua 3, 10,
  120; Robert 76; Sarah 10, 11; William 10.

GAMMELL. James 45, 46, 52.
GARLAND. James 51.
GARROT. William (of Louisa Co.-92), 93, 118.
GARTH. Thomas 82, 96, 97.
GEORGE. William 79, 80.
GILBERT. Henry (of Hanover Co.-54), 55.
GILES. Nathaniel (of Bartimore County in
  Maryland -70), 71.
GILLIAM. Auther 44, 45; Mary 10, 11;
  Richard 10, 11, 42, 44, 45, 109, 110.
GILLUM. Elizabeth 70, 71; John 36, 37, 56,
  70, 71; Peter 23, 61; William 83, 100.
GILMON. John 80.
GLASS. David 85.

GOLDSBY (GOOLSBEE). Charles 53; Johanna 7;
  Thomas 7, 114, 115; William 71, 72.
GOOCH. Line 20; William 12;
  William Junr. 78, 79.
GOODALL. Charles (of Orange Co.-106), 107,
  114; Elinor 106, 107, 114.
GOODE. Joseph 98.
GOODMAN. Charles 104.
GOUGE. William 80.
GRAVES. David 42; Joseph (of Rowan Co.- in
  North Carolina -105), 106; Thomas 11.
GRAYHAM (GRAHAM). Arthur 118;
  Francis 104; Jno. 88.
GRAYSON. William 33, 58, 61.
GREER. John 63.
GRENOLD. Robert 32.
GRILLS. John 47, 48, 74, 109.
GRIMES. Francis 73.
GRUBBS. Higgason 69; Thomas 21, 22, 69.

HADEN. John 48; Joseph 18, 19, 20.
HAGGARD. Nathaniel 94.
HALL. John 122.
HAMMOCK. John 106.
HAMNER. Elizabeth 65; Jeremiah 45;
  Nichs. 110; Samuel 45, 65, 69;
  William 45, 65.
HANDCOCK. John 59, 60.
HARBOUR. Thomas 13.
HARDIE. Robert 15.
HARGIS. John 12, 25, 26; Penelope 25, 26.
HARLOW. Joel 34, 35; Nathaniel 115, 116;
  William 34, 35.
HARRIS. Christopher 21, 22, 69; Lucreasia 91,
  92; Robert 21, 22, 69, 91, 92; Tyre 21, 22, 69;
  William 95.
HARRISON. Andrew (of Goochland Co.-82), 109;
  Benjamin (of Goochland Co.-16), 82; Jane 109;
  Sarah 16; Thomas 29, 82; William (of Gooch-
  land Co.-55), 56, 82, 83, 90, 91.
HARVIE. John 84, 120.
HAWKINS. John 122.
HAZELRIGG. Abel 58; Richard 58; Sally 58.
HENDERSON. Bennett 24, 40, 82; John Junr. 50,
  78, 79, 80, 103; William 64, 65.
HENRY. Patrick Junr. 38.
HENSON. John 82, 104; Judith 104;
  William 60, 61.
HEREN. William 60, 61.
HICKMAN. Edwin 11.

HIGGINSON. Thomas 119.

HILTON. James 14, 15; Lucy 15.

HINES. James (of Amelia Co.-41); Marimiat 41.

HOLLAND. Corner 118; George (of Goochland Co.-18), 19; John Junr. (of St. James Northam Parish in Goochland Co.-12), 13, 14; Martha Junr. 13, 14.

HOMES. Stephen 96, 97.

HOOPER. William 119.

HOPKINS. Arthur 23, 106, 113; James 23, 24, 106, 113; William 12, 23, 24, 106, 107, 113.

HORD. Mordecai 39.

HORRALL. William 65.

HORSLEY. John 119; Rowland 116; William 119.

HOWARD. William 5, 49.

HUCKSTEP. Samuel 79.

HUDSON. Capt. 44; Charles 46, 61, 63, 66, 82, 108; Land of 10.

HUGHES. Line 33, 59; Stephen 85, 109.

HUMPHREY. William 18, 19, 21.

HUNTSMAN. Josias 27; William 27.

INMON. Hezekiah 93, 94; Jane 94.

IRVING. Charles 47, 48.

ISBEL. James 32.

ISRAEL. Michael 35, 98, 99; Sarah 98, 99.

JEFFERSON. Thomas 39, 81.

JENKINS. Samuel 58.

JERDONE. Francis (Mercht. of Louisa Co.-75), 76.

JERRY. Thomas 1.

JOHNSON. Andrew 60; Betty 112; Christopher 9, (of Bedford Co.-112), 113; Delmus 59, 60; Frances (of Orange Co.-114); James 18, 19, 20, 21; John 6, 114; Mary (of Orange Co.-114); William (of Buckingham Co.-6), 34.

JONES. Elizabeth 21, 22; James 109; John 25, 39, 40, 47, 48, 92; Michael 25, 26; Mosias 5, 39, 69, 77, 88, 94, 95; Richard 41; William 8, 9.

JORDAN. Matthias 88.

KEATON. Margaret 86; William 86.

KENNERLY. James 78.

KEPPER. William 123.

KERR (See CARR).

KEY. George (of Bedford Co.-34); Henry 103; John 34, 83, 100; Martin 83, 100; Mill Swamp 34; Mr. 118.

KIDD. Webb 57, 66.

KINKEAD. Andrew 33, 58; David 8; Elizabeth 8, 9, 35, 36; John 8, 9, 33, 35, 36, (Farmer-58), 59; Mary 33; Winifred 8.

KING. John 85.

LAMBERT. Charles 53, 54, 66, 103, 104; Chris. 71; David 53; George 53.

LANCASTER. John 74.

LANGFORD. Thomas 74, 75; William 47.

LEA. Joseph 113.

LEAK. Mark 65, 107; Revd. Samuel 65.

LEATHERDALE. Line 74.

LEE. William 68.

LEWIS. Charles 66, 93; Charles Junr. 81, 82; Charles Lilburn 81; David Junr. 35, 41, 50, 51; Jane 55; John 39, 114, 115; John Junr. (of Halifax Co.-96), 97; John Junr. 114, 115; Line 118; Nicholas 34, 39, 113; Robert 28, 29, 39, 46, 51, 52, 55, 95; William 17, 74; William Terrell 6, 7, 84, 85, 94.

LINDSAY. Reuben 9, 34.

LITTLE. William 50.

LOCKHEART. Elizabeth 41.

LOGAN. Betheah 8, 9, 36; James 8, 9, 17, 36; Robert 8, 9, 17, 18, 36.

LOVALL. George 68, 71, 72.

LOWRY. Line 20.

LUDWELL. Richard 94.

LYON. Elisha 57; John 88; Mary 57; Nicholas 57; Peter 57.

McALESTER. Hector 4.

McCLEASTER. Neil 27.

McCONNALL. Ann 85; John 84, 85.

McCORD. Agnes 9; Benjamin 9; William 68.

McCULLOUGH (McCULLOCK). Isabella 89, 90, 111, 112; Thomas 3, 89, 90, 111, 112.

McGEHEE. William 81.

McKENZIE. Entry of 83.

McNEELY. James 22; Michael 22, 70; Robert 22; William (of Amherst Co.-22).

McWILLIAMS. Andrew 57.

MABE. John 43, 44; William 43.

MacRAE. Philip 77.

MARKS. James 115; John 120.

MARSHALL. Gilbert (of Augusts Co.-57), 58.

MARTIN. Ann 90; Benjamin 90; Charles 23, 57, 71; George 33, 44; Henry 24, 72, 77; Henry Crumpton 82; Hudson 6, 77, 106; James 62, 90, 106, 113; John 6, 12, 47, 48, 61, 62, 77, 82, 106, (of Henrico Co.-119), 120; Mary 120; Samuel (Mercht. of Whitehaven - 29), 55, 82, 109; Susannah 88, 89; Thomas 72; William 88, 89, 104.

MARYLAND. Baltimore County 70.

MASSIE. Charles 1, 2.

MATLOCK. Nicholas 12.

MAUPIN. Daniel 73, 74; Gabriel 122.

NAURY. Land of 74.

MAXWELL. Ann 42, 43; Bazeleal 42, 43; William 42, 43.

MELTON. Richard 59, 60; William 65.

MEREDITH. James 107.

MERIWETHER. Land of 11, 34, 39; Mildred 68; Nicholas 39, 74.

MICHIE (MECHIE). John 66, 67, 76; Pat: 77; Robert 67, 76, 77, 104, 115; William 52, 67, 95.

MIDDLETON. Robert 28, 29.

MILLER. Robert 24, 31.

MILLS. David 57, 121; Line 74, 114; Mathew 50; Nicholas Senr. (Will mentd.-118).

MITCHELL (MICHELL). William (of Goochland Co.-55), 56.

MOODY. Edward 48.

MOON. Jacob 36, 37, 64, 67, 68, 71, 72; Jacob Junr. 45; William 45, 67, 68.

MOORE. Jno. 35, 42, 84, 100, 101, 105; Jno. Junr. 84, 100, 101; William 47, 48, 102.

MORAN. Elijah 80, 81; John 72; Nicholas 72; Sarah 72, 73; William 80, 117.

MORRISS. Hugh 122; Hugh Rice 121; John 108.

MOSLEY. James 13, 14.

MOSS. Alexander 94.

MOUNTAIN: Blue 50, 69; Blue Ridge 17; Grannies Hill 63; Great 91; Green 3, 10; Little 39; Payne 115; Piney 64, 78; Ragged 1, 37, 94, 108, 109, 121; Scratch Face 119; South West 43, 83, 96, 100, 106.

MULLINS. John Junr. 86, 87, 89; Mary 68; Matthew 68, 69, 74.

MUNDAY. Samuel 60, 61.

MUNFORD. Robert 41.

MURRAY (MORROW). Alexander 17; Thomas 17, 18.

MUSICK. Abraham 27, 57; Terrell 58.

NAPIER. Patrick 40, 48; Thomas 41, 48, 121.

NASH. Henry 13, 14; John 107.

NELSON. Coleman 61; Line 64; Solomon 70, 117.

NICHOLAS. John (of Buckingham Co.-10), 11, 54, 55, 95; John (Court Clerk -28).

NIGHTINGALE. Matthew 64.

NORIES. William 31.

NORTH CAROLINA. Rowan County 105.

NOWLIN. David 22, 23, 61, 94, 117; Mary 22, 23.

OGG. John (of Orange Co.-16), 17, 75.

OGLESBY. David 122, 123; Jacob (of Amherst Co.-122), 123; Shadrick (of Buckingham Co.-122, 123; William 122, 123.

OLD. John 4, (of Province of Pennsylvania -37), 44, 45.

OVERTON. Samuel 106, 107.

PAGE. Robert (of Amherst Co.-93), 94.

PAYNE. John 98; Robert (of Pittsylvania Co.-109) William 77, 101, 106.

PEMBERTON. Rebecca 121; Thomas 121.

PERKINS. Thomas 118.

PERRY. George Junr. 110.

PETTITT. Wm. 118.

PHILLIPS. Old Line 86; William 101.

PLACES: Buffalow Meddow 37; Hercules Pillar 105; North Garden 121; Rich Cove 42, 66.

POINDEXTER. Joseph (of Augusta Co.-77), 78.

POWELL. Robert 106.

POWERS. Thomas (of Goochland Co.-28), 29.

PRICE. Daniel Junr. (of Henrico Co.-28); Edmund (of Cumberland Co.-107); John 99; Meredith 118.

PRINCE. John 36, 37, 65; William 48.

PYE. Joseph 58.

RAGLAND. William 83.

RAMSAY. Barbara 83, 119; Bartholomew 111.

RANDAL. Henry 46.

RANDOLPH. Henry 32, 101; John 117.

RAY. Andrew 45, 46, 52, 104, 105; Jane 73, 76, 77; Mary 52, 105; Samuel 73, 76, 77.

REID (READ). James (of Amherst Co.-24), 25, 43; Thomas 50.

RENNOLDS. Richard 85.

RICE. Charles 16; Edward 16; Edward Junr. 16; Nicholas (of Louisa Co.-117); William 16.

RICHARDS. Thomas 83.
RIGHLEY. Thomas 110.
RIPPEN & CO. George (Merchts. of Glasgow-4).
RIPPITO. John 115.
RIVER. Doyles 25, 86, 89, 91, 92, 99;
  Hardware 10, 44, 65, 68, 71, 79, 92, 93, 110,
  117, 120, 122; James 6, 7, 11, 16, 37, 73, 76,
  78, 82, 98, 106, 109, 116; Linches 38;
  Meachams 21, 22, 31, 33, 36, 40, 45, 46, 50,
  52, 66, 72, 95, 96, 102, 108, 111; Moreman
  31, 66, 68, 69, 85, 105; North 11, 121;
  Rivanna 11, 27, 28, 73, 81, 90, 104, 108,
  119; Rockfish 2, 93; South Hardway 80.
ROAD. Adams 29; Fitzpatricks 64;
  Ridge 22; Rockfish 3, 40; Three Chopt 79.
ROATHWELL. Clabon 106.
ROBINSON. John Esqr. 58; Munford 101.
RODES (RHODES) -39; Ann 114; Clifton (of
  Louisa Co.-68); David 94, 95, 113; John 85,
  90, 111; John Junr. 105; Sarah 105.
ROSS. David (of Goochland Co.-26), 118.
RUN: Bisket 53, 109; Blue 96, 97;
  Keys Mill 83, 100; Marsh 78; Michams 3;
  Stocktons 51; Stony 27; Turkey 112.

SATTERWHITE. Francis 110.
SCOTT. John 10, 11, 107.
SEWELL. John 117, William 117.
SIMONDS (SEMONDS). Ephraim 38, 114.
SHARP. Edith 29; Robert Junr. 29;
  Robert Senr. 29, 79; Susannah 79.
SHAW. James 113.
SHELTON. Henry 96, 97; Lucy 85, 86;
  William 21, 22, 85, 86.
SHEPPARD. David 81; John 18, 19, 20, 21.
SHIELD(S). John 51; Thomas (of Augusta
  Co.-30), 31.
SHIFLET. John 74.
SHILTON. Clough 4.
SIMPSON. Samuel 44.
SIMS. William 33.
SINTER. John 116, 117.
SMITH. Adam 30; Betty 72, 73; Daniel 24,
  33, 44, 74, 97, 106, 108; John 33, 72, 73;
  Joseph 11; Mary (Burk-119); Obediah (of
  Chesterfield Co.-118), 119; Thomas 33, 69,
  70, 74; Thomas Senr. 33; William 12, 72, 73,
  108.
SNEAD. Jacob 118; Mary 118.
SNOW. Elizabeth 114; Tristan (of Orange Co.-
  114)

SOUTHARD. Jno. 65; William 72.
SPENCER. John 41, 42, 74; Rosanna 41, 42.
SPRADLING. David 38.
STAPLES. Christian 62; David 62.
STATHAM. Charles 75, 76.
STEPHENS. Line 122; Majr. Joseph 18, 19,
  20, 21.
STEVENSON. Thomas (of Augusta Co.-5).
STITH. Mr. 83; Revd. William 114.
STOCKTON. David 63, 96; Prudence 87;
  Samuel 15, 51, 87; Sarah 96; Thomas 15.
STONE. Elijah 102; Hezekiah 102;
  Marbel 101, 102; William 102.
SUDDARTH. William 83.
SUMPTER (SUMTER). William 33, 77, 78, 91.
SWANN. John 36, 37, 57, 64, 65, 72.

TALIAFERRO. Samuel 46.
TANDY. Jane 34; William 11, 12, 34, 35.
TAYLOR. James 120.
TEAS. William 35, 36.
TERRELL. Henry 40; Joel 27, 32, 34, 36, 37,
  46, 56; Reubin 90, 108, 112;
  Robert 89, 90, 111, 112.
TERRY. Thomas 83, 84, 100, 101.
THOMAS. George 37; John 1; Michael 47, 48.
THOMPSON. George 40, 41, 48, 81; Joseph 48;
  Robert 16, 17, 74, 75; Roger 40, 41, 48;
  Waddy 75, 76.
THURMAN. Philip 80, 82, 104.
TILLEY. Henry 50, 51, 74.
TINCKER. Samuel 33.
TINSLEY. Richard 24.
TOOL. John 94.
TRACT: Dry Branch 106, 113; Mount Samuel 29;
  Stocktons Mill 51.
TRAP. Martin 103; Mary 103.
TRENT. Peterfield 56, 57, 64.
TUCKER. William 90.
TULEY. James 88.
TURK. James (of Augusta Co.-8), 9.
TURNER. Francis 2; James 57, 71; Terisha 65.
TWYMAN. William (of Culpeper Co.-102).
TYREE. Jacob (of Amherst Co.-66); Mary 66.

UPTON. Thomas 7, 8.

VENABLE. Line 19, 20.
VICE. William 116; William Junr. 73.

WADDY. Line 104.

WAKEFIELD. Elioner 1, 2; Henry 1, 2;
  Henry Junr. 1, 2; John 1; William 1, 2;
  William Junr. 1.
WALKER. James 87; John 39, 63, 84, 97, 118;
  Line 33; Thomas 32, 33, 39, 47, 48, 74, 96,
  97, 112; Thomas Junr. 97, 120.
WALLACE. Adam 22; Andrew 24, 113;
  Michael 32; William 21.
WARE. John 82, 83.
WATSON. James 106; William 37, 45, 57, 71,
  77, 106.
WATTS. David 106; Jacob 64, 91, 115, 121,
  122.
WETHERRED. Francis 65.
WEBB. Corner 114; Foster (of New Kent Co.-
  37), 38, 121, 122; John (of Hanover Co.-37),
  38, 59, 60, 121, 122; Judith 37, 38, 121, 122.
WEBSTER. Giles 36; John Lee (of Baltimore Co.-
  in Maryland -70), 71.
WHARTON. John 65, 68, 72.
WHEELER. Benjamin 27, 28; Benjamin Dod 28;
  Micajah 28.
WHITE. Benjamin 10, 11, 44, 45, 120;
  Jeremiah 61; John 108; William 59, 60.
WHITESIDE(S). David 3; Elizabeth 87; William
  (of Amherst Co.-87), 102, 112.
WHITLOCK. Nathan 78, 79.
WILBURN. Richard 83, 88.
WILKINSON. John 37, 44, 45, (of Baltimore Co.
  in Maryland -70), 71, 83; Land 36.
WILLIAMS. John 18, 19, 20, 21;
  William (of Goochland Co.-98), 99.

WILLIAMSBURG. Patents from 4, 6, 7, 72, 102, 111.
WILLIAMSON. John 48, 117.
WILLS. Elias 90; Keturah 39.
WILSON. Mary 63; Richard 63, 97; Spring 97;
  Whilfd. 113.
WINGFIELD (WINKFIELD). Charles 23, 78, 79,
  94; John 79, 80.
WINN. John 98; John Junr. (of Hanover Co.-97),
  98.
WINSTON. Anthony 55; John 54;
  William 89, 90, 111; William Overton 54.
WITT. Abner 77; Ann 77.
WOOD(S). Abner 58, 59, 70; Ann 52;
  Archibald 30, 31, 63, 108, 109; Henry 78;
  Isaac 90; James 22, 25, 26, 31, 32; John 17,
  42, 50, 63, 90, 108, 109, 112; Joseph 1, 31;
  Josiah 49, 67; Lettis 63; Lucy 25, 26, 31, 32;
  Michael 35, 51, 52; Nathan 31; Patrick 31;
  Richard 3, 24, 25, 43, 46, 49, 70, 98, 99, 108,
  109; Samuel 22, 84; Susannah 109;
  William 22, 35, 42, 51, 70, 72, 73, 90, 98, 99,
  108, 109; William Junr. 90.
WOODSON. Abra. 121; Benjamin 62; John (of
  Goochland Co.-41), 42, 63, 98, 99; Jonathan 119;
  Rene 40; Tucker Junr. (Deputy Court Clerk -12)
  55, 56, 84, 109.
WRIGHT. Thomas 17.

YANCEY. Jeremiah 115.